BEYOND THE BOX

BEYOND THE BOX

How Hands-On Learning Can Transform
A Child and Reform Our Schools

A Mother's Story

Paula Lazor

www.mascotbooks.com

Beyond the Box: How Hands-On Learning Can Transform A Child and Reform Our Schools

For more information, please contact:
Mascot Books
620 Herndon Parkway, Suite 320
Herndon, VA 20170
info@mascotbooks.com

Book Design by Morgan Alessi
Author Photo by Anna Carson DeWitt

Library of Congress Control Number: 2018909219

CPSIA Code: PRFRE1018B
ISBN-13: 978-1-64307-001-8

Printed in Canada

To my family.
You are all my shining stars.

▪ TABLE OF CONTENTS ▪

Foreword   11

Prologue   15

CHAPTER 1   PANDORA'S BOX   19
CHAPTER 2   STORM CLOUDS   29
CHAPTER 3   MELTDOWN   37
CHAPTER 4   WIRED AND TIRED   49
CHAPTER 5   MIXED SIGNALS   63
CHAPTER 6   ROCKIN' ROUND THE CLOCK   83
CHAPTER 7   ANYTHING BUT SPECIAL   97
CHAPTER 8   A TOUGH TRANSITION   117
CHAPTER 9   INTERLUDE   129
CHAPTER 10   COLLEGE MEDIA NEWS SERVICE   145
CHAPTER 11   THE NEW SCHOOL   153
CHAPTER 12   NARCOLEPSY AND
             THE NEW GAME PLAN   163
CHAPTER 13   W-L INTERLUDE   173
CHAPTER 14   TWICE-EXCEPTIONAL   189
CHAPTER 15   BEST SCHOOL YEAR EVER   195
CHAPTER 16   ADVOCACY FIRST STEP:
             NARCOLEPSY   201
CHAPTER 17   A MATTER OF PRINCIPLE   209
CHAPTER 18   A SQUEAKY WHEEL FOR THE
             TWICE-GIFTED   219
CHAPTER 19   NOW WHAT?   225
CHAPTER 20   ISAEP   239
CHAPTER 21   BEYOND THE BOX   253

Epilogue   269

Resources   279

About the Author   283

Acknowledgments   285

▪ FOREWORD ▪

Somehow, my generation came to imagine the time between middle school and retirement like a long, slightly uphill, gentle bicycle ride. But career options and job opportunities are circumstantial, sometimes even accidental, and are rarely long-lived. For today's learners, academic choices and careers are much more complicated than for their parents' generations.

Today's workplace is increasingly technical and increasingly global, and our jobs and roles can change quickly due to international competition and customers' demands, new technologies, new regulations, changes in contracts or grants, and political winds.

Post-secondary options are changing under scrutiny. Lifelong learning, both informal and formal, is more and more frequently required as workers are expected to regularly add new skills and earn new certifications. A growing number of education leaders expect that in the future, traditional college enrollment will decline, while lifelong learning, multiple occupations, necessary technical certifications, and other alternative, more flexible associations with higher education become common.

Even now, the shortage of skilled workers is sometimes remedied through community college partnerships, but not all communities can support that. Parents are understandably worried about what is happening and will continue to happen when their young adult children cannot find highly engaging, meaningful opportunities or the means to support their desired lifestyles.

Every parent dreams that the lives of their children will be better than their own; instinctively, those parents support what they know worked for them. For many years, that has meant academic tracks focused on college preparation, and not enough explicit focus on real skills, confidence-building experiences, encouraging creativity, and real inquiry-driven explorations. How can we overcome the reliance on traditional college preparation, which emphasizes oversubscription to AP courses rather than the skills employers tell us are in short supply? Parents often aren't even told about other options by counselors or educators until there are problems that need to be solved.

Paula has invested in these important topics like few others. As a parent, she discovered alternative programs and professional and technical career education opportunities for students. She knew there were many terrific examples of what works for today's diverse students and thinkers, and that she could raise awareness of the importance of the hands-on, project-based learning available through these opportunities. She knew other parents needed to know, and after volunteering on committees that supported non-traditional school initiatives, she expanded her role as a communicator.

I monitor education blogs that suggest that parents usually participate most actively in support of their first children during the elementary school years, but their engagement diminishes from there. Many elementary parents are curious and supportive of school transformations—but we need those parents to be aware of and advocating for high school reinvention, too. Parents will be a necessary force to reorient high schools away from the memorization and regurgitation of standardized learning and high-stakes exams and toward curricula that include real problems, projects with products or working models, authentic audiences, and student autonomy within their classrooms and programs.

I don't have my own kids, but as a career and technical education teacher (animal science) and biology teacher (including AP Biology) mostly working in alternative programs over the last twenty years, I've come to know several thousand really fascinating teenagers on a first-name basis (many alternative program teachers go by first-name), as well as many of their parents. I've met some really, really wonderful parents. When they understood my approaches to hands-on, project-based inquiry, they often became real partners, helping to create opportunities for all my students to find their own paths to meaning and advanced citizenship.

"Inquiry" has been a buzzword in education jargon for decades, often used to mean the pursuit of problems or questions identified by a teacher rather than students' questions or a community need. My thoughtful school colleagues were all tuned-in to individualizing education, striving to bring out the best in kids who were often not thriving in traditional school environments. Even in career and technical education, though, students went from task to task and project to project without ever applying those skills outside of structured environments.

The model of *I Do—We Do—You Do* was helpful for modeling and teaching skills, but many teachers have begun taking those skills to the next level. Today, we encourage teachers to train for skills and teach for understanding, then ask, "What do you want to do with these new skills/ tools you have?" Interestingly, I find that some elementary teachers do this best. They're already teaching multiple subjects to the same students, and they tell me it's simply more fun to teach this way. But when high school teachers embrace hands-on, project-based learning, they can change lives. Their students become self-aware, broadening the scope of their identities and discovering the foundations for self-advocacy.

Inquiry-driven project-based learning in Career and Technical Education (CTE), science, and math classes has certainly evolved to reflect the importance of Science, Technology, Engineering, and Math (STEM), habits of mind (including technical skills, comfort with data, design-based problem-solving, embracing new understandings, embracing new tools, and communicating technical concepts). But even today, scientists, engineers, and the teachers of these subjects create an aura of exclusivity. Science fairs and other competitions are appealing to those already predisposed to science and with access to resources and mentors, but these competitions probably turn many more people away from academic pursuits and careers in technical subjects than towards. We could, at least, supplement science and engineering fairs (which are rarely fair to engineers!) with festivals and expos for sharing students' individual interests and work with the community—less "judging," more encouragement!

In my lab, I guide more than 4,000 students and teachers in technical college and career exploration, and the foundations of computing, engineering, and creative robotics. Young people visiting me today will likely still be working full-time 50 years from now. Looking at them, I am frequently reminded about something no teacher, parent, or other concerned adult should ever forget: *people may not remember what you did or said in a particular class or setting, but they will remember how you made them feel.* Every educator can decide to make young people feel like special, smart, capable, and valued citizens who are contributing to something bigger than themselves.

Whether schools focus on project-based learning, problem-based learning, or other forms of *student-centered*, inquiry-driven instruction, this book helps us to recognize how we can provide learners with a combination of technical skills, communication skills, and the strategies for building a network of others who know about their interests and skills. Through her son's five-year journey to find the right program, Paula discovered that all students can benefit from calculated risk, recovering and learning from mistakes, and becoming self-aware problem-solvers, confident in self-advocacy and enlightened citizenship.

I look forward to how this book will launch new discussions, new explorations, and expand meaningful, transformative school experiences to all.

▪ Jim Egenrieder ▪

▪ PROLOGUE ▪

It was a golden day in early November 1998 when Matt, our adventurous eleven-year-old son, made his first outdoor climb. Watching him prepare to ascend a cliff above the fast-moving Potomac River, I had to keep reminding myself that he knew all the basics; he had been practicing them for weeks with the other members of Sport Rock, an indoor climbing gym in Northern Virginia. The day of reckoning had finally arrived.

My husband Tom and I had initially been wary about letting him literally climb the walls, but while we'd winced through those first few months, our son had confidently learned the ropes. As I realized many years later, it was the ideal sport for him. Ascending a summit like a spider deftly moving across its web was both a physical and mental challenge. He had to study the rock formations and crevices to decide which equipment to use and how to position his body, but all the effort was worth it. Harnessing every muscle fiber and brain cell to reach the top of a precipice was exhilarating for Matt. He was able to focus on one thing at a time, at his own pace, and he had no one to compete with but himself. Now, at least indoors, it was as if he had scaled mighty boulders all his life.

Nonetheless, when Matt stood at the base of that fifty-foot rock face, I said a few prayers quietly to myself. Yes, I believe that God is with us at all times—*but how much did our Higher Power know about carabiners?*

When it was time for him to ascend, Matt tied himself to his rope with a figure-eight knot, then secured the rope to his brown leather harness. The boys were doing top-roping; it is considered the safest method for beginners because the climber is always protected by the rope anchored above. As he moved slowly toward the top of the cliff, I kept reminding myself that he had a belayer on the ground below him, watching his every move. His partner knew when to slacken or tighten the rope to keep Matt from falling or catch him if he fell.

Tom and I sat on the ledge above with several equally nervous parents. From our vantage point, I could not see Matt until he neared the top. He was about five feet away from it when he came into view; I pulled out my camera, slung the strap gingerly over my neck, and held it at the ready.

Matt was concentrating very hard, studying each nook to choose his next grip while positioning his legs against the rocky ledge for balance. I wanted to take a picture of him facing me, but I also wanted to make sure I did not disturb him.

Finally, Matt stopped for a minute to rest. I could see his blonde bangs hanging below his helmet, his harness strapped snugly over his gray fleece sweatshirt and black pants, and I knew this was the moment I wanted to capture.

"Matt," I called to him quietly.

Our son slowly looked over at me, unaware until that moment that I had been watching him. Our eyes locked, and he broke into a broad grin.

As Matt beamed at me, I quickly took my first shot, then the shutter clicked again and again. I knew he had to finish his climb, but I must have taken a dozen pictures before I put the camera down.

It's been nearly twenty years since I took those photos. I've kept one on our refrigerator, and even alongside dozens of other family gems, it is that picture of Matt, grinning broadly as he neared the summit, that tugs at my heart the most. Scaling the cliff that day, Matt was the happiest I would remember him being for several years to come—years that were as rocky as the ledge he climbed on that crisp, sunny afternoon.

■ ■ ■

Looking back at that special moment in time, I realize why it still stands out so vividly in my mind: Matt's climb up the cliff had clearly demonstrated his strengths and how much he could accomplish when given the right equipment. Unfortunately, as we would discover over the course of many years, the tools offered in traditional classrooms did not work for him.

Tom and I never doubted that Matt was a bright child, but as his backpack grew heavier in middle school and he was expected to juggle several subjects at a time, his academics suffered. With the additional complication of the sleep disorder he developed in the eighth grade, Matt's world imploded.

What followed for our family was an emotional rollercoaster ride. Matt moved from program to program during our five-year journey to find the right one, and we discovered that he was not alone. We learned of too many children who were not being taught in the ways that they were able to learn. In those instances, it was not the students who were failing— it was the schools that had failed them.

There are schools out there that recognize the multiple intelligences in all of us and have devised academic programs that recognize and value them. These programs can be obscure, expensive, and difficult to access, and without the strong support and advocacy of our family, Matt never would have been offered these opportunities. Through long uphill battles, though, desperate for answers, we tried one after the other.

Finally, when it seemed all possible alternatives had failed, Matt found the right one—much like mountain climbing, it was a program that played to his strengths and enabled him to learn by doing. After all, shouldn't education be an exploration that sparks the interest of all students— regardless of academic level, regardless of learning disabilities or learning styles? Shouldn't all children learn about the world around them, to help them see the connection between academics and their lives, and to find and use the tools that will empower them to use those talents for the betterment of society? This path was a lifesaver for our son, helping him to make the connection between his academics, his life, and his future career. Through the things he accomplished, once given the right tools, he gained hope and direction and transformed his life in ways that still benefit him daily.

Matt's story goes beyond the transformative power of hands-on learning. It is a story of hope, and a lesson in life to never give up on someone you love. Thankfully, our story had a happy ending, but only because we learned how to navigate a complicated and confusing maze of special education rules and procedures. Without the personal trials our son endured and our subsequent parent advocacy, Matt never would have stumbled into the program that has helped him build the life he has today. Just like the day our eleven-year-old son climbed confidently above the mighty Potomac River, Matt now has the professional skills and belief in himself to succeed in his career and lead a fulfilling life. We hope that sharing this knowledge will help others to advocate for education programs that are built on students' strengths, rather than their perceived "learning deficits."

▪ CHAPTER 1 ▪

Pandora's Box

Nothing was scarier than Matt's dark green backpack. It looked possessed, as if a whirling dervish had burrowed its way inside, tossing papers like confetti from his three-ring binder.

The contents were the perfect reflection of his eighth-grade mind—swirling with ideas, but not in any apparent order. When he remembered to bring his worksheets home from school, Matt frequently had trouble finding them in his bag. When he did find his homework, he often forgot to complete all of it. When he did complete his assignments, he often forgot to turn them in the next day.

So, on his first day back to Swanson Middle School from winter break in January 2001, I couldn't help but wonder if he had everything he needed to start the New Year right—or if he would even get to class on time.

"Hurry, Matt, or you'll be late!"

I looked at my watch while I waited on the brick front stoop of our small colonial home, stamping my feet to keep warm. Even though it was a sunny morning, the air outside was so cold that I felt like I was breathing icicles.

Matt slowly gathered up his books and homework and stuffed the muddled mess into that dreaded backpack in the hallway. Slinging the bag onto his back like some turtle reuniting with its shell, he headed out the door.

We had started a daily routine to get Matt to school before the tardy bell. I would follow him part of the way with our black miniature schnauzer, Lucky. Matt loved Lucky, and although he wasn't thrilled with having me in public view, he didn't mind it when our little dog accompanied us. Lucky and I just needed to stay about ten feet behind him and turn around a block before he reached "hell" (his favorite word those days for middle school).

I couldn't say I blamed him. So far, Matt's experience as an eighth grader could have been written by Dante. He couldn't stay awake in his classes, and his constant sleeping had led to a steady and notable decline in both his grades and his self-esteem.

To my surprise, as we neared the mom-free zone, Matt turned around and gave Lucky and me quick kisses goodbye. Perhaps he was in good spirits because he had been off from school for nearly two weeks and now believed it was possible to make a fresh start with his classes and grades. It hadn't been the first time he'd held out hope and, unfortunately, it wouldn't be the last time he would see those hopes dashed.

When Matt came home from school that afternoon, he seemed happy to have survived another day. But once the family dinner ended, another evening of homework awaited him, and it didn't take long for his mood to change.

With the smell of meatloaf and broccoli still lingering in the air, Tom cleared the plates and began to wash the dishes in the sink, and our daughter, Matt's older sister, Emma, headed upstairs to study. Matt sat down at the dining room table to begin his math assignment, fumbling around in his backpack until he found his book.

I looked in on him about five minutes later. He had propped his chin on the upturned palm of his left hand, his bent elbow and upper arm acting as the supporting beam. I wasn't sure if he was concentrating hard or if he had fallen asleep.

"How is the math going?" I asked cheerfully, as much to check on whether he was awake as to find out if he was working.

Matt glanced up at me with a distant look in his eyes. "I can't focus."

Matt's focusing problems had begun in elementary school. His first-grade teacher had noticed he had difficulty following directions and staying on task without a lot of supervision. These issues came up repeatedly at meetings with his teachers and school specialists in those early years; they said he had difficulty concentrating on his homework and organizing tasks, that his attention wandered, and that he frequently lost necessary items, like books and pencils.

Matt often daydreamed throughout the day and, although he was a cooperative student, he appeared at times to tune out classroom activities. He would do that on the soccer field, too. He was much more interested in staring at cloud formations than watching his teammates kick the ball down the field.

The problems persisted, so Tom and I had taken him to a pediatric neurologist. After the examination, the doctor diagnosed him with mild attention deficit hyperactivity disorder; he had the predominantly inattentive type, marking his behavior as more distracted than overstimulated. Tom had assured me that he'd probably had the same problem as a child—only that, back in the fifties, his teachers had simply checked the box on his report card that read "Doesn't pay attention."

Matt also had delayed auditory processing. That meant that when a teacher spoke to him, it would take a few seconds for him to understand what had been said. By the time Matt sorted through the information, the teacher had already moved on to the next lesson point. Consequently, he would give the correct answer, but to the previous question, confusing both him and his teacher. Not surprisingly, Matt often had difficulty keeping up in class, which only worsened as he grew older and the homework load grew heavier.

That evening, like so many nights before, I sat down to help Matt with his math. We would spend hours reviewing concepts and practicing the multi-step formulas that challenged him, but no matter how well he grew to understand the material at home, he would go to class, take his test, and fail it.

Later that night, I found Matt in bed, unable to fall asleep, and I noticed a crumpled-up sheet of paper on his nightstand. I asked what it was, and he grabbed it in a panic. When I asked to see it, he reluctantly handed the paper to me. It was his progress report.

One bright spot earlier in the school year had been his grade in English class. He had started the quarter with a mock job interview and nailed it. I still remember how professional he had looked, dressed smartly in the suit he had worn at his grandmother's funeral. His English teacher told me how he had done everything by the book—shaking hands firmly with the interviewer, making direct eye contact, and speaking confidently about his abilities to fill the make-believe position.

It was this type of hands-on work that he was particularly good at doing. In grade school, he'd proudly displayed his mythology project: twelve computer-drawn pictures of *The Odyssey* that he had taped to a scroll and then recorded a story about, courtesy of our Fisher-Price cassette player.

His fifth-grade teacher had recognized his adeptness with computers and audio-visual equipment, so as the school year had drawn to a close, she'd put him in charge of running the slideshow for the graduation ceremony. Matt had helped to select the slides highlighting the students and school activities.

For the grand finale at the very end of the program, with more than fifty children and their parents looking on expectantly, Matt had slipped in a picture of one of his classmates making rabbit ears behind the school principal.

Parents and teachers alike erupted in laughter. Fortunately, the principal had a sense of humor; he'd even told Matt's classmate, who had turned several shades of red, to stand up for a round of applause.

Matt's playful humor had certainly endeared him to family and friends, but I also think it had helped him balance all his efforts to get his schoolwork done. In elementary school, most of his efforts had something positive to show for them. But second chances for taking a forgotten test or turning in missed homework were not options for Matt in eighth grade.

The essays and spelling quizzes and grammar tests had come, steadily whittling away at his high English grade until, like in many of his other subjects, his abilities weren't reflected in the final assessment. Now, looking down at Matt's progress report, I saw that his English grade had plummeted from an A to 53.6 percent. I also noticed that he'd scribbled his own comment on it in big, bold strokes: *"You earned it. You piece of shit."*

I was stunned by the hateful words. Matt had been frustrated about school over the past few years, but I had seldom seen him lash out so harshly at himself.

"I might as well start making friends with the seventh graders." He sounded utterly resigned to repeating eighth grade.

This was not the Matt we'd known in elementary school. By the second grade, his ability to process information had tested solidly in the average to high-average range, though those same exams had shown a significant discrepancy between his ability and achievement. As a result, the school had identified him as learning disabled, and with that designation came a host of services that had helped him immensely. He'd become eligible for special education services and an Individualized Education Plan (IEP).

To help Matt keep on track, his second-grade plan spelled out several accommodations for his teacher to use, such as a reduced workload and placement at the front of the class so he could be given subtle cues for paying attention and finishing his assignments. Because he had problems following instructions more than one step at a time, his teachers throughout grade school had laid out directions for him, one-by-one, in chronological order, and they coached Tom and me on how to do this at home.

In fact, one Sunday afternoon, the grade school reading specialist and Matt's teacher had visited us at home to cue us in on homework assignments for Matt's next reading level. Tom and I were incredibly fortunate to have had so much support for Matt's success that school teachers even paid house visits. To this day, I think many of them not only recognized Matt's potential, but that the traditional method of teaching was not the right match for him.

Matt had seen an occupational therapist throughout elementary school for fine motor skill challenges. It had been handled well in earlier grades, but by fifth grade, it was increasingly clear that he was having trouble forming letters for his written assignments or even using scissors to cut paper. His writing was legible when he only had short writing assignments, but with longer ones, the manual exertion wore him out. As his workload grew, the school decided to provide him with an "alternative keyboarding device"—the Alphasmart. During a time when students rarely even used rudimentary word processors, Matt was issued a computer, and his work improved noticeably. His responses were lengthier and of much better quality when he typed them. Even though the Alphasmart helped him to write longer and better-quality pieces, it would glitch sometimes, and Matt would lose all his work! Initially, he thought the computer was a very cool thing, but after a while, it made him feel self-conscious because it made him stand out from the other students.

The school took a collaborative approach with each student, tying in the observations of the teacher with the specialists outside the classroom and the parents. Too often, IEP meetings at public schools can become battlegrounds, with parents pitted against teachers and specialists to determine the best services for the child. Tom and I felt that we were part of the team, and very lucky that our relationships with the elementary school teachers and staff were so good.

Unfortunately, by the time Matt reached eighth grade, he no longer felt like the teachers and specialists were his supporters. In fact, to him, they appeared to be part of some unholy alliance out to sabotage him.

Matt sat in bed that night growing increasingly upset. Like too many other nights, he was teary-eyed and clenching his fists over and over again. I tried to reassure him that it was the middle of the term and he still had time to improve his English grade, but my encouragement wasn't working.

"Is anything else bothering you?" I asked.

"I was bored in English class today, so Amy told me to write a note," he said.

"What did you write?"

"It wasn't a note. I drew a picture, and the teacher snatched it from my desk near the end of class."

Matt wasn't known for his artwork. In fact, the last time I remembered him making anything at all was in grade school, when he'd brought home glazed ceramic gargoyles. Tom and I later placed them strategically behind the piano, next to his sister's baked Sculpi pottery, on the bottom two shelves of the bookcase in the living room.

"So, what did your teacher say to you?"

"Nothing." He shrugged. "I took it from her desk after class ended."

I was exasperated. It was too late to get into a discussion that night about his behavior. "We'll talk about this tomorrow."

I spoke to him as firmly as I could, but I was always torn about what to do when he confessed to doing something wrong. After all, he could have lied about this or not told me anything.

■ ■ ■

When I headed into our bedroom after Matt's late-hour outburst, Tom came upstairs.

"What's wrong?" he asked, always sensitive to changes in my moods or uncharacteristic quietness.

Maybe it was simply the build-up of another disappointing day that had started so normally, or the long night of struggling with Matt to do his assignments. Or maybe it was the accumulated sadness of seeing such a happy boy turning into such an unhappy teenager. I began to cry softly.

Tom held me close and tried to comfort me. "I know this is hard on you. But you are a good mom and you are doing your best. Everything will be okay."

Emma must have heard my muffled crying. I heard her voice from the hallway: "Mom, I am taking you out on a date on Saturday! Let's go out for lunch or tea."

I smiled and said I would be happy to have a girls' day out with her. This wasn't the first time she had tried to cheer me up when I grew upset about Matt; she appeared to be concerned by how his behavior was affecting me.

Emma headed back into her room. As usual, she was staying up past her bedtime to finish her homework. An eleventh grader in a rigorous academic program, she had an essay due in a few days on *Metamorphoses.* No doubt she would do well on it, as she had in every other subject. In another year, she would be heading for college and, like so many of her friends, she was shooting for a 4.0 average to get into a top-tier school. She always studied hard, and fortunately for her, there was no gaping hole between her ability and achievement.

This success sometimes made it difficult for Emma to understand why Matt wasn't doing well in school, too. Emma had become skeptical of her younger brother's school complaints and had told me more than once that he was simply trying to get out of doing his homework. When her brother had a heavy workload like she did, she'd advise him to simply hunker down, get it done, and not cry about it.

I thought back to one night, when Matt was sitting at the dining room table, immersed in choosing pictures from a photo album for a fifth-grade autobiography assignment. He had made sure he found photographs of himself at all ages, beginning with one happy in his stroller, his tufts of blonde hair and sparkling green eyes drawing smiles wherever he'd gone.

Matt had looked up at me from his pile of pictures with a wide grin on his face. "Look at this one, Mom!"

I'd walked from the kitchen to look at the photo he had chosen. It was a picture of him and Emma posing at their pre-school playground. They'd both stood facing the camera as they'd held onto a set of parallel bars, each with their right legs extended behind, as if they were synchronized skaters on an ice rink. That picture so perfectly reflected their dynamic at the time—Matt following his big sister's lead, and Emma happy to have him mimicking her every move.

That had all begun to change once Matt had reached middle school. As his assignments grew harder and his grades fell, he was no longer able to follow in his sister's footsteps. Matt compared his school struggles to Emma's academic success, and like many siblings of high achievers, Matt began to feel like a failure.

Tom and I had encouraged him to pursue interests outside of the classroom that he was good at doing. When he'd taken an interest in rock climbing in sixth grade, we'd enrolled him in an indoor climbing club. He'd learned the ropes quickly and was soon helping other new students with their techniques, but his sense of accomplishment on a climbing wall had not bolstered his confidence in the classroom. Matt's school life, much like his disorganized backpack, resembled Pandora's box. No matter how hard Matt tried to keep everything in order and under his control, the lid had already burst open.

▪ CHAPTER 2 ▪

Storm Clouds
(1998–1999)

Sixth grade arrived like a slow-moving storm. The workload was noticeably heavier, and it took its toll on Matt—not only academically, but emotionally and physically. First, there were headaches and stomachaches, then the asthma that he had struggled with since he was a toddler started flaring up. All of these maladies translated into a growing number of missed school days, which in turn led to lower grades, which led to growing anxiety, and consequently, more headaches and stomachaches. It was a vicious cycle.

Tom and I met with Matt's sixth grade teachers, counselors, and specialists at an IEP meeting in late January 1999. We sat in a small interior room as we waited for the meeting to start; it was not unlike the ones from his grade school years, but this time, I felt more confined.

One of the first teachers to speak was Mrs. Gallagher, who had Matt for two subjects: English and social studies. She gave him a mixed review, noting that he was a bright boy, but "not participating in his education." Other members of the staff also focused on his participation, stressing that our son needed to learn to advocate for himself.

According to school records from this January meeting, the IEP goals focused primarily on advocacy. Matt was directed to ask teachers for clarification of oral or written directions if he did not understand, request additional time when needed to complete classwork, and "initiate appointments" with teachers for after-school help.

The last goal seemed to be particularly unrealistic to us. For Matt, a child who had reached his limit with school by the time the final bell rang, the last thing he would want was more school.

Halfway through the meeting, Matt's class came back from a field trip at the school's environmental science center, the Outdoor Lab. His counselor, Joan Murphy, corralled Matt into the meeting instead of his last class of the day.

When Matt walked into the room, Tom and I could see the difference in him immediately. He grew very quiet and wouldn't make eye contact with anyone. It was difficult to get more than yes-or-no responses from him when the staff asked him how he liked school and whether he had any questions about his classes or schoolwork.

Although Matt was not responsive to their questions, Tom and I felt fortunate he had teachers and guidance counselors who wanted him to succeed in school. We knew it took them many hours to prepare an IEP, including specific classroom accommodations for him and goals for him to achieve during the school year.

Once Matt came home that evening, he was back to his old self. He excitedly told Tom and me how much fun he'd had at the Outdoor Lab, and explained their "survivor skills" assignment in great detail. He proudly announced that he'd caught a salamander and successfully lit a fire with the third of five supplied matches.

This was the son we knew, animated and happy about making new discoveries. He looked at us with a sparkle in his eyes, talkative and confident about what he was good at doing. This fit an all-too-familiar pattern: happy and in his element when he could learn by doing, but unsure of himself and hesitant to learn when he had to sit in a classroom all day.

In early March, Matt received another disappointing progress report; he was failing math and had a D in science. The science grade seemed especially discouraging, since he was not getting credit for three labs in which he said he'd done his work, but his lab partners had not turned it in.

In math, on several occasions he seemed to understand the concepts when we worked on his problems at home, yet he repeatedly failed his tests at school. Only much later, reading literature about ADHD, did I realize that children with ADHD commonly have problems with memory retrieval. He had not forgotten what he'd learned; he'd simply had problems calling it up from where it was stored in his brain.

When left to his own devices, Matt would convince us he'd completed his assignments and turned in his homework to his math teacher. If the teacher was absent, then he'd tell us he'd handed in his schoolwork to the substitute. We didn't question his explanations at the time—that would come later.

■　■　■

One night, Matt dissolved into tears; all of his friends had made the honor roll, whereas he wasn't able to get any grade better than a C. Tom and I grew concerned that he was being stigmatized for this by his classmates.

I first noticed signs of alienation in early March, when Matt asked for thirty-five cents to call me at lunch time so he could "talk to someone." He explained that most of his friends bought lunch and didn't get to their seats for about twenty minutes, leaving him sitting alone. He told me some of his classmates had asked him why he'd become so quiet during lunch period.

"I only have about four civilized conversations a month," Matt told me.

Tom and I started grasping at straws to find ways to make him feel better about his social life at Swanson. I told him sixth grade had been tough for Emma, too, and that kids mingled better beginning in the seventh grade.

■ ■ ■

One bright spot during Matt's trying days at school was Sportrock, the indoor climbing facility I took him to on Saturday mornings. Unlike school, climbing was something he loved to do, and he was good at it. I'll never forget one cold, blustery morning in early February 1999, when I watched Matt scale an incline that jutted outward, then crack-climb halfway up a forty-foot wall by wedging his arms and legs into the man-made rock face. He also came out of his shell with his fellow climbers. It was so encouraging to see him chatting easily with the other boys.

A neighbor once told me that if a child is passionate about something—especially when they are doing poorly in school—it was important to do all you could to help them pursue their dreams. Even though school was beating him down, we began to see Matt's success in rock climbing as a way to build him back up again. With that in mind, as Valentine's Day neared, Matt said he wanted a new pair of climbing shorts. There was nothing in Matt's size on sale at his favorite sports store, so he chose some crimpers (small climbing holds) and a package of beef jerky instead. Not exactly a traditional Valentine gift, but we knew that in Matt's eyes, they beat a box of Whitman's candy.

Matt's joy of climbing also brought out his sense of humor. One Saturday morning, we took him to a climbing competition that two other boys named Matt were registered for. They had to pick nicknames, and Matt picked "Fabio," a famous male model at the time.

Other sorts of outdoor sports attracted Matt, too. His favorite one in the winter was snowboarding. In mid-March, Matt joined his friend Sam and Sam's father for an outing at Ski Liberty, a nearby resort in Pennsylvania which featured a snowboard park. Not usually an early riser on weekends, by 7:00 in the morning on the day of the trip, he had all his gear packed in his sister's Nike bag and had hopped into his boots, quickly brushed his teeth, and (after a last-minute return for his sunglasses and ChapStick) was on his way.

When Sam's dad dropped Matt off at the house after his day on the slopes, he told us that our son was a natural-born athlete and that he had been soaring over the snowboarding ramps and sailing down the mountain runs just as well as the more experienced boys. He'd also wisely rented a helmet—a smart move, since he'd fallen several times after somersaulting!

Perhaps Matt's developing abilities outside the classroom made him more confident in school; all we knew was that, by the end of the school year, not all of his academic efforts were for naught. There were occasional successes. As the school year progressed, he proudly announced he'd gotten a B on his social studies project on Ethan Allen. He also worked hard on his science project and finished with flying colors—a day early! Tom and I were really proud of him for sticking to the task, though it had taken frequent reminders along the way.

■ ■ ■

Usually, Matt's school anxiety lessened considerably over the summer, but that year it was still an underlying presence throughout the hot days of late June, July, and August. It seemed that his relief from finishing sixth grade dissipated much too quickly—particularly when he began to fear we were nearing the end of the world.

Matt was not a fatalist but, like most children at twelve, he was impressionable. I don't know exactly where our son had first heard the prediction by the sixteenth-century philosopher Nostradamus that the world would end in July 1999; I suspect it might have been on the Discovery Channel, which he watched often. Whatever the source, Matt grew more upset with each passing day of the season he normally found relaxing, until finally, he started getting sick.

On July 3, I took Matt to see his pediatrician, Dr. Goldman. The screening for strep throat came back negative, and after he felt Matt's stomach area and tested for tenderness, the doctor assured me that whatever was brewing wouldn't require surgery. Interestingly, he told us the most common cause for stomach pain was stress.

Matt had been asking me about Nostradamus' prediction, having initially heard the world was to end on July 1. I tried to reassure him, to no avail. Finally, it occurred to me that if I could find a more authoritative prognosticator than myself, maybe he would quit worrying about Armageddon.

I remembered a Bible passage which, loosely paraphrased, said that no one but the Heavenly Father knew when the end of the world would come. In July 1999, Google was less than a year old and I had never heard of it, so I went directly to the source. Thankfully, one of the versions of the Bible at our house listed several topics and applicable verses, and within seconds, I nailed down the verse: Mark 13:32. Matt looked relieved, but only partly so.

That was when Emma's ingenuity sprang into action. As Doomsday grew closer, in Matt's mind, his big sister came up with a great idea that was much more convincing than mine. After an afternoon at the library, Emma came home and told Matt that she'd come across an article on Nostradamus, and that he had predicted the world would end on July 7, 1999. It was now mid-July, more than a full week after the predicted demise of Mother Earth.

After Emma's revelation, Matt's stomach pains began to subside. It looked like the pediatrician had been right; once he realized it was not curtains for the world, he could sleep peacefully through the night.

However, that reprieve lasted no more than a week, and Matt's symptoms continued intermittently throughout the summer. Tom and I became more and more convinced that Matt's stomachaches, coughing, and tight chest were stress-related, particularly after Emma ventured that they sounded like the anxiety attacks she'd had at the beginning of the school year.

Emma had hidden her anxiety from Tom and me so successfully that we used to joke that Matt was our high-maintenance son and Emma our low-maintenance daughter—little realizing that, like so many siblings of children who require extra attention, Emma felt invisible at times. Sometimes children hide or downplay their anxiety from their parents in order not to worry them. Over time, they might overcome those fears and be the stronger for them. But, they also run the risk of those fears worsening if they continue to keep them pent up inside.

■ ■ ■

In August, Matt went to a Sportrock camp at Carderock Park, located on the Maryland-Virginia border overlooking the Potomac River. There were only nine kids in the camp, and he was the only one who was an advanced climber, so, to his delight, the climbing instructors pulled him aside for separate instruction. While the other children learned the basics, Matt was free to learn new skills separately with his own instructor, Susan, essentially his own personal trainer. This certainly boosted his morale.

Tom and I were so happy that Matt's skills and abilities were being recognized. Unlike school, where he was identified by his academic weaknesses, at the climbing camp, Matt was recognized for his strengths.

Matt would have been one unhappy camper, I'm sure, had he been lumped in with the novice climbers. The boys and girls learning basic skills were only in fourth grade, and Matt said they were pretty immature—an interesting observation from someone whose fifth-grade teacher had made the same observation about him. (However, in fairness to Matt, the teacher had added that virtually all fifth-grade boys were immature.) He told us that a few of the boys only climbed once the entire day because they'd misbehaved, whereas he had climbed all day long.

Matt was even allowed to bring more of his own climbing gear on the second day, which he pulled together after dinner. What a sharp contrast this was to his lack of organizational skills in school! Compared to the messy abyss of Matt's backpack, his gear bag was neatly assembled. He had placed items that he probably wouldn't need, such as extra chalk powder, at the bottom of the bag, along with a stuff sack of small bundles of slings, coil webbing, and daisy chains; stacked above that was more climbing gear on carabiners.

I couldn't begin to identify all the essential items that he placed on top, although I recognized his helmet and first aid kit, understandably crucial items to have at his disposal. Of course, he packed more than he needed, since the camp provided all the essentials; I think he wanted to show everyone how much gear he owned, and having it neatly assembled was a matter of great pride.

It was a fun week for Matt—one that he always looked back on with a smile. He learned new skills and assumed a leadership role among the aspiring young climbers.

But the feeling of a normal, healthy life did not last long.

■ ■ ■

We had friends over for dinner on the deck at the end of the August. Sitting under the night sky with the summer sound of cicadas, the conversation and wine flowed easily, and it was one of those magical gatherings.

After everyone left, though, Matt's stomach pain returned. I looked at the calendar; school began in less than two weeks.

Matt awoke the following morning with a pounding headache and upset stomach. I found him sprawled out on the family room sofa, lying flat on his stomach, in no shape to sit through 9:30 Mass. When I asked whether he was coming, he said he didn't want to cry during church, so Emma and I left him watching *Rugrats*. Tom, a devout fan of the Sunday morning news programs, stayed home with him, but by the time Emma and I returned from church, he'd come up with an idea for the whole family—a Sunday afternoon matinee.

Matt brightened up a bit at those prospects, even though his headache didn't go away immediately. However, he began to feel well enough to venture outside early in the afternoon to go biking with his friend Sam. By the time he came back and we all jumped into the car to head to the movies, Matt was his bright, cheerful self. His headache had disappeared.

Matt's last few days of summer appeared to be happy ones, at least from the outside. He had occasional bouts of anxiety, but for the most part, he spent his time skateboarding and biking with friends. Even his first day of seventh grade went smoothly, though it wasn't long before the cycle of headaches and stomachaches, missed school days, and anxiety began again. Little did we know that after the first few rocky months, his school world would implode.

PAULA LAZOR

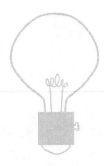

■ CHAPTER 3 ■

Meltdown
(1998)

It was only the second day of seventh grade, but we were already crossing our fingers. Unlike sixth graders, who were supported by a team of teachers, seventh graders were expected to work more independently on a much heavier load of homework each night from day one.

So here it was, day two, and Matt already felt like he was falling behind. No sooner had he painstakingly worked through his pre-algebra problems, growing more frustrated by each one because he had to solve so many of the same kind, then it was time to turn to his writing assignment. Matt dug through his backpack, looking for his worksheet. A moment later, he burst into tears, more overwhelmed by trying to find the assignment than actually doing it.

Like the previous year, our daughter came to the rescue. Wise beyond her years, Emma cheered him up and organized his binder and accordion folder, so he was all set for the rest of seventh grade. Or so we hoped.

After seeing every piece of paper in its proper place, Matt diligently finished all his assignments. Matt was much more organized about his homework the following day, too, when every assignment was in its folder or the correct section of his binder.

■ ■ ■

During the first few relatively calm weeks of school, I fondly remember enjoying some quiet time in Old Town Alexandria, on Saturday mornings while Matt was at Sportrock. I walked along the cobblestone streets under blue skies, the crisp early autumn air invigorating me as I passed the restored, colonial-era homes or watched the sailboats cut the air while I munched on a bagel with cream cheese and sipped cinnamon coffee from a local bakery.

Like so many times ahead, there would be moments and even sometimes days when life seemed so normal. This was especially the case on Friday evenings and Saturday mornings, when schoolwork was not looming immediately overhead. Looking back, I now know it was the calm before the storm.

■ ■ ■

Those first few weeks of normal school days barely lasted through September. Matt's anxiety level was slowly intensifying, and by early October, he was having major digestive tract problems, often unable to fall asleep until the wee hours of the morning because of stomach cramps. I would stand vigil with him in the family room until some ungodly hour, when I could finally lead him upstairs.

His inability to sleep would lead to half-days of school or completely missed ones. On one of the occasions when he stayed home all day because of acid reflux (a.k.a. heartburn), I found him feeling much better by the time I arrived home from the office.

He explained that during the day he had looked up an article on acid reflux, which recommended regular exercise, especially walking (as well as avoiding caffeine, alcohol, and tobacco).

"Why don't I see if this works?" Matt said, with a hopeful tone to his voice.

I warily allowed him to go for a walk. He returned claiming he felt better, and credited the exercise as the reason for his quick comeback.

Looking back, I am surprised Tom and I didn't question these near-miraculous recoveries (which always seemed to coincide with the end of the school day) sooner. Similarly, I wonder why Tom and I didn't suspect the timing of the aches and pains when Matt would make it to school, but call later in the day from the nurse's office.

When phone calls from school persisted, I asked Matt one morning to put me on the line with the school nurse. I then asked her what she did in similar cases.

I think she noticed the frustration in my voice, because she responded reassuringly, "When there is no fever and just a stomachache, I have a child rest for twenty minutes and go back to class."

So that was what we did. The first few days that he tried these naps, a much happier Matt returned home from school. Once the novelty of a twenty-minute school break ended, however, Matt's ailments resumed. We had no doubt this was school-related stress.

■ ■ ■

In addition to keeping Matt in school, we were also having problems simply getting there on time. I recall dragging Matt from the sofa one morning shortly after the tardy bell so I could drive him to school, which was thankfully only a few minutes away.

My drop-off time coincided with driving Emma to high school. Her classes started later than the middle school's, so despite Matt's late arrival, she would make it on time—barely. There was no mistaking her annoyance about this.

After I let Matt out at the Swanson parking lot, Emma and I both noticed him wincing as he walked up the stairs to the school's front entrance.

"Mom, I am sure Matt is in pain, but I doubt he is hurting as much as he lets on," Emma said. "I think he is exaggerating this just to get attention."

Emma's tone of voice had changed unmistakably, and that comment stuck in my mind all day.

As usual, when Matt first came home, he was in good spirits, and his professed pain had disappeared. After dinner, I warned him about being late for school in the days ahead, and observed that all of these stomachaches and headaches seemed to be related to going to school.

"Matt, I know you believe that school is the main culprit, but if you continue to miss it, you will simply create more stress by falling further behind."

Matt looked at me without saying a thing. Then he reluctantly sat down at the dining room table and reached into his backpack very slowly, as if there were a snake inside ready to attack him. I noticed the look of resignation on his face as he pulled a few worksheets from his bag. If papers could have bitten him, I bet they would have.

■ ■ ■

Every year in mid-September, my friend and her husband held a "Bratfry" at their home. They provided the sauerkraut, bratwurst simmered in beer, and hot dogs and hamburgers on the grill for upwards of fifty people. It was a potluck meal, so all the guests brought side dishes and desserts. There was no shortage of food to eat.

Tom and I joined a table of friends who I knew from my reporting job. The wife of one of my colleagues taught ninth grade gifted children in Fairfax, Virginia, and I happened to mention that Matt had recently received an invitation to join an after-school program to her.

"That's probably an SOL prep session in disguise," she warned.

The State of Virginia required public school students to take and pass standardized tests (Standards of Learning, or SOLs) in math, English, science, and history in order to graduate.

Critics of this high-stakes testing, which included many of the teachers required to give the exams and the parents of many students who had to take them, opposed the exit examination as the sole measurement of a pupil's academic ability. Our teacher-friend was among those who believed SOLs were an inappropriate assessment method. She also was skeptical that teaching Matt to the test would do any good improving his grades or likelihood of passing the exams.

"Does that mean he will be putting himself farther behind for future SOL tests?" I asked her.

"If need be, so be it. Perhaps he will be more mature and capable of 'catching up' in a few years, or, even better, they'll change the ridiculous standards."

Ironically, Emma called the SOLs "a joke" because she was taking much harder exams in the International Baccalaureate program (IB) program. In her view, the state-required standardized tests were not worth preparing for because they did not apply to what she was studying.

Passing the standardized tests was a worry for Matt, but at least he wouldn't face them until the end of the year. It became increasingly apparent that there were more immediate concerns.

■ ■ ■

One evening, I looked at his assignment book only to discover his English teacher had written a note to Tom and me. Matt had not handed in five homework assignments, and he had an autobiography sketch due in a few days that he had not started.

I looked at the autobiography instructions. He was required to provide recollections from his first days in pre-school, kindergarten, and grades one through six. I shook my head in disbelief, wondering how many children could actually recall events spanning such a long time, especially before they'd started grade school.

When Emma heard about Matt's assignment, she took him aside and offered him advice that only an older sibling who has been through the homework wringer can give: "Just make something up."

I couldn't help but think that, in this case, she was right—especially for a child whose IEP noted he sometimes had problems with memory retention. However, as tempting as Emma's "solution" turned out to be, there had to be another way to fill in the blanks.

There was one obvious option: photo albums. And we had a ton of them. So even if Matt couldn't rely on remembering particular moments in his early childhood years, he could write about those captured in the photographs.

After the first few weeks of relative normalcy at Swanson, Tom and I had become very disappointed with Matt's school performance— not because of his lack of trying at home, but because of the lack of monitoring when he got there. How could his resource teacher be so clueless about how far behind he was in English and about the assignments he had done but not handed in?

■ ■ ■

That evening, Matt once again dissolved into tears. "I feel like a failure! All I ever get are Cs."

Handling grades in our household was tricky. While Tom and I would always congratulate Emma on her high GPA (she would later become one of the valedictorians in her senior class), we would invariably ask her not to talk about her grades in front of Matt. We were concerned that it would only make him feel worse.

Although we never compared Matt to Emma, we knew that alone was not enough to keep Matt from measuring his grades to her As and Bs. He so wanted to make the honor roll, just like his sister.

It was years before Emma told us how much that had hurt her and how resentful she was about it: "I just wanted to be able to celebrate my report card with my family." It was such a balancing act for Tom and me, trying not to shortchange Emma of the attention she deserved for her successes.

■ ■ ■

At the end of September, it was back-to-school night at Emma's high school. For us, it was mostly a social gathering with other parents, since there were no academic issues to discuss with teachers or guidance counselors.

I could see why one teacher was her favorite—not only did Emma like American history, but the teacher allowed the students to sneak in candy and soda, Emma told me later, with a mischievous look in her eyes.

A few days later, in sharp contrast, it was back-to-school night at Swanson. For Matt's classes, we became intimately acquainted with his teachers and the school services staff every year. Tom and I spoke with Matt's seventh grade school counselor. She assured us she would advise the teachers to give Matt a little latitude about homework when possible while he worked out his transition problem. We requested a meeting with Matt's teachers and school staff in early October.

The overall team seemed to be very supportive and willing to give him extra time to hand in his late homework, as long as he kept up with his current assignments. This was no consolation a few days later, however, when he couldn't find yet another misplaced book he had been reading for his Civil War studies. All these misplaced books and assignments were taking their toll on Matt.

"I'd like to be optimistic and think things will get better once he catches up, but another part of me says it is going to be a long school year," I told Tom while Matt was in the basement finishing a science assignment one evening.

■ ■ ■

Only a few days later, I found myself sitting next to Matt on his bed as he sobbed into his pillow. He was absolutely miserable at school, and he felt like a failure in French and just about every other subject.

He then told me what really bothered him: "It's the way they set up the classes as advanced, normal, and 'other.' They put me in 'other' for all of them."

A few days after, Matt worked himself into another frenzy at bedtime when he realized he wouldn't finish yet another assignment on time. This led to tears about how insensitive many of the kids were at school.

"My lab partners sometimes yell at me for not listening. They make fun of me and wave their hands in front of me because they say I'm zoning out and daydreaming!"

I began wondering if having Matt talk out his problems with Tom or me was enough.

"Maybe Matt should see a professional counselor. He really gets worked up, and his frustration level has escalated since the parent-teacher conference," I told Tom one evening at bedtime.

We wanted to address this as soon as possible, before he turned his frustration into anger and gave up on school altogether. Increasingly worried about Matt's emotional well-being, we made an appointment with Dr. McClintock, a pediatric neurologist. The doctor was low-key and kindly, good traits to have around a child who was stressed out by school. After I explained how overwhelmed Matt had become with his schoolwork, his trouble sleeping, and his frustration with being placed in less advanced classes, Dr. McClintock made an intriguing suggestion.

The doctor focused first on Matt's poor sleep cycle. He recommended phasing in an earlier bedtime and awakening him during weekends about fifteen minutes earlier than normal. Only after trying this new approach would he consider a prescription drug and even then, it would be a medication for attention problems, not to treat anxiety. In his view, if Matt could concentrate better in school and on his homework, it would lower his anxiety and improve his academic performance.

We tried Dr. McClintock's suggested sleep schedule, but we did not see any improvement. After a few weeks without success, the doctor prescribed 15 mg of Adderall to help him focus on his work.

At first, Matt did not notice any improvement. In fact, he lost his appetite, and it upset his stomach and made him dizzy. About a week later, however, we noticed that Matt had begun to work on his assignments patiently, in one-hour periods of time rather than the usual fifteen to twenty-minute spurts, when he was often distracted by the white noise of the television.

I also noticed that Matt's work was of much better quality, with none of the usual written scrawl or run-together sentences. Instead he typed everything out on the computer and it only needed minor editing.

■ ■ ■

Matt was taking band class at the end of the day. He was in the percussion section. Unlike his other classes, where he was seated all the time, Matt moved around to play various percussion instruments, including the triangle and cymbals. He said his dream someday was to own a drum set.

We noticed that whenever he talked about band practice, he spoke with self-confidence. This was also true of his skateboarding—although his love for pushing himself on a narrow wooden board proved to be hazardous one day, when he fell and landed on his left middle finger. Even though it hurt him, he seemed delighted by the novelty of needing to keep his left middle finger extended.

After an evening band meeting for parents, I had a chance to talk to Matt's band director and tell him what a big difference it had made for Matt during his difficult transition to seventh grade. I told him how his bandmates had welcomed him with open arms and really made a difference in how he felt about himself in class. Mr. Norris brightened when I shared this with him. He said that was how he saw the band—as a family that looked out for each other.

■ ■ ■

I began to hope that the Adderall was working. Unfortunately, just like other promising approaches, it proved to be only a temporary fix. Matt's improvements at school did not last, and once again, we faced long battles with homework and tears.

Matt continued to spend hours each night struggling to complete his homework; I was often seated right next to him for when he needed help on a math problem or writing assignment (his two hardest subject areas). One night, I found him crying in front of the computer as he worked on a Civil War composition.

"The days are so long and the evenings too short," he said, looking up at me with tears trickling down his cheeks. "Before you know it, it's bedtime and you have to start all over again."

In mid-November, I took Matt and Emma out to lunch, and all

seemed to go well until our ride home. As Emma and I chattered away about colleges she was considering looking at the following year, Matt sat quietly in the backseat of the car. He eventually broke the silence.

"I'll never go to college," he said softly.

My heart dropped.

When we got home, I asked Matt to get out the leaf blower, a chore he normally enjoyed; this time, he simply went through the motions. Then I suggested we take a bike ride to Glencarlyn Park, his favorite place for climbing rocks. I'd hoped this would cheer him up; instead, I was struck by the sadness in his eyes as he half-heartedly agreed to go.

Normally, Matt loved to race as fast as he could on the rolling hills of the bike path, leaving me easily a few good hundred feet behind him. This time, he rode slowly, only a short distance ahead of me. It was as if he had given up.

At bedtime that evening, he said he couldn't fall asleep, and he began to cry uncontrollably. The crying spell lasted long past midnight, so long that Tom suggested calling our health insurance company's twenty-four-hour nurse line.

It was reassuring to hear the nurse's calm voice. "Try making him some hot tea. Children often find that very comforting," she suggested.

It was nearly 2:00 in the morning before Matt calmed down enough to sip his tea. By the time he was able to fall asleep, the digital clock on his nightstand read 3:30.

I let Matt sleep in the next morning, and he woke up in fairly good spirits, particularly since part of the school day had already passed. However, when it came time to go to class, Matt began to cry again and simply wouldn't budge. At a loss, I decided to take the afternoon off from work to be with him.

One key factor in my ability to be with Matt during his school absences was the flexibility of my job. I was a reporter who specialized in covering domestic policy issues. I was extremely busy and worked long hours during the height of the congressional session, particularly in the areas of tax, budget, and health care law; however, I was able to take time off to be with my son during work days that did not require hour-to-hour coverage. A few skills that I'd honed as a reporter turned out to be invaluable in the years ahead: my ability to do research, write in clear, concise sentences, and ask precise, persistent questions, challenging school officials when necessary.

Of course, none of these skillsets were on my mind as I watched Matt on the floor of the living room that afternoon, working on a new knot for his climbing rope. He also tried to read *Harry Potter*, but couldn't concentrate. He rallied enough mid-afternoon to suggest we return to Glencarlyn, where he could use his climbing equipment at his favorite bouldering place.

I watched him scale the wall of rocks under overcast skies; there was an unmistakable chill in the air, a portent of the winter to come. When we walked back to the car, brown leaves rustled underneath our feet, and there was the comforting smell of wood smoke in the air.

I stopped for a few seconds and stared at the nearly bare-limbed trees silhouetting a faint pink sunset. Despite life's unforeseeable turns, I reminded myself to be mindful of its unexpected moments of beauty.

Matt did not have a crying spell that evening, but he refused to go to school again the next morning. He told me he was afraid to go back because he had been having "blue periods" during the day and he was afraid he would start crying in class.

At my wit's end, I called Dr. Goldman, who gave us the name of a child psychiatrist. Our question earlier in the school year of whether Matt needed to see a therapist had just been answered.

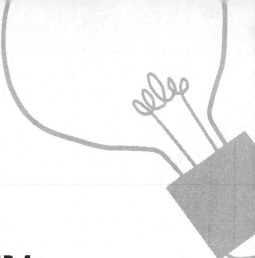

▪ CHAPTER 4 ▪

Wired and Tired
(1999–2000)

Matt began to see a psychiatrist the very next day. We had not expected it to happen so quickly, but the doctor recommended by our pediatrician had a cancellation in the morning. And so began Matt's weekly meetings with Dr. Welch.

When Tom and I first took Matt to Dr. Welch's office, we liked him from the start. The mild-mannered psychiatrist seemed to be well-suited for his profession. He was soft-spoken and had kind brown eyes.

Dr. Welch spoke kindly to Matt when he introduced himself. Not surprisingly, Matt was very shy, making very little eye contact and mostly offering yes and no answers when the doctor asked Matt about what had brought him there. It wasn't easy for a twelve-year-old to feel comfortable talking to a middle-aged man, though the doctor mostly nodded and played cards with him. Dr. Welch later explained to us that it was his way of putting his young patients at ease and helping them open up about what was troubling them. This strategy could take a long time, and sometimes, he cautioned, it would not work at all.

After it ended and Matt got into the car with us, he didn't mince words about his feelings.

"So, what do you think?" I asked him as he slid into the backseat.

"I think the whole thing is weird."

"How come?" Tom asked as we pulled out of the parking lot to head home.

Matt paused for a moment. "I don't like the way he paused after every answer I gave him to his questions."

I could tell by the sound of his voice that he was upset and irritated.

Tom then explained, "Dr. Welch does that because he is a good listener and wants to give you time to add extra information."

I think Tom's answer made Matt feel a little differently about his new doctor, even though it would still take time for him to get used to talking to a professional therapist. All in all, for a first visit, we thought it went relatively well.

Matt was in good spirits that evening, at least outwardly, although he later told me he'd still felt sad. He plodded along with his science homework and even showed enough interest to ask to camp out in the backyard so he could see a once-in-every-thirty-three-years display of stardust.

The thought of Matt staring into the night sky to catch a glimpse of the ephemeral trail of an ancient asteroid brought tears to my eyes. At times, I knew he felt so alone in a school world that didn't seem to understand him.

■ ■ ■

Matt was not the only child overwhelmed by school. I had recently found a parent group that met once a month in the juice bar section of a nearby organic food store to discuss issues arising from having children with learning disabilities. I decided to go to their next gathering.

I felt a mixture of hope and wariness when I walked into that grocery store. I wanted to explore every avenue of help I could find, but I also wanted to be realistic about discovering any grand solution to Matt's school woes.

There were several light wooden booths and tables adjacent to the beverage area, and the many windows and hanging potted ferns gave the room a warm, open feel. About a half-dozen women in their mid- to late-thirties were chatting easily with each other when I approached and introduced myself.

They welcomed me and then began sharing the latest challenges with teachers and homework and whether they had been successful in advocating for the specific education accommodations unique to their children's learning needs. One parent advised that the key to dealing with the school system when one approach had not worked was to ask, "So, what are you going to do about it?"

I mentioned that Matt's math teacher was resistant to cutting the number of algebra problems by half because she thought he might miss a concept.

"Then she should choose problems that ensure all the concepts are included, even if it means selecting the specific problems herself," advised one mother.

I left the group at the end of the evening feeling like these moms could be an invaluable source of support and information based on their many years of experience navigating the special education system.

Once I returned home, I told Tom about the challenges facing many of these parents and their children. Several kids had multiple disabilities—Asperger's syndrome, obsessive compulsive disorder, and other conditions with exotic sounding names. In comparison, Matt's learning issues seemed mild. This wasn't much comfort, but at least it made me feel a little relieved (if somewhat guiltily) that we weren't facing learning challenges of the same magnitude.

■ ■ ■

One evening after school, Matt grew particularly agitated and wanted to do something unrelated to homework. Tom and I had noticed in recent days that Matt's heartburn had returned with a vengeance, and he'd grown angry about his schoolwork more often and would frequently go down to the basement to beat on his drums.

I agreed to take a pre-dinner walk with him. During our walk, Matt disclosed that one of his classmates ran away from school (Matt didn't know why) and was later found at one of the county libraries.

I got the feeling he didn't blame him. Our son was not about to fly the coop, but some evenings he was simply too upset to focus on his work and get it done; the stress of the school day had just worn him out.

Matt had the perfect description of how he felt on those days: "Wired and tired." And unfortunately, for a good portion of the school year, he felt that way quite often.

■ ■ ■

The first parent-teacher conference day with Matt's seventh grade teachers and guidance counselor was held in early December, and couldn't come soon enough. In the twenty minutes allotted to us, we managed to hear encouraging words from some of his teachers: Matt was holding his own in American studies class, and he seemed to be coming out of his shell, at least in band, where one teacher saw him joking with the percussionists. The guidance director had also observed him talking at lunchtime with other students.

Tom and I also met with Dr. Welch one morning in early December. He thought more sessions were in order to try to get to the root of Matt's feelings of inadequacy. Thankfully, he said, Matt's social anxiety was lessening. Dr. Welch also told us to tell the teachers to continue to keep the pressure off about the homework.

During this period, we tried several different medications to treat his anxiety, some more effective than others. The combination of drug therapy and doctor visits was getting mixed results, and Matt's moods continued to fluctuate. Still, there were things to be hopeful for.

■ ■ ■

One evening in mid-December, Matt grew more frustrated over a homework assignment than usual. We didn't hear him at the time, but he went down into the basement bathroom and vented his anger in a way he never had before.

I was packing lunches the next morning when Emma came into the kitchen wrapped in a white bath towel. She walked quickly down the basement steps, in a hurry to take her shower. A few seconds later, she ran back up.

"Mom, come look at the shower," she said breathlessly.

Puzzled, I followed her quickly into the basement bathroom and looked at the white-tiled wall inside the shower. The soap bar holder and surrounding tiles dangled from the wall.

I looked at Emma in disbelief, then hurried up the basement stairs.

It had to be Matt. I remembered how upset he had been the previous night. This time it was bath tiles, but what if he began to turn his anger on others—or himself?

I had just made it back to the kitchen when I heard Matt's footsteps on the second floor, walking down the stairs from his bedroom. When he reached the bottom of the stairs, I stood there ready for him.

"Matt, what did you do!?"

He looked at me, but before he could answer, I told him to walk down to the basement and go into the bathroom. I followed behind him as he walked slowly toward it.

Instead of walking into the room, however, he suddenly halted.

He already knew the damage he had done.

Matt shook his head. Tears brimming, he said, "I'm so sick of school and I'm so tired of spending every night on homework. No matter what I do, I always fail."

I was deeply disturbed about how he had handled his anger, but at the same time, it was clear he was reaching his limit on how much he could take at school. At this point, though, I knew it was time to be a disciplinarian.

"Matt, what you did was wrong. Breaking things isn't the answer," I said firmly. "The next time you are so angry about something, don't go and break something. Talk to me!"

"I'm sorry, Mom," he said, with a hollow sound to his voice.

Judging from the distant look in his eyes, I wasn't sure he believed a single word that he said.

■ ■ ■

After this disturbing episode, I decided to talk to Matt's school counselor. Her suggestion caught me by surprise: if Matt was that overwhelmed, maybe Tom and I should consider homeschooling.

I knew one woman who homeschooled her child, and I had no idea how I could possibly do it with a full-time job. I also knew that, at least in the D.C. area, there was a stigma attached to homeschooling—thoughts of parents fearful of exposing their children to secular teaching sprung to mind. While I knew this wasn't the case for every child, I had never seriously considered homeschooling as an option.

Then again, I thought of one of Matt's classmates in his confirmation class at church. Kevin was so mature, self-confident, and sociable when I spoke with him after class. He had been homeschooled for several years, although, in his case, it was not due to any learning challenges. His parents were in the Foreign Service, and because of how frequently their family moved, they thought homeschooling made the most sense.

Although the circumstances were different, I began to ponder the idea of having so much flexibility in Matt's daily schedule. Kevin only spent about four hours a day on his subjects, and then spent the other half of his day going to museums or practicing piano.

I decided to off-handedly mention homeschooling to Matt to see how he felt about it. I thought he might find the alternative way of learning appealing, particularly since it could mean fewer hours of school lessons and the opportunity to go on field trips. Even though I had no clue how I could possibly teach him at home, I thought I could at least toss the idea out there as a possible option.

He nixed it right away.

"I want to be with my friends and don't want to be by myself all day," he told me. He added that the few kids he knew who stayed at home were "different," and that he didn't want to be looked at the same way.

I knew his blanket statement about homeschooled children was not true, but I must admit, I breathed a sigh of relief. I couldn't imagine quitting my job and being at home all day either.

■ ■ ■

It was about this time that we hired a house painter to do several rooms in our home. Bill Peters was a very friendly man, easy to take a liking to right away. I struck up a conversation with him on a day that Matt was home due to a bad stomachache.

Bill had noticed Matt sitting in the family room before he headed up to Matt's bedroom to paint it a pleasant blue with white trim. I explained that he wasn't feeling well, and half-jokingly noted that middle school had become Matt's least favorite subject.

"I never thought any grade of school was fun—except for my senior year," the house painter observed, breaking into a wide grin.

Yet, here he was with a successful business.

"The key is to find something you love to do and find someone to pay you for it," Bill said.

In Bill's case, he not only loved what he did, he was his own boss.

■ ■ ■

There continued to be one exception to Matt's anxiety about school: band practice. The second week of December, he came home and proudly told Tom and me that he had a solo in the holiday concert.

"I'm playing cowbells during 'Matador,'" he said excitedly.

On the evening of the performance, Matt looked so handsome in his black pants, white shirt, cummerbund and bow tie. When I said goodbye to him in the hallway leading to the band rehearsal room, Matt looked back at me with a nervous smile. But sure enough, after days of practice in what undoubtedly was his favorite seventh-grade class, Matt played the cowbells right on cue.

Unfortunately, the stage nervousness that he had overcome during the performance (and which hadn't stopped him from eating pizza beforehand or a load of cookies at intermission) finally got the better of him. Instead of heading back to his seat for the orchestra and symphonic concert, Matt headed hurriedly toward the school entrance and told me he wanted to go home.

"I don't feel well," he said, with a pleading look in his eyes.

At first, I thought he had a stomachache from all the goodies. Later, however, Matt told me he'd grown too anxious to stay, even though leaving the concert meant he'd missed the band party after it ended. Regardless of the real reason, we took him home.

Matt was in a stupor the next morning, and too weepy to consider school. I called Dr. Welch, and he advised keeping him home and restarting one of his anti-anxiety medications.

I had no luck getting Matt to do his homework, so I decided to take him on a trip to the animal shelter, hoping that the break would make him feel better enough to start his assignments. Interestingly enough, what actually snapped him out of his mood was his ability to put together Emma's new bed frame later in the day, after she and Tom were unable to figure it out.

"If they had only shown more patience instead of arguing with each other," Matt explained to me, sounding more like a parent than a child. He then proudly showed me how he'd fixed what the two of them had done wrong, and admitted it made him happy that he could solve the problem that they weren't able to.

"Competence makes you happy," Dr. Welch observed at Matt's next appointment.

Unfortunately, this was just a brief reprieve from his usual feelings of frustration. More often than not, I would hear upsetting reports from Matt after school.

"My science teacher got mad at me today. She said she called on me a lot of times, but I didn't answer." Matt tearfully went on, "When I was in English, the teacher said I wasn't paying attention, and someone threw a pencil at me!"

As the Christmas drew closer, I couldn't see how he would meet all his homework assignments before the break unless I helped him *a lot*. Even then, he might not be up for it and would possibly fail his exams.

Sometimes I wondered how Matt and I could continue our daily study routine. I remember how emotionally exhausting it was to mark every day by the number of homework assignments that were due. All my own free time revolved around Matt's homework—would he need my help that evening? Had I double checked his backpack that morning to make sure all his assignments were in it? Even though they were his responsibility, I felt like they were looming over my head, too, until he completed them.

■ ■ ■

I was shocked when Dr. Welch first mentioned it as an option: "Hospitalization."

The sound of the word triggered memories of a dear aunt's institutionalization in the early eighties, and how her son went against the facility rules to have her home for Christmas Eve.

Dr. Welch wasn't talking about a state-run psychiatric institution, thankfully, but a local hospital that provided short-term stays for children and adolescents struggling with emotional problems. While they were there, the hospital worked with the school system to keep them on track academically.

Nonetheless, I was very relieved at the conclusion of our morning appointment in mid-December, when Dr. Welch assured Tom and me that he did not think intensive therapy would be the best route to take—at least, not yet. Instead, he wanted us to once again drop one medication, adjust the time of taking another, and add an anti-depressant to the mix. My head would spin sometimes from trying to keep track of all the changes in Matt's medicines and dosages.

Matt was supposed to go to school that day after the morning session with Dr. Welch, but he fell apart in the car and at home, to the point that I told him we would wait it out a day so that he could have a better night's rest. His mood was better off and on throughout the day. He certainly relaxed and became more affectionate once he knew school was not looming. He even joked when I assured him that he would feel better in the long run.

"Yeah, about fifty-six miles long," he said with a weak smile.

■ ■ ■

Although Matt's mood improved over the course of the day, Emma was none too happy when she found out her brother had once again missed school.

"I don't feel sorry for Matt," she told me in the kitchen. The look on her face and tone of voice gave away her mixture of hurt and resentment.

It was so difficult to find enough time to spend with Emma when I was often consumed by trying to keep Matt afloat. Performing this balancing act could have developed into a firestorm of accusations between us, or even between her and Matt. With Emma, though, if there was a tinderbox lit inside of her, she usually kept it to herself. She only occasionally complained to me about her brother.

For my part, I tried to set aside time for just the two of us throughout our family trials with Matt, but those times together were much too fleeting. Emma nearly always worked independently on her homework assignments, though one memorable evening, I was able to keep her from pulling an all-nighter.

It was shortly before midnight, and Emma was still not up in her bedroom. I was a night owl and normally did not go to sleep until later, so I headed down to the basement den to see what she was doing. I found her sitting on the carpet with a drawing pad and several crayons scattered around, working madly away.

She had to make two copies of illustrations and color each of them for a book report on literary legends (she had chosen the tale of Robin Hood), but she was beside herself because she was only halfway through the first copy.

Why on earth the teacher didn't simply ask the students to Xerox a second copy was beyond me, but seeing her near tears, I offered to help. We colored pictures of Robin Hood, his band of Merry Men, and Sherwood Forest well into the early hours of the morning.

■ ■ ■

An equally daunting challenge was finding ways for Emma and Matt to spend time with each other. Even if Matt and Emma had been close-knit, it would have been difficult for him to compete with her numerous school activities, homework, and girlfriends. Plus, at age fifteen, most girls don't want to spend time with a younger brother, whether he's having difficulties in school or not.

However, we did find one common interest that at least temporarily created a bond between them.

For the past several months, Emma and Matt had been lobbying for a puppy, and their persistence finally paid off. Shortly before Christmas, we picked out a black miniature schnauzer from a breeder at a livestock farm in White Plains, Maryland, a rural area about thirty miles from our home.

The only name the four of us could agree on was "Lucky" (not a particularly imaginative one). Both Emma and Matt were elated about having their new puppy and spent many hours playing with Lucky. Matt even cheerfully took care of him before school, laying out bowls of food and fresh water a few minutes before grabbing his bag and heading out the door.

■ ■ ■

Despite the excitement of a new dog, Matt's happiness at home was counterbalanced by stressful days at school. He came home early a few days after the puppy purchase, complaining of a stomachache. When I asked how the day went, he said, "Sucky."

Tom and I wondered more and more if he would need intensive therapy after the holidays. School simply seemed to overwhelm him so much, and his interim progress report didn't help matters. His grades were okay, but he was still expected to hand in all his makeup work and do a cell project presentation the next day!

I had a reassuring conversation with the counseling director. She assured me that the staff was there to support him and us. She even told us they could let this semester go by ungraded, if needed.

There were only a few more days before winter break. One of the days, Matt's class had a field trip scheduled to visit a local university and watch five short holiday plays. I thought he would be excited about this trip—at least as excited to skip class as to go on the outing.

I was wrong.

He had started out the day okay enough, getting up and eating his warm banana waffle, but by the time I returned from dropping off Emma at high school, he was sobbing quietly to himself and huddled up in a ball on the family room couch.

I made the all-too-familiar phone call to the school to tell them Matt would not be attending. After that, I called Dr. Welch and left a message.

I returned to the family room. Matt hadn't budged, still curled up like an infant in the womb, not ready to be born.

I padded to the sofa and looked down on my son, at a loss for words. I had been grasping at straws for so many days. I tried to find a reason for him to go to a school that beat down harder and harder on him every time he set foot in the door. Could I honestly tell him that if he went to school, he would do better in his classes, or that his grades would improve? Did I actually believe that this would set the groundwork for a successful future career? How could I tell him any of these things when I doubted them myself?

The best I could think of was only four words, a brief sentence fashioned because there was absolutely nothing else to say. As I bent down closer to him, I spoke my words softly:

"Do it for me," I told Matt. "Do it for me."

Matt turned around and looked up at me, as if my eyes alone held the answer. Then he ever-so-slowly uncurled his body and rose off the sofa.

Reluctantly, Matt walked over to his backpack, which was leaning against the wall in the front hallway. He put on his winter jacket, black woolen cap, and warm gloves. I grabbed the car keys from a straw basket in the kitchen.

As he hoisted the canvas bag over his shoulder, he looked back at me.

When he spoke, I could hear the resignation in his voice.

"I'm ready to go, Mom."

Then he walked out the door.

▪ CHAPTER 5 ▪

Mixed Signals
(2000)

C hristmas break at last. Just like previous years, Matt was in good
spirits while we visited my family in Pennsylvania over the holidays.
And with no schoolwork immediately hanging over his head once we got
back home, he was calm and happy, especially playing with our brand-
new puppy.

On the afternoon of New Year's Eve, Matt joined Tom and me when
we took Lucky for a sunny walk in the park. The three of us planned to
go to a friend's home for a party that evening while Emma spent the night
out with her girlfriends.

As we were just about ready to go, Matt noticed some itchy red welts
all over his back and arms. Certain they were hives, Tom suggested we
stop at the emergency room on our way to the celebration so that Matt
could get a cortisone shot.

Not surprisingly, the holiday hospital staff was sparse; as a result,
to the great disappointment of us all, Matt wasn't released until a few

minutes before midnight. The television was on in the emergency room lobby, and we could hear the countdown as the giant silver ball slowly made its dramatic descent at Times Square.

"Ten…Nine…Eight…Seven…"

I glanced around at the few stone-faced patients waiting to be seen.

Suddenly, the year 2000 flashed on the TV screen. As the crowd roared in New York, Tom and I kissed, and then Matt joined us in a great big bear hug.

By the time we left the hospital, it was too late to drive to our friend's party, but we hadn't eaten dinner, since we had expected to dive into plenty of food once we'd gotten there. Facing no particularly good choices, we decided that pizza would be our best hope. We scouted the few pizza joints in our neighborhood, but each one we passed was closed. Realizing it was an exercise in futility, we made our way home.

As Tom pulled into the driveway, he tried to find the humor in it all. As soon as we all stepped out of the car, the moment of inspiration came to him.

"Sucky New Year!" he exclaimed at the top of his lungs.

And he was right. It certainly was an unusual way to ring in the year 2000.

In retrospect, it seems so clear that Matt's hives that evening were symptoms of his anxiety—the anxiousness borne from the reality that school was only a few days away.

■ ■ ■

Matt's anxiety and academic problems intensified almost as soon as he walked through the school door after winter break. Just in the first week back, Matt forgot his social studies book with an SOL review assignment in it.

Matt confided that he sometimes lost his train of thought, or nodded when people talked to him without actually following the conversation, and a good friend had begun kidding him about having a girl's voice and being spoiled because he could come to school so late. I told Matt that he needed to toughen up a bit about the teasing, but I wondered to myself how the year could possibly get better. Tom and I knew our primary goal was to get him through the rest of seventh grade without feeling like a failure.

■ ■ ■

There was one saving grace for Matt early that semester: his science project, the once-a-year assignment that kept teachers guessing how much of each exhibit was the student's own doing and how much involved "parental supervision."

In Matt's case, it was one take-home assignment he worked on enthusiastically by himself. He immersed himself so completely in his project that one night, he voluntarily turned down an invitation to play basketball or go to a movie in order to work on it. I fondly remember Matt even smooching me a few times as he worked patiently on his display board. As much as he struggled with assignments, we knew he always looked forward to doing hands-on work.

Still, Matt was not thrilled about every one of the project's requirements; his good spirits faded when it was time to do his oral presentation. The evening before it was due, he practiced his talk in front of Tom and me. He started out just fine, but dissolved into tears shortly after I asked a question about his procedure.

"I can't do this. I get nervous standing up in front of a class," he cried.

Knowing how hard he had worked on his project and how defeated he could feel if he froze in front of a classroom full of his peers, I decided to write a note to his science teacher. I asked her to exempt Matt from giving the oral report and just have him discuss the project informally with her, perhaps during a lunch period.

Matt looked relieved when I mentioned my idea to him. Unlike so many homework assignments that he did at home and then forgot to hand in the following day, Matt said he remembered to give my note to his teacher right away.

It was all for naught.

I wasn't terribly surprised. I had not been optimistic that the teacher would settle for any alternative presentation, no matter how hard Matt had worked to collect the information. I'd met Mrs. Deville at a few IEP meetings, and her teaching philosophy seemed to be as rigid as a scientific formula; she wouldn't stray from it, regardless of extenuating circumstances.

I asked Matt about his presentation as soon as he came home the following afternoon.

"It went okay," he said, but he sounded disappointed.

Matt earned a C on his oral report, but that was only part of his overall grade. The remainder was based on a paper about the results of his project, and once again, he shone. Matt readily worked on the final science paper, earning an A on the second version of his rough draft.

His final grade for the project was an A-. It was clear that when Matt could apply what he'd learned to an actual project—when he could see the link between academics and what he could produce from that knowledge—he succeeded.

■ ■ ■

As the new year slipped into February, there were good and not-so-good days. During these up-and-down periods, I had to remind myself to take breathers, even if only for a few moments at a time.

One of my favorite parts of the weekday was walking the puppy before I got ready for work. Lucky saw something new and exciting every day, whether it was a garbage truck or a piece of paper. When I was out looking at the world through the eyes of our dog, my mind could wander on all things not-Matt-related.

The sidetracking was therapeutic for me, but I would grow exasperated sometimes with Matt when I found him playing with Lucky instead of doing his homework. One evening and one time too many, I saw Matt take a puppy break and I grew exasperated.

"Oh, Matt Michael!" I said.

He always knew I was really upset when I called him by both his first and middle name.

"I'm sorry. I won't do it again," he said, running downstairs and into the bathroom. He came out a few minutes later visibly upset and wiping away tears.

"This happens to me all the time. I can't keep up with everything," he said.

Seeing his tears, I felt badly for him; any anger I had felt melted away.

"I know it's hard to do your work. Just remember, your family loves you," I said.

Matt looked at me and calmed down. His understanding and acceptance seemed exceptionally adult. We hugged, and after some encouraging words, he calmly finished his social studies and some of his math.

■ ■ ■

It was subtle at first, but Tom and I began to notice an improvement in Matt's attitude about school and homework during the first few weeks of February. He even began to see some humor in his anxiety over schoolwork. When his guidance counselor worked with his teachers to scale back his homework to manageable amounts for the evenings, Matt deadpanned, "It's really been a big help paying off the teachers."

In late February, I met with Matt's core teachers and received good reviews: he was more engaged in most of his classes and he participated more in class discussions. One of his teachers still complained of missing assignments, but when I checked the list, I saw it was all work he had done on time, but had not handed in.

How wonderful it was to have some normal days again, without tears from Matt over homework, stressed-out, wakeful nights, or stay-at-home spells.

■ ■ ■

Dr. Welch noticed the changes, too, and concluded in February that Matt's mood had stabilized to the degree that it was no longer necessary for both Tom and me to come to every appointment. By mid-March, Dr. Welch noted the steady improvement in Matt's social anxiety in school and decided to keep his medications at the same level.

After that session, Matt told me it was becoming a lot easier for him to talk in school. He began spending time on weekends skateboarding with some of his schoolmates; it was such a relief to see Matt's circle of friends expanding again.

In fact, the only thing that he didn't like about his regular sessions with Dr. Welch was the difficulty he had keeping them from his friends. He told them he had drum lessons during the week. (His real drum lessons were on Saturdays.)

Matt gave his science teacher the same excuse when she told him he had to attend a meeting after school. Not knowing he actually had a doctor's appointment, she told him that if he didn't go to the meeting, he could not go on a class canoe trip. When Matt told us about his predicament, we quietly explained his real after-school commitment to Mrs. Deville. It was resolved before the trip and Matt was able to join the rest of his science class on their outing.

This incident made me think about the stigma he feared for seeing a psychiatrist, an aspect of his life that he rarely talked about. While everything on the surface seemed to be going smoothly for Matt, I wondered if beneath it all, he thought there was still something wrong with him. I'm sure it was hard enough for him to deal with the day-to-day challenges of school—trying to keep up with his work while seeing other classmates succeed and spending every night struggling over his homework—but on top of that, he had to see a shrink.

■ ■ ■

Then there was the papaya.

In early April, Matt had to write a paper about vegetation that grew in tropical climates, and he chose to write about a papaya. He accompanied Emma and me to one of the branch libraries one chilly afternoon so he could check out some books on his assignment. I tried to make this a brief visit, since Emma needed to get back home to work on her own schoolwork.

Matt had no luck with his online search, but while he was on the computer, I found four good print sources. I was still leafing through the rainforest books when Emma came over to me in the children's section.

"You know Matt is looking at snowboarding books," Emma commented.

In retrospect, I realize this was one of many times I helped him to do his work, thinking it would help shave some time from what was bound to be another long homework assignment.

Consequently, since he had run a search for the right subject online, I let him leaf through books on the wrong subject briefly. In my mind, it was lesson enough for him not to be allowed to take the contraband books home. While Matt might have excelled in getting sidetracked, I was running a close second on rationalizing it.

■ ■ ■

Matt had two full weeks to finish his project, and because it involved hands-on work, he was engaged. He completed—*on time*—an essay about the papaya, enthusiastically gluing a picture of the juicy fruit he had found online to his title page. He patiently finished the bibliography and report cover.

But what he most enjoyed doing was making a model of the papaya. I remember him sitting on the kitchen floor with his watercolors and stack of newspapers, slapping one layer of pasty paper at a time to a mold of the tropical fruit fashioned out of playdough. He also used real seeds from a papaya he had bought at a neighborhood grocery store. He painted the outside a dark green and the inside of it shades of pink.

His diligence and pride in his work reminded me of when he was a small child, showing me the photos he had selected for his grade school autobiography. I imagined how pleased he would be to hand in the work he had spent hours creating, and wished there were more assignments where he could work with his hands.

A few days later, Matt returned home with his essay and papaya.

"How did you do on your project?" I asked, smiling broadly.

Without any expression on his face, Matt replied in a flat voice: "I got a C."

"Why?" I asked, dumbfounded.

"Mrs. Deville said I was supposed to build a model of the plant. Not the fruit."

I suppose some children would have been so angry that they would have thrown away their papaya. Matt simply set it down on the kitchen table and walked away.

I was angry about what I perceived as the teacher's insensitivity. *Surely she knew about Matt's difficulty following directions and his record of incomplete assignments. He spent hours writing and putting together his report. Didn't that count for something? He spent hours making an amazing, life-like model of the fruit, sliced open to reveal its juicy pulp.*

I walked briskly into the living room where Matt sat on the sofa, immersed in a television program.

"I can't believe Mrs. Deville would give you a C. You worked so hard on this!"

I'd thought that my outrage over this might at least make him feel better about his low mark, but Matt just looked up at me. He remained silent and expressionless. It was clear, regardless of how he really felt, that he didn't want to talk about it. Had he simply resigned himself to working hard at home and not succeeding at school?

■ ■ ■

In late April, it was time for another in our endless series of IEP meetings. There were a few strengths included in the report: the teachers recognized Matt's general knowledge and that when he participated in discussions, he asked good questions and demonstrated good verbal expression.

In general, Matt's organizational skills and writing had not improved, but he was much happier with his classmates and applying himself at home. Teaching him to advocate for himself in class and remember to hand in his work were still major hurdles.

Although there was some improvement, the frequency of Matt's tardy arrivals and absences was still concerning. There were nearly twenty-five infractions, all combined. The sheer number surprised me, but they had become such a common occurrence that they simply had blurred all together.

Matt's inattentiveness in class was still an issue. In an attempt to say something encouraging, one of the teachers at the meeting noted that recent studies had found that everything clicked between the ages eighteen and twenty-one for boys with ADHD and poor organizational skills, as long as they were kept on the education track.

Matt was only a few weeks short of his thirteenth birthday.

Great—only five to eight years to go.

■ ■ ■

While there were still ups and downs in Matt's progress as May wore on, we noticed he was doing a lot of assignments at home on his own, without any prodding or assistance. When I mentioned this to Emma one evening, frustrated, she quickly replied, "You mean how everyone usually works."

Matt took up a lot of my time, and sometimes that took a toll on Emma and our mother-daughter relationship. Tom and I would attend every crew competition and school concert, and we always made a point of eating dinner as a family, but Emma and I rarely had special one-on-one moments. I tried to set aside time for just the two of us, but like many parents with children who have disabilities, I missed opportunities. When those special times did occur, though, I cherished every minute.

There were simple, unexpected moments, like the one day in early February when an unpredicted snowstorm swept along the East Coast, closing down the federal government and all local schools. It was nasty weather until nightfall, when Emma took a few moments' reprieve from her own studies to take a walk with me. On our way home, she plunged into the snow flat on her back, then, waving her arms up and down, made a snow angel. I smiled as she reminded me that even the most sophisticated tenth graders weren't too old to play in the snow.

During many hard times over the years, I reminded myself of Emma's Mother's Day card. It was two pages long! She wrote a long list of what she wanted to say thanks for, including making her lunch every day, packing her crew snacks, waking her eight times in the morning without raising my voice, waking her up at four in the morning and driving her to crew, playing with her hair, making rules because I cared, telling her she deserved things, teaching her values, giving her strength and teaching her to value her strengths, reading her Nancy Drew until one of us fell asleep, staying up until two in the morning to help her color in pictures, giving her the appreciation of sunsets and being outdoors, making her feel like the best, teaching her to be humble, crying at the end of cheesy movies and anything involving little kids at church, making her happy, never being angry at her for too long, being the best mother ever, and making her proud to be my daughter.

I laughed and cried when I read the list. What a sweetheart she was to have found the time to write all of this on a busy weekend, revealing her thoughtfulness and sensitivity as well as her honesty, humor, and her beautiful ability to express herself. Whenever I felt that I wasn't the best housekeeper or journalist in the world, I remembered this card, because trying to be the best mom and raising such caring children beat all the other pursuits, hands down!

Though they happened all-too-infrequently, our special mother-daughter outings were incredible experiences that I still treasure. Emma has always been beautiful, inside and out, and watching other people delight in her company has always made me exceptionally proud. One evening during the Christmas holidays in 1999, I took Emma to a special holiday show downtown, and a friend who was at the performance took a picture of the two of us standing in front of a beautifully decorated Christmas tree. She remarked how grown-up and beautiful Emma had become; I made sure to repeat the compliment to Emma later, as I showed her a copy of the picture.

One evening in mid-May, I thought of a special gift I could give to Emma for her sixteenth birthday: a train trip to New York for a weekend that summer, just the two of us, doing whatever she wanted to do. Tom thought this was a great idea, too. I was so excited that it was hard to keep it a secret until her birthday on June 7, and I was delighted in mid-July, when it was finally time to take Emma to the Big Apple.

It was pouring buckets when our Amtrak train arrived at Penn Station, but we made the best of it. After checking in at the stately Mayflower Hotel, we sought shelter in several department stores.

Thankfully, the weather cleared by the evening, so we dined outdoors in Little Italy. I thoroughly enjoyed eating pasta, sipping red wine, and conversing pleasantly with my lovely, poised, sweet daughter. Afterwards, we walked along the streets illuminated by strings of white lights, making sure to stop at a few vendors who seemed to specialize in knock-off Rolexes and designer bags. Emma bought a "Gucci" watch for ten dollars, a dramatic markdown from the regular price of $5,000. We limited ourselves to a few more purchases, including two silver necklaces that seemed to be legitimate.

On Sunday, Emma and I woke up to sunshine streaming through our windows overlooking Central Park. We took a leisurely morning stroll through the southern part of the park, walking by the lake and gazebo as we looked across at the castle before brunch time at the Russian Tea Room, where we feasted on scrumptious cheese blintzes, mixed fruit, and sliced cinnamon apples. We spent the afternoon enjoying the bustling crowds and even posed in front of the marquee announcing it was the last week of *Cats*.

Emma and I both were reluctant as we headed back to the train station for our ride home. Looking back on that weekend in New York, I must admit it was the last time for a long time I would give her the undivided attention she deserved.

■ ■ ■

Matt's birthday is on May 25, thirteen days ahead of Emma's. When they were younger, that meant holding two birthday parties within two weeks of each other and breathing a sigh of relief when both of them were over. As they got older, we celebrated with dinners out instead.

This year was a special one for Matt, since he was officially becoming a teenager. When the big day arrived, he was determined to celebrate every minute possible—even staying up past midnight to welcome it in.

"Three more minutes and I'll be a teenager!" Matt said when I came into his bedroom at 11:57 on May 24. I stayed at his bedside, and we joked until 12:01.

"Two more years and I can get my permit," Matt said with a grin. "Three more years and I can get my license. Eight more years and I can drink and drive!" he joked.

I think the excitement got to him; his stomach was too upset to dig into his Baskin & Robbins' frozen mud pie. It remained in the freezer, although Matt took it out once to "admire it."

■ ■ ■

The following weekend, Matt took an overnight band trip to Hershey, Pennsylvania. I still remember how excited and cute he looked before he left, snuggling for a few minutes with Lucky on the kitchen floor before grabbing the backpack that held his change of clothes. I thoroughly enjoyed that Saturday morning myself; I volunteered to register runners for a 5K race sponsored by the middle school to raise money for the homeless.

When Matt alighted from the bus again that afternoon, he was holding a huge stuffed animal that he'd won at the amusement park. Unfortunately, he also disembarked with the flu bug that bit many of the students on the trip. I had no doubt the first few days he stayed home from school that he was genuinely ill. However, as the week progressed, his flu symptoms went away, replaced by the all-too-familiar headaches and stomach pains.

The string of school absences meant he was falling behind in his classwork, which only exacerbated the stress that undoubtedly caused all his body aches. At one point, he even claimed that his back and neck hurt so badly he couldn't move them. Recalling the issues Emma had experienced with a compressed nerve in her neck, Tom and I decided to have Matt checked out by a chiropractor.

As a precaution, Dr. Ames took x-rays of Matt's spine (which Matt mistakenly referred to as "electroshock therapy"). Afterwards, the doctor asked me to accompany him to an adjacent room to look at the results. Except for a few slight curvatures, the neck looked fine. In other words,

Matt's pain in the neck was likely due to a pain in his head, otherwise known as anxiety or stress.

Dr. Ames recommended, in extremely diplomatic terms, that Matt resume some of his outdoor activities. "The fresh air would be good for you," he coaxed.

■ ■ ■

Matt seemed in fine spirits later and even took his skateboard out before dinner. Emma had a band concert that evening, something Matt wasn't overly eager to attend. Since he had several makeup assignments to do, I asked him to do one of his easier ones while we were gone.

When we came home, I stopped in the bathroom. I was surprised to notice fine clumps of blonde hair in the sink. Puzzled, I walked into the family room to ask Matt about it, thinking perhaps he had decided to give himself a trim.

As a tribute to turning thirteen, Tom and I had allowed him to dye his hair a light shade of blonde, much like the color it had been when he was a toddler. I'd figured this was a harmless enough indulgence on my part; it wasn't like he'd wanted to sacrifice his locks to the Goth look.

He was lying on his left side on the sofa; I walked over and asked him to get up. Tom and Emma had come into the family room, too. To our horror, when he sat up, we saw that Matt had pulled out a strip of his hair from front to back about two- to three-inches wide—too wide for a comb over.

Matt began to whimper. After we calmed him down, he told us he'd done it because he'd grown frustrated and angry about schoolwork. I was afraid the problem was deeper than that; fearing that he might do something to harm himself, I called Dr. Welch. He did not answer, so I left a frantic message.

Dr. Welch called back shortly and told me not to panic. Matt's hair pulling was more than likely due to sheer frustration over his school problems and anger at himself rather than any desire to hurt himself. He suspected Matt had been pulling his hair for a while, noting he had worn a baseball cap for the entirety of his last session.

Slightly reassured by this, our next concern was how his classmates would react when they saw him. Emma saved the day with an alibi. She suggested that he tell everyone he had tried to frost his hair, but left the peroxide in so long that it had burned the roots.

Apparently, his classmates bought his "burnt roots" story.

Matt asked to go to a hair salon after school to see if they could repair the damage. He was leaning toward having a buzz cut, but when I picked him up later, I was stunned to see his new look. He had decided that rather than a buzz cut, he would have his entire head shaved so it would all grow back at the same time.

The stylist, to my chagrin, said there was a possibility that Matt's hair cells were damaged and that the hair might not grow back.

"Then I'll have to use Rogaine," Matt joked, seemingly unperturbed by the prospect.

Matt's bald pate even became a source of inspiration for two of his school assignments. For his magazine ad project, he chose the hair renewal product; for his school assembly on the seventies, he decided to play "Kojak," a popular television show character in that era about a bald New York City police detective known for carrying his trademark lollipop while solving violent crimes.

Thankfully, Matt's hair pulling never happened again. Looking back, I remember thinking it was simply a small dip in his progress, probably set off by the stress of getting sick after a band trip.

■ ■ ■

In mid-June, Matt almost missed the Kojak skit because he felt too anxious to perform on stage. With a little gentle nudging from Tom and me, he made it to school. I held my breath as he walked on the stage, dressed in a dark suit and sucking on a lollipop. He remembered all his lines, and Tom and I were so proud of him.

Despite his successful performance, Matt resisted going to school the next morning, curling up in a ball until nearly ten. I told him if he didn't get to school at a reasonable hour, we would not go to the ski liquidator shop to fix his skate wheel and he could not play after school with his friends. There were consequences to his choices; those consequences were not punishments, but the results of his voluntary decisions, a message echoed by Dr. Welch.

■ ■ ■

Matt's seventh grade school year ended with mixed results. Thanks to scaled-back homework, makeup assignments, and extended time to do them, he was able to complete the year with average grades.

However, I realize now how analogous Matt's papaya project and his Kojak character were to his seventh-grade experience. The time and concentration that it took for him to painstakingly shape and color the pulp of that delicious fruit was not recognized or valued by his teacher, even though he had applied what he'd learned about the tropical plant in his presentation and written report. On the other hand, Matt's hair-pulling could have devastated him, but instead, his quick mind and natural sense of humor prevailed, and he saved the day with Kojak, a hands-on solution.

■ ■ ■

One evening shortly after the school year ended, I asked Matt where he was on a scale of one to one hundred, with one hundred being the most anxious.

Matt paused for a moment to give the question careful thought, then he looked at me and answered, "Seventy-five."

I was very puzzled; I'd thought there would be notable improvement in his anxiety level since his major stressor, school, was over for ten weeks.

A few days later, we talked to Tom's sister, who was the principal of a school for emotionally disturbed children. Joyce did not seem overly concerned about Matt's anxiety problems. She said she found it surprising only in that he seemed to be so happy whenever she saw him. "You'd never know it to look at him."

■ ■ ■

While some of Matt's anxiety was puzzling, there were also instances when it was understandable.

One Sunday morning, I slept in until 9:30. It was too late for us to attend our usual service at church, so we went to another church instead, arriving halfway through the sermon.

We'd no sooner sat down in our pew when I realized the pastor had raised what was likely to be a touchy subject with Matt (particularly given his prior reaction to Nostradamus' end-of-world predictions). The sermon was all about death.

"Death can come at any time," the pastor declared in a surprisingly upbeat voice. "Why, think of all the people who live recklessly and die young just so they will have a beautiful corpse." He then added that he looked forward to presiding over the funerals of many in the parish—"Old and young alike!"

Emma and I exchanged glances at the last comment. Then I looked at Matt; I could tell right away the priest's words had blown him away. His face was as white as a bleached sheet. He looked at me, expressionless, and asked to leave—quickly.

Emma remained until Mass had just about ended. While we waited, Matt and I talked about how the priest needed to work on his delivery. I thought of much more light-hearted subjects, and told him about a friend of mine who was in her late sixties but looked about twenty years younger. When I told him the problem she had finding boyfriends since, at her age, they were either married or unavailable, he piped in, "Or dead."

Well, at least he managed to find some gallows humor in the demise of young and old alike.

■ ■ ■

On the Fourth of July, our family went to downtown Washington to watch the fireworks. I drove into town early in the morning and parked close to where we would view the fireworks and also to the bridge we would use to skedaddle out of town once the pyrotechnics had ended. We had learned this trick to avoid the post-event traffic jam from years of experience.

It was hot and sticky outside that evening, and almost as soon as the show started, Matt began to feel anxious. Tom and I looked at each other, then back at Matt's ashen face. Emma, on the other hand, was oohing and ahhing over every spectacular display.

"Emma, honey, we have to go," I told her.

A look of surprise, then disappointment, spread over Emma's face. She glanced over at Matt and realized why we were making such a quick exit. She sighed, shook her head, and without saying a word, joined us as we walked around the jammed crowd of spectators all looking upward at the incredible light show in the evening sky.

Our plan to escape from the noise backfired. As we headed quickly to the car, the boom of the fireworks reverberated between the government office buildings, echoing the sounds even louder than they had been on the grounds of the Mall.

Once home, Matt unwound by setting off his own fireworks at a neighborhood park (they were far quieter) before cuddling with the dog until bedtime.

The sound of fireworks bothered Matt a bit again the next day when he heard them being fired off from a distance in the neighborhood.

When I mentioned the fireworks episodes to Dr. Welch at Matt's next appointment, the doctor posited there were several factors at play: "It's likely that Matt preferred the ones at the park, not only because there was far less noise, but because they were under his control."

We decided to stay away from the D.C. crowd the next year, knowing that Emma would be old enough to go downtown with her friends if she wanted.

■　■　■

Matt was not wracked with anxiety for the entire summer. In August, his confidence and leadership skills once again soared during a week of Sportrock camp. In the middle of the week, he came home beaming: he had climbed the highest of any of the campers.

The class had a wonderful ratio, with seven students and two instructors. Matt thought all the kids were nice, and unlike the previous year's novice grade schoolers, this group was older and comparable to his skill level. What a difference we could see in Matt when he could be among his peers, participating as an equal or, in this case, even outshining some of them with his climbing techniques! His instructors marveled at how nimble he was scaling each rock and what a natural he was at figuring out the best route to climb and how to position himself as he scaled each cliff.

Yet Matt never bragged about being better than anyone else in camp. He was simply excited that he was good at something he loved to do and that he could share this passion for climbing with others.

■ ■ ■

On my birthday at the end of July, the family took me to an Italian café for dinner. I ruminated about how fortunate I was to have such a loving family. Even though we had our rough patches, overall, it had still been a year to be thankful for. God never promised us a rose garden.

My birthday was on the last day of July, the eve of the most relaxing month of the year. August was the slowest month for my job, so I usually took two or three weeks off, one of which we spent at Bethany Beach, Delaware. It was a perfect quiet getaway for families, yet close enough to Rehoboth Beach, with its busier boardwalk and greater selection of restaurants and shops (attractions that grew greater as the children grew older).

■ ■ ■

As much as our family loved beach time, school loomed in the not-too-distant future once we returned. Right before eighth grade began, Dr. Welch offered a few tips on building Matt's self-esteem while holding him more accountable for his actions. He suggested that Tom and I should tell Matt that no matter what his label was at school, he was always special to us—not because of ADHD or any other diagnosis, but because he was our son. Dr. Welch also emphasized that I needed to lay off the homework assistance. "That sends the wrong message all around."

Maybe that means I could have more of a personal life during the school year and even take up piano lessons, I remember thinking.

It didn't take long for me to realize, however, that eighth grade would turn out to be one of the most demanding years of Matt's life—and, consequently, mine.

▪ CHAPTER 6 ▪

Rockin' Round the Clock
(2000)

Matt had barely started eighth grade when a new problem arose: he wasn't able to stay awake in class. This wasn't just an occasional nodding off during a lesson—this was full-blown body jerks and a head-down-on-your-desk, deep sleep that pulled Matt in within minutes of sitting down in his chair.

Falling asleep at night was also a disaster for Matt. By the end of the first week, he was awake until five o'clock in the morning. I even resorted to giving him a strong jolt of coffee before school, just to get him out the door on time.

Barely a week passed before we received the first phone call from Matt's guidance counselor. Mrs. Murphy told us she was already getting complaints from Matt's teachers about his excessive sleepiness and how difficult it was to teach his classmates while he slept soundly in the room. They were also understandably frustrated that an inordinate amount of *their* time each day was spent trying to get Matt to stay awake—time that could have been used to teach the rest of the students.

I couldn't blame them. Once again, Tom and I were at a loss for what to do.

■ ■ ■

As luck would have it, we had already scheduled Matt's annual exam with Dr. Pearl, his pediatric neurologist. Dr. Pearl's practice was affiliated with Children's Hospital, a highly respected medical center in Washington, D.C. I felt very fortunate that we lived in an area that had such excellent medical care.

We'd seen Dr. Pearl at the start of each new school year to check whether any changes in medicine were in order ever since Matt had been diagnosed with a mild form of ADHD in second grade. The doctor had no reason to expect anything besides another low-maintenance visit when he saw Matt for his yearly appointment; other than having his low dose of Ritalin tweaked a few times over the years, Matt had not required additional medical treatment.

We entered the large gray stone medical building and took an elevator up to the second floor. When we walked into the pediatric office, I noticed children of all ages. Most of the older ones were sitting down and leafing through kid's books and magazines. The younger children were either nestled on their mother's laps listening to stories or they were playing with toys on the floor.

Looking at our son, with his dyed blonde hair gelled to punk-rock perfection, his easy smile and funny comebacks whenever I joked with him, you would never have suspected anything was going wrong for him.

After a few minutes in the waiting room, a nurse emerged from the inner sanctum and called Matt's name. Once in our assigned space, Matt boosted himself onto the examining table and waited patiently for the doctor to arrive.

A few minutes later, Dr. Pearl whisked into the room. He looked to be in his mid-thirties, but despite his youthful appearance, he had an air about him that made his patients feel like they were in the hands of a well-seasoned expert—which they were. He was holding Matt's medical records in a cream folder; unlike Matt's thick special education file, this one was relatively thin and appeared to contain only a few written reports.

"So, Matt, how have you been?" Dr. Pearl asked as he leafed through Matt's papers.

"Good," Matt said pleasantly.

"So, what grade are you in now?" Dr. Pearl asked.

"Eighth," Matt said, but I noticed how the tone of his voice had changed slightly. Once a person mentioned school, no matter how innocuously, Matt's light-heartedness evaporated.

"Matt has been having trouble staying awake at school," I said, trying to strike the right balance between showing concern and looking worried.

"So, what has been happening these past few weeks at school to make you want to sleep through it?" he asked Matt in a good-natured way.

The child specialist continued his line of gentle questioning, and in a short period of time, Matt volunteered that he had no trouble staying awake when he walked in the hallway with his friends between classes or when he ate lunch in the cafeteria. He also had no problem in seventh-period band, where he played drums loud enough to wake the Grateful Dead.

"It happens after I sit down in class and put my binder on the desk," Matt explained. "I start to feel very, very sleepy. The next thing I know, the teacher is waking me up."

For a teenager, Matt was pretty open about how he spent his days, whether they were good or bad. How he *felt* about his days, however, he kept to himself.

Dr. Pearl then turned to me. "What time does Matt go to bed at night?" he asked.

"Matt is a night owl. In the summer, he stays up past midnight, but now that school has started, I try to get him to bed no later than ten-thirty," I said.

"And how is that working?" Dr. Pearl asked.

I sighed. "Not very well." I explained to him how Matt's nocturnal hours were worsening.

Dr. Pearl looked down at the notes he had been taking, then he looked up and smiled, almost as if he had just figured out the last word in a

Sunday *New York Times* crossword puzzle.

"I think I know what's going on here," he said.

Matt and I leaned forward, anxiously wondering what the verdict might be.

The doctor attributed the excessive sleepiness to school phobia and a school avoidance disorder (not sleep apnea or narcolepsy, two debilitating sleep disorders that afflicted his father) before he offered a solution we'd never heard of before.

"Right now, Matt's biological clock is out of order," Dr. Pearl explained. "His body's bedtime appears to be about three in the morning. If he isn't falling asleep at ten o'clock every night by Veterans Day weekend, I want him to try something called 'chronotherapy.'"

Chronotherapy? Even the name sounded soporific.

Dr. Pearl explained that the treatment was used to help people with delayed sleep-phase syndrome.

An estimated 7-16% of adolescents have delayed sleep-phase syndrome.[1] The sleep pattern of someone with the disorder is out of synch with the person's circadian rhythm, and sleep is delayed by at least two hours beyond the socially acceptable or conventional bedtime. Scientists believe the sleep disorder may be an exaggerated reaction to the normal shift of the internal clocks that is seen in adolescents after puberty, but the exact cause is not completely known. One certainty, however, was that it was not willful behavior, according to medical experts.

Under chronotherapy, the patient gradually adjusts to an earlier bedtime by pushing the bedtime forward four hours every day, Dr. Pearl explained.

We must have looked perplexed.

Thankfully, Dr. Pearl put it in simpler terms: "I call it 'Rockin' Round the Clock.'"

He explained how it worked. The first night, Matt would go to bed at four o'clock in the morning, followed by nine hours of sleep. The second

---

1.   Cleveland Clinic, *Delayed Sleep Phase Syndrome (DSPS)*, https://my.clevelandclinic.org/health/diseases/14295-delayed-sleep-phase-syndrome-dsps.

night he would stay awake until eight o'clock in the morning and wake up at five o'clock that evening. This pattern would continue until the sixth and final day. Dr. Pearl assured us that by the sixth day, Matt would be able to fall asleep by ten o'clock at night and wake up at seven o'clock in the morning feeling refreshed and alert from nine hours of sleep.

Matt listened carefully. I noticed Dr. Pearl sparked his interest as soon as our son realized that Rockin' would mean missing several classes throughout the school week.

Chronotherapy, Rockin'…I didn't care what Dr. Pearl called it. We just prayed that it would work.

Between our office visit and Veterans Day, Dr. Pearl told us to make Matt get out of bed every morning at seven o'clock, regardless of the amount of sleep he'd had by then. We were to continue this regimen seven days a week, combined with light exercise and the use of a full-spectrum lighting fixture that imitated sunlight.

■ ■ ■

We tried the new routine that evening and the next morning; we were not expecting a miraculous difference, and we were right. Matt slept through the school day and, as usual, was alert and happy once he arrived home.

That evening, one of our favorite cousins came over for dinner at five o'clock. Alan had been Tom's best man at our wedding, and he frequently flew from Chicago to D.C. for business conferences. He and Matt always enjoyed teasing each other during his visits.

At six o'clock, we ate dinner. At seven o'clock, we ate dessert. At eight o'clock, Alan left. Five minutes later, Matt fell fast asleep on the basement rug.

In frustration, I went over to him and shook his shoulder as if I were throwing a pair of dice; they seemed loaded, and not in my favor.

"Matt, get up!" I insisted.

He looked at me heavy-lidded and slowly got to his feet. I brought him a glass of water and asked him to sit down at the dining room table, where he often worked on his assignments. Matt half-heartedly got out his pencil and began to fill out a geography worksheet. He didn't even attempt his math, but soon enough, it was ten o'clock and time to get him into bed.

Had it not been so late, I would have helped him with the first few math problems. Given the hour, I wrestled with my conscience a moment before deciding to complete a few graphs in his algebra assignment on linear equations, in hopes he could finish the rest in his study hall the following morning. It wasn't the first time I would do parts of his homework; I even tried to imitate his handwriting. I feared that if he failed his classes, he would have to repeat eighth grade.

As I began writing the correct answers to the equations that evening, I paused for a moment with one of Matt's pencils poised in my hand, then reluctantly continued on. What I didn't realize at the time was how doing the work for Matt affected his self-esteem. I saw it as a way to prevent him from failing; Matt told me years later that it had reinforced his belief that he couldn't succeed on his own.

Matt's sleep-deprived nights and his constant napping in class continued, as did his unfinished homework assignments. Exasperated by what appeared to be a never-ending cycle, Tom and I did not wait until November to try chronotherapy. We reasoned that the longer we waited, the further behind Matt would be in school.

And so, the first day began.

■ ■ ■

Day One

Matt's bedtime began at four o'clock in the morning. I checked on him at three o'clock; he was thoroughly engaged in watching extreme sports on TV, so I slipped back to sleep upstairs. Tom went downstairs at four-thirty to remind him to go to bed. He was already a half-hour behind his bedtime schedule, and it was only the first day!

Despite his pre-dawn bedtime, Matt woke up quite easily at the prescribed time of one o'clock in the afternoon and headed to school in time for math class. His resource teacher had left him a list of missing assignments; it was not an overwhelming amount to catch up on over the weekend. Even with his unusual sleep schedule, I was optimistic Matt would be able to get his homework done by Monday.

Day Two

Fortunately, the eight o'clock in the morning bedtime for Day Two fell on a Saturday. That made it possible for me to get some uninterrupted sleep, too. Matt's wakefulness at night since the beginning of the school year had been taking a toll on me. Regardless of how little sleep I'd gotten, I still had to wake up shortly after six o'clock each morning to get the children out the door on time for their classes; by mid-afternoon, I was nodding off in front of my laptop as I tried to write a story for my job.

Understandably, when I tried to stay up through the night, I drifted off to sleep about four o'clock in the morning—only to wake up in a panic when I noticed Matt had conked out beside me. There was still an hour to go before his eight o'clock bedtime!

"Matt, wake up!" I shouted, getting up abruptly from the sofa and nearly tossing Lucky off my lap in the process.

Tom and I had agreed from the beginning of the sleep therapy treatment that I would be the one to be with Matt during his waking hours—not an easy task when they were the ungodly hours of the morning. Keeping in mind Tom's own sleep problems, we had decided that it would be best for him to be the one to keep normal hours, so when Matt awoke in the afternoon, right according to schedule, Tom took him to drum lessons and I rested.

How could Rockin' possibly work when I was too sleep-deprived myself to monitor him?

Day Three

The Sunday shift went smoothly. I even tried my hand at mowing the lawn while Matt was on a noon to nine o'clock at night sleeping schedule. Whenever I could, I tried to preserve some form of normalcy in my own life, whether it was doing a few household chores or taking our dog for a lengthy walk.

On Sundays, there was church, and then after the morning Masses, members of our church fixed a full breakfast. Our congregation has several thousand worshippers from all around the metropolitan area, dozens of whom stay for the weekly breakfast. I had known many of the people there for several years, and there were a handful of us mothers who often shared our family news and parenting advice, especially when any of us faced difficulties with our children.

During my personal trials with Matt, many of those conversations were invaluable. No matter our children's personal challenges—and they included mental health problems, physical disabilities, substance abuse, and poor friend choices—a common message shone through:

Never give up on your children and love them unconditionally. They might resent you or rebel against you, but underneath it all, your children know you have their back.

Meanwhile, Emma continued to keep up the frenetic pace of her school days. Like most teenagers, our daughter's world revolved around her girlfriends, her after-school activities, and her hours of homework each night. While she knew we had put Matt on a special sleep schedule, she didn't ask many questions about it. She thought Matt had simply found another way to attend school as little as possible.

Day Four

Matt's sleep schedule required him to be in bed at four o'clock in the afternoon on the fourth day. Since he had to be awake all Sunday night, he was understandably drowsy at school all day. Just as he was about to hit the sack, Matt remembered that he had forgotten his geography book and worksheet.

Usually when Matt forgot anything at school—and remembered that he'd forgot—I would make him go back and fetch the missing materials. This time, because he had to go to sleep by the prescribed hour, I decided to head to his middle school for him.

I had to ask Matt for the combination to his school locker. I am lousy with combination locks, and I hoped I would be able to open it once I got there. Matt sleepily told me the numbers before crashing on the sofa. I decided to lead him up to bed after I'd gotten back from the school.

Classes had ended a few hours earlier, so the hallway was empty. I walked to Matt's locker and tried to open it. I rattled the lock. I shook the door. It simply wouldn't budge.

Shaking and rattling a locker in an empty hallway in the late afternoon drew the attention of a teacher as he left his classroom for the day. He looked over at me—no doubt trying to figure out why a middle-aged woman with short, dark, spiky hair appeared to be breaking into a student's locker.

"May I help you?" the teacher asked.

I looked up at him somewhat sheepishly as I explained my son had forgotten his homework but was unable to come back for it.

The teacher, who appeared to be in his early thirties, had short-cropped brown hair and was wearing a blue windbreaker, jeans, and running shoes. He was trim and athletic-looking; in fact, he looked like he probably ran track but didn't eat enough carbs.

"These things happen," he said, smiling. He extended his hand. "Hi, I'm Tom Feeney."

I recognized the name immediately; Matt must have talked about his geography teacher at least a dozen times since school had started.

I introduced myself. "I'm Paula Lazor, Matt's mom."

Feeney looked surprised. "How is Matt doing?" he asked. There was a note of concern in his voice.

"He's sleeping right now. That's why I'm here. Normally it's his job to come back and get anything he forgets," I explained. "Matt should be able to complete his work on time soon. In a few days, his sleep schedule will be back to normal."

Now Mr. Feeney *really* looked confused. It was evident that the guidance office, which was supposed to inform all of Matt's teachers about his temporary schedule, had not told him. It made me wonder how many other teachers were not aware of the sleep plan.

When I explained how Rockin' worked and the goal behind it, Matt's instructor was very supportive. He seemed more than willing to work with Matt to keep him engaged in the classroom. I was so happy I had run into him.

After our fortuitous introduction, he said goodbye and I got back to the business at hand, shaking and rattling the lock until the door finally opened.

The inside of Matt's locker was as messy as his backpack. I managed to find the missing book and worksheet; clutching them to my chest, I hurried home.

Day Five

The next morning, I mentioned to Matt that I had met his geography teacher.

"Mr. Feeney had to wake me up a lot last week," Matt said. Then he casually added, "One time he asked me to stay after school to talk to him a minute."

I was surprised that Matt had not mentioned this to me earlier. I stopped and gave him my full attention. "What did Mr. Feeney say?"

"He asked me if I had a bedroom of my own to sleep in at night," Matt said. He paused a moment, then, almost as an afterthought, he added, "He also asked me if I had a father."

I was stunned. Unfortunately, this wouldn't be the last time that teachers would draw the wrong conclusions about Matt. Too often, it was assumed he was simply faking sleep to get out of classwork. And apparently, at least one of his teachers thought there was something on the home front—perhaps a chaotic family life—that kept him awake at night.

It was lucky that Mr. Feeney and I had run into each other, and it was a relief to know our meeting had ended his misconceptions about our family situation. Perhaps we had even developed an ally.

Meanwhile, Matt and I had to go to bed at eight that evening and wake up halfway through the night. I could hardly wait.

Matt was able to stay awake, but after settling under the throw and eating breakfast, he kept putting off his homework. I had hoped he would finish his assignments quickly, so I could go to sleep for a few hours. Instead, he pronounced he was too tired to do any of it.

I was beside myself. I looked at my teenage son and suddenly felt like

Emma had been onto something. It seemed like her brother *was* milking his sleep therapy for all it was worth.

"Get off the damn sofa!" I shouted. "You can at least paste pictures into your geography notebook!"

One of Matt's easiest assignments was keeping a notebook of newspaper and magazine clippings and photos about current events. Even if he wasn't mentally alert enough to work on a linear equation, he certainly could handle a pair of scissors and apply some Elmer's glue to a piece of paper.

Matt jumped up. He hated confrontation, and when faced with it, he always chose flight over fight. As he left the room, I suspected he was heading to the basement den.

"Don't you dare go down and play video games!" I screamed after him. "I want you to come back into this room right now!"

Matt returned, his face flushed with anger, but didn't say a word. Instead, he snatched a pair of scissors from the top of the computer desk and stomped over to the magazine rack in the family room. He grabbed a few news magazines that were mixed in with several issues of his *Popular Mechanics*. About fifteen minutes later, he had cut and pasted several news stories and photos into his notebook.

"Now can I go downstairs and play on my PlayStation?"

"You've got to be kidding, Matt. If you are awake enough to play games, then you should be able sit down and do your math."

Not surprisingly, he was upset with me (and hopefully at himself) for the rest of the night.

Understandably, Matt had trouble staying awake at school when he got there the next morning. However, to my surprise, he was pretty alert when he came home. He even did some homework! Since the sixth day, when his bedtime had started at midnight, Matt had just about gotten back to a normal schedule.

Day Six

Matt awoke easily Wednesday morning and said he felt alert all day in school. Tom and I were practically ecstatic when we saw the difference in him. We agreed—the key was to stick to the sleep schedule, weekends, too! That night, to celebrate the successful end of Rockin,' I took Matt to East Coast Board Shop for his reward: new ball bearings for his skateboard.

Finally, it seemed that things were going our way. Just as Dr. Pearl predicted, once Matt reached the final day of the sleep cycle treatment, he fell asleep at ten o'clock at night and woke easily at seven o'clock in the morning.

It was heartening to put Matt to bed that first night. He looked at peace and content—such a difference in less than a week!

The following day was back-to-school night at Swanson. For the most part, I liked Matt's team of eighth grade teachers. When Tom and I arrived in Matt's geography class, Mr. Feeney walked over and greeted us warmly.

"I have noticed a big difference in Matt. He participated in class today. I have never seen him so engaged and alert," the teacher noted, smiling broadly.

About five minutes later, the school bell rang, ushering us to Matt's next classroom. This time it was study skills, a study hall that had schoolwork support for students who needed some assistance keeping on track with their assignments.

This was a crucial class for Matt. His teacher was Mr. Brent, an amiable man in his late-thirties with a shock of gray hair and calm gray eyes behind his wire-rimmed glasses. Mr. Brent was responsible for making sure students wrote down their daily assignments and brought the necessary school books home. Too often, Matt forgot to do the latter.

"Matt needs to work on his organizational skills," Mr. Brent told us matter-of-factly. "Personally, I like Matt. He is a pleasant young man and his sense of humor is way beyond his years. He is also very knowledgeable about subjects that interest him."

Matt often floored us with his knowledge about the intricacies of rock climbing, the equipment necessary for scaling a cliff, and how each piece fit together to prevent him from falling. Matt also was fascinated with fixing things, from clocks to bicycles. Our son was much more likely to have acquired his knowledge from his own tinkering or the Discovery Channel than from reading a textbook.

"Matt is also very sociable," Mr. Brent noted. He called him a "floater," noting how easily he moved from group to group in the cafeteria, accepted by everybody, no matter where he sat.

Tom and I felt a tremendous sense of relief after the open house. Matt's prospects for the rest of the year had sounded very encouraging now that he was getting enough sleep at night and staying awake in all his classes.

That night, he told us that he felt a lot less anxious in school, too. When he went to bed, he fell asleep almost immediately. Tom and I dared to hope that we had found a solution.

But the very next day, Mr. Brent left a message saying that Matt had several missing school assignments. Unfortunately, he did not identify them.

So much for catching up over the weekend. I began to feel the tugging sensation in my stomach that I so often had when Matt could not keep up with his work and fell further and further behind. *Is it possible that his success is already slipping away?*

That weekend, as usual, he was a bundle of energy. On Sunday, he and his friends spent the afternoon building skateboard ramps at a local park, but that evening, Matt came down with an upset stomach. It was the all-too-familiar complaint he had almost every Sunday evening on the eve of his return to another week of school.

I tried to remain hopeful, but a sense of dread swept over me. *Can this possibly be happening again?*

Monday dawned, and we kept Matt home from school after he'd had a fitful night of sleep. I made sure his time was not too alluring; I called Mr. Brent and tracked down his missing homework. He spent the day doing makeup work as well as his current assignments.

Matt's stomach problem dissipated Monday evening, but he stayed awake until close to two o'clock in the morning. On Tuesday, he was once again fighting sleep in school. By Wednesday, the day-long sleeping returned.

For the next several days, I went through the motions of getting

Matt off to school at the regular time, hoping that if I acted like it were just another normal day, it somehow would become one. Tom and I had wanted so badly for Rockin' to return Matt's life to normalcy, but after those few days of promising results, our hopes were dashed. It simply hadn't worked.

Matt was a puzzle. His behavior baffled everyone, including those who knew and loved him the best—his family.

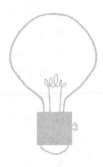

▪ CHAPTER 7 ▪

Anything But Special
(2000)

I n late October, Matt and I gathered around a rectangular table in a small, windowless room with Mrs. Murphy, Mr. Brent, and Mr. Feeney, acting as a teacher representative from his core classes.

Matt could barely keep his eyes open. Mrs. Murphy intervened and offered him a bottle of water, which he slowly steered to his lips.

The purpose of the meeting was to review Matt's latest IEP. Earlier in the month, a special education eligibility committee had met to assess whether Matt had a learning disability that required a continuation of IEP services. Not surprisingly, the committee determined that a disability still existed, but this time, there was a significant change in the nature of that disability. Part of the identification was the same ("Other Health Impaired"), but there was also an addition to it: "Emotionally Disturbed."

"This is not a clinical definition," Mrs. Murphy had assured Tom and me. "It just means that Matt's emotions—his falling asleep in class, even though he tries to fight it—get in the way of him functioning in the classroom at his grade level."

We certainly couldn't argue about his inability to function in class. He could not stay awake in the classroom, so he was missing vital information, and consequently, failing several of his courses.

When I raised my pen to sign the IEP form, Matt sat there, expressionless. *Is he simply not paying attention or is he deliberately tuning us out?*

I began to grow teary-eyed. "Emotionally disturbed," to me, conjured visions of a book I had read in college when I'd started out as a special education major. It was titled *P.S. You're Not Listening* by Eleanor Craig.

Even though it had been more than twenty years since I'd read the book, I still remembered the severe emotional disorders displayed by the children in it. One child was very violent, while another believed he was a ghost and that inanimate objects were alive. All the students had been placed in a single classroom and were taught by one teacher, Eleanor Craig, the author. I swallowed hard at the thought of Matt being placed in a class with children who had disturbing behavioral problems.

Seeing that I was growing upset, Mrs. Murphy patted my arm and handed me a tissue. Then she nudged Matt.

He had fallen asleep.

■ ■ ■

While Tom and I observed warning signs about Matt's well-being on the home front, his special education files tracked even more alarming signs at school. Wendy Karr, the school psychologist, had noted in a September 22 report that Matt did not seem "invested in school," and that socially and emotionally, he continued to struggle with issues of self-esteem and self-competency.

Significantly, the records also showed the results of a "self-report" by Matt. He'd denied having commonly experienced emotions—for example, when he'd read the statement, "I sometimes get mad," he'd answered "false."

The school specialist had concluded that the number of these types of responses indicated that Matt tended to engage in denial strategies to manage his emotional distress, which could lead to denying himself access to help or accommodations. This was the best explanation I had read yet on why Matt did not speak up for himself.

Karr believed that "a structured system of consequences and rewards [could] help Matt develop a sense of being able to manage his academic workload and to see the results of his efforts." She also recommended that the school staff establish ongoing consultation with Matt's private therapist, something Tom and I readily agreed to.

About a week after Ms. Karr wrote the report, we had a chance meeting in the hallway at school.

"I'm glad I had the chance to see you in person," she said kindly. "It's so much better than simply writing up a report about your son. Matt is a very bright child," she noted, "but also someone who doubts his ability to succeed in school."

She suggested some positive strategies to keep him awake in the classroom, from getting up and moving around (teacher permitting), to flexing his hands and rotating his feet to keep him alert.

Although well-intended, Ms. Karr's suggestions seemed like an invitation to Matt's classmates to tease him for being so fidgety. Even if teachers had supported the ideas, I doubted Matt would agree to do anything that he thought would draw more negative attention to himself. He was already doing that when he fell asleep!

■ ■ ■

There was another approach, strongly recommended by Dr. Welch, that was a far cry from the school therapist's positive reinforcement suggestions. As the doctor put it, Matt had to learn the consequences of his actions.

Beginning the second week of October, Matt had to complete his classwork assignments before leaving school for the day. Consequently, his guidance counselor required him to be pulled out of the cafeteria to eat his lunch and do his homework in the guidance office if he hadn't finished his morning assignments before the lunch period.

Our first stab at parent advocacy was when Tom and I decided to protest that decision. Lunch was the only time of day besides band when he felt like a normal, happy kid.

The guidance office reluctantly agreed, although his guidance counselor noted that Matt had worked on his map assignment the previous day without falling asleep. When Dr. Welch found out about the change we'd requested, he complained to us. We reluctantly agreed to let the guidance office resume the practice.

Then they intensified the consequences-to-actions approach by pulling Matt out of band, the only class he liked and did well in. He could not return until he was earning a C-average in every subject—no small feat, given that he was failing almost every core class. Consequently, Matt never returned to the only class where he'd felt like he fit in and was accepted by everyone.

The final straw was when he was required to complete any unfinished assignments before leaving school for the day. While Matt had dutifully spent his lunch hour in the guidance office, one day in early November, he rebelled against staying after school.

Tom and I didn't realize what had happened until later that evening, when Matt volunteered that he had cut out after school rather than stay to do his science homework.

"Why did you do this?" I asked. I was exasperated by his behavior, but once again, my anger was mitigated because he had been open and forthcoming with us.

"I couldn't stand being in school a minute longer," he said, his voice trembling as he defended himself.

Later that evening, Tom and I talked about Matt's behavior.

"I think all these classwork catch-up sessions, being pulled out of lunch with his friends, being removed from band, and staying after the school day ends are pushing him to the limit," I fretted. "If this continues, I think he'll walk out before school is even *over*."

■ ■ ■

Matt's after-school flight did not go unnoticed. We received a call from the assistant principal's office that Matt was to be placed in ISAP (In-School Alternative Program) the very next day. In-school suspension consisted of sitting in a classroom under the watchful eye of a supervisor the whole day, except for lunch in the guidance office. Students worked on their class assignments or, in Matt's case, fell asleep.

Following his day-long ISAP, Matt had to stay after school for two hours to finish his science homework. I came to pick him up and found him in the hallway looking like he'd had the wind knocked out of him.

■ ■ ■

There were a few approaches that initially offered a glimmer of hope, though they all turned out to be fleeting dreams. In hopes of getting Matt to finish his work, his resource teacher set up a point system for him; each time he completed an assignment, he would earn a checkmark on his point sheet. Once Matt earned enough points, he would be recognized for his achievement.

I liked his resource teacher, and Tom and I appreciated the incentives system that he had devised. Mr. Brent was low-key and didn't seem to rattle easily. He had a lot of patience and a dry sense of humor, which couldn't hurt in a job like his. He assured me he wanted Matt to succeed.

The idea was to use positive reinforcement to get Matt to complete his work, and initially, he did well.

For about a week—then Matt lost the point sheet.

No matter how many approaches the school took in its consequences strategy, success evaded Matt.

■ ■ ■

Tom and I decided to talk to Mrs. Murphy about the growing mound of incomplete homework assignments and our concern Matt would give up the idea of getting anything done altogether.

The guidance director reluctantly decided to start Matt off with a clean slate since, she agreed, he had been digging himself into a deeper and deeper hole.

"Tell him to focus on current assignments and not makeup work, although some of the missed work will need to be completed if current or future work was built on it," she warned.

It was one of many times during the school year that the guidance office said it would work with Matt's teachers to cut back on his makeup work, but the message never seemed to reach all of the instructors. Many of them required him to hand in the missing assignments anyway.

■ ■ ■

As hard as it was to accept the reclassification of Matt's learning disability, it did not come as a complete surprise. Ever since his brief period of success with Rockin', Matt's sleeping pattern had caused him increasing distress.

Earlier in the semester, Matt had come home from school absolutely mortified. Normally, he would drop off his backpack and run over to a friend's house to practice skateboarding tricks on his makeshift plywood ramp. That afternoon, though, Matt walked into the family room while I was on the computer, reading through my company emails. He slumped down on the sofa and didn't say a word.

"What's wrong, Matt?

Matt hesitated a moment, then came over to my desk.

"I fell asleep in math again this morning. I woke up when some of the kids started throwing pencil erasers at me."

I was angry this happened to him, but I was also at a loss for what I could do. "What did your teacher do when this happened?" I asked him.

"She was out of the room."

Matt was not about to tattle on his classmates, and I did not think the solution was to confront his teacher. It was hard to find a balance between being an advocate for your child and an interfering mom. I decided to call his guidance counselor the next day. This would at least be a point of discussion for our next meeting with Matt's teachers.

In the meantime, I had a son looking at me, waiting for a reassuring word. So I gave him the best answer I could muster: I hugged him.

Later that semester, Matt called me at work after school, crying. It was one of many times that I'd wished I could be at home with him when school upset him.

It wasn't a classroom incident this time. It was the school's Halloween ball, which was for band members only. Because the guidance office had transferred him from band to a study skills class, he couldn't go. Once again, he felt ostracized because of his lack of success in school.

"Why study if I am going to end up falling asleep during the test anyway?" This became a recurring question from Matt each night as we sat down for yet another few hours of homework. I tried to convince him that it was his job to prepare for tests, and that at some point he would step out of this classroom stupor with the knowledge waiting inside of him.

■ ■ ■

In the middle of these challenges, I had my annual physical. My doctor took a holistic approach to medicine; she spent as much time (if not more) talking to her patients as she did examining them. She listened sympathetically to my situation with our thirteen-year-old son.

"The worst age is usually fourteen," she advised.

I shook my head, then said none-too-convincingly, "Maybe we are getting ours over a year early." But then I added, with a weak smile, "Or the best is yet to come."

■ ■ ■

When Tom and Matt went on a Boy Scout camping trip in late October, I asked Emma to have a lunch date with me at La Madeleine, a small French restaurant.

It was unseasonably warm, nice enough to sit outside. Of course, I couldn't help but remember the last time we'd eaten outdoors there, nearly a year prior. That had been the day that Matt's depression had hit full-force, triggered on the way to the restaurant as Emma and I talked about colleges.

I didn't mention this to Emma. Too many of our conversations revolved around Matt's problems; I wanted this to be her day to talk and do whatever she wanted.

That evening, I surprised her with a candlelit dinner in the kitchen. We dipped into appetizers from a special Lebanese restaurant, including our favorite, baba ghanoush. Not one to experiment in the kitchen, I amazed her (and me) by making a cucumber-yogurt salad with toasted cumin seeds. It was so special to have some uninterrupted time with her.

Time with Emma, whether alone or as a spectator at one of the activities she participated in, was nearly always illuminating. I remember working at the concession stand for Emma's marching band at the high school football game, one of the rare times when I was involved in a school activity with other parents.

While we did not normally watch the game, Tom and I always made a point to arrive before half-time to see our daughter perform. There was something reassuring and inspirational about watching several dozen teenagers in matching blue-and-gray uniforms marching in formations without crashing into each other.

If only we could find a way to keep Matt from having so many collisions in the classroom.

■ ■ ■

Matt, after spending hours outdoors hiking on marked trails, cooking dinner over an open fire, and making s'mores, came back from the camping trip in great spirits.

Their next Boy Scout outing was very different. Instead of open skies and a wooded hillside, the boys, wearing their crisp scout uniforms, saw the confines of the county jail. Tom told me later that Matt had listened attentively to the police officer's ninety-minute talk and asked intelligent questions.

We were stumped as to how Matt could be so alert and perceptive during a lengthy presentation outside of school, yet so disengaged in the classroom. Emma had once warned us that Matt was using his sleep problem to save face in school; that way, if he failed his courses, he could blame it on his sleep problem, not himself. *Is there simply some underlying fear of failure that his work wouldn't be good enough and he would fail if he tried?*

■ ■ ■

In mid-November, Swanson held a career day. I took Matt to school in a very light-hearted mood. I asked him what sessions he had chosen.

"Stuntman and FBI Agent," Matt said happily.

Only having classes in the afternoon was clearly a great relief to him, too. While I was glad to see the joyful look on his face, I wondered whether Matt would stay awake through both sessions.

Well, Matt did more than stay awake. I received a call early in the afternoon from the assistant principal. Mr. Robinson said Matt was among several boys who'd asked the FBI agent "inappropriate" questions, and that he would be placed in ISAP the next day.

Some of the boys had asked questions like, "Did you ever kill anyone with your gun?" or made comments like, "If you haven't killed anyone, then you are not a hero." Matt, after looking in the FBI officer's bulletproof vest pocket, had repeatedly asked if the agent had things Matt could keep, or if he could try on the agents' handcuffs.

Matt looked bewildered when he came home that evening. He told us he had been called into the principal's office.

"I don't know what I did wrong! I was excited about seeing an FBI agent and I asked a lot of questions, but I raised my hand each time," he said tearfully. "I wasn't acting silly," he insisted.

He offered me his reason for wanting to wear the handcuffs: earlier in the year, there had been a school assembly for the DARE program to combat illegal drug use. "Kids were allowed to try on handcuffs and I never had the chance," he explained.

Even if Matt's impulsive behavior made sense to him, Tom and I knew we had to stand our ground. Tom cancelled an invitation for the following evening to see a Wizards basketball game that had been extended to him and Matt by a good friend. Even Matt's crestfallen face was not enough for us to change our mind.

■ ■ ■

When Emma found out about the incident at the dinner table that night, she offered her view of ISAP.

"Kids get thrown into that all the time at Swanson and W-L," she said, unperturbed by Matt's upcoming detention. "There was one guy who got ISAP for making up a school announcement on the PA system one morning."

"What did he say?" I asked.

"He said there would be an after-school Tic Tac Toe tournament."

Tom and I couldn't help but laugh. We knew Emma meant well by playing down the punishment, and we were grateful. Nonetheless, in my mother's mind, I felt like school was hard enough for Matt. ISAP was supposed to be for willfully poor behavior, but our son didn't seem to know what he'd done wrong. I knew he had to accept the punishment, but I also wondered if he was simply acting on impulse, where good judgment could have been checked at the door.

■ ■ ■

Sitting in my office the next day, I thought a lot about Matt spending yet another day in detention. I called him at home shortly after he had left school for the day to check and see how it had gone and to get some more answers. When I questioned him, Matt grew increasingly upset and defensive. He denied his teacher's complaint that he had "badgered" the agent.

"Geez," he kept repeating in a high-pitched voice, until finally, he exclaimed, "So you don't believe me either!"

I began to wonder if I should have waited until I got home before raising this touchy subject again, but it was too late.

Matt suddenly said, "Ooh," and the phone line clicked.

I repeatedly called back, growing worried when he didn't answer the phone. My fears were confirmed when I received a voicemail from Tom that Matt wasn't home.

Unsure where he'd run off to, I quickly left work. I made it home in less than thirty minutes, thanks to good subway connections and a cab. To our relief, though, Matt had simply scootered to the deli a few blocks away. He returned shortly after I'd paid the cab driver and walked into the house.

Matt remained distant and hurt until I managed to talk him into joining me after dinner to run an errand. Matt hugged me sweetly and apologized after I announced we'd be stopping afterwards for ice cream at Baskin-Robbins. I thought at the time that it was a relatively innocuous reward compared to club seats at the Wizards' game. Looking back, though, I wonder how often I was simply rewarding him for bad behavior.

■ ■ ■

November 28 was report card day, but, despite another late night, Matt headed off to school in good spirits. Of course, a strong cup of java and zipping down the hill on his skateboard no doubt helped.

That afternoon, Emma was the first to hand us her report card. She had received As in everything but English and French, but those Bs counted as As as well, since they were in advanced level classes.

Matt, as he'd feared possible throughout the semester, had flunked math and English.

He seemed to take the grades fairly well, at least from the outside. At the dinner table, he even kidded about getting an A in failing. Tom and I had exchanged glances at his joke, because we knew he assumed Emma aced all her subjects. As usual, we were careful not to bring up her excellent grades in front of him, although we always made a point of praising her when he wasn't within earshot. We always gave her a little gift card, too, so she could buy her favorite CD or see a movie with a friend.

Later in the evening while Emma was in her bedroom studying, Matt sat at the dining room table working on his vocabulary words. I sat next to him, ready to quiz him on each definition. Tom came over to us and stood behind Matt, resting his hands on his shoulders and giving them an affectionate rub.

Both Tom and I could see how diligently Matt was copying the definition of each word into his notebook. We knew it had to have been hard for him to continue working, night after night, only to bring home a report card that didn't reflect the effort he'd expended.

"Hey, Matt. About your report card," Tom said.

Matt stopped writing and looked up at him.

"Just remember, what you brought home is from your first grading period, and you are showing improvement now."

He looked up at Tom and gave a slight smile. At least he knew we had his back.

■ ■ ■

One step forward. Two steps back. After our pep talk with Matt about his report card, Mrs. Murphy and the assistant guidance counselor pulled Matt and eight other students from class the next day to tell them they would be monitoring them because they were not working hard enough.

Thanks a lot, guidance. Just as we tried to rebuild Matt's confidence at the start of the new grading period, they were pounding it out of him. I decided to get to the bottom of Matt "not trying hard enough" in his classes.

■ ■ ■

A few days later, at my request, Matt's math and science teachers called me. They both seemed to be patient and understanding, although, to my surprise (and dismay), the math teacher said Matt might do better "at a slower pace"—in special education. She suggested the best route for him might be to take a makeup class in summer school.

After I hung up, I called my mother for her thoughts about summer school.

I grew up in a hard-working, blue-collar neighborhood. In my hometown, high school diplomas and GEDs were socially acceptable, in stark contrast to the highly educated D.C. area, where you were expected to aim for a four-year college or, at minimum, a two-year associates degree. (In the entire time that Matt sat with us at IEP meetings, technical schools or career training programs were never mentioned as options, and certainly not a GED.) Both of my parents had earned high school diplomas during the Depression—something my mother's older siblings had not been able to do, since they'd had to quit school and go to work at age sixteen to help support the family. Many of my friends and I were the first to go to college.

Mom knew hardship and the value of an education, but she'd also seen her brothers able to get jobs in the local factories and hone skills that paid well enough to get their own children through high school.

"I think summer school would be a mistake. It's important for Matt to have a break," Mom said without a moment's hesitation. "Of course, that is my opinion," she added, not wanting me to feel pressured in any way.

■ ■ ■

Feeling very frustrated, I ran into my neighbor, Paul, one morning during my walk with Lucky; he had encouraging words about Matt's situation.

Paul told me bluntly that he'd struggled with ADHD as a child and an adult. "I learned through the school of hard knocks and worked my way up to a well-paying job."

His son, Mark, also had attention problems and had struggled with school for several years. Now he was in his senior year and finally doing great academically after transferring to H.B. Woodlawn, an alternative high school program in Arlington.

"H-B," as it was popularly known, distinguished itself by allowing students a greater voice and more choices for designing their own education plans tailored to the way they learned. Some students did independent studies or, for example, produced films instead of the usual PowerPoint demonstrations. The school held a weekly town hall on the premises, where students and teachers could exchange ideas about the curriculum and how the school should run in general.

The faculty-student relationship was collegial—students were on a first-name basis with their teachers. To keep the class sizes small on their allotted budget, H-B required all staff, including those in the administrative office, to teach.

The highly rated alternative school was in such high demand that there was a student lottery to enroll.

Mark thrived in the drama and theater classes offered. In a traditional curriculum, these classes would have been electives. For Mark and other students like him, though, these classes needed to be given equal weight to the typical "core" requirements. Mark's passion for working creatively motivated him to work hard in his other classes. Paul noted that once Mark had enrolled in H-B, his grades did an about-face; he was even taking AP classes and getting As in math and science.

Tom and I had heard about H-B and its different approach to education, but had never visited. Our impressions had been that it attracted many "artsy" students and that they were given a lot of leeway to design their own programs. Trusting our instincts, we decided not to pursue it as an option for our son. If Matt was eligible to get in, the program would require a lot of self-direction and student independence; it simply did not seem to be the right match.

■ ■ ■

When I told Paul about Matt's academic troubles, he had a good way of describing what Swanson was trying to do with our son: "It's like offering a dog treats if he is able to learn how to fly. The treats aren't going to make any difference if he can't fly."

Not long after talking to Paul, it dawned on me that the school should have been providing a program that taught Matt the way he learned, in a stimulating environment where he could stay alert and engaged. Only then could he achieve his academic goals.

Matt wasn't failing school; school was failing *him*.

■ ■ ■

Ellen, my work colleague, owned a talk radio news program and college media news service. When I confided in her, she gave me a pep talk.

"He'll turn out fine as long as he doesn't get mixed up in drugs," she said in her classic candid manner. "The main thing is to keep him interested in activities he likes and does well or excels in.

"I did miserably in seventh and eighth grade and ended up at McLean Hospital," she said matter-of-factly, referring to the renowned psychiatric teaching hospital affiliated with Harvard Medical School. Ellen revealed that she had not been placed in a psych ward at the hospital; she described her program as more like a boarding school for bright teens who didn't fit the mold.

She highly recommended the Lab School in Washington, D.C., an innovative school at the cutting edge for teaching nontraditional learners. Using an "arts-based curriculum," the internationally recognized school specialized in educating students with learning differences, including dyslexia, ADHD, and related language-based learning difficulties. She said the staff would work with Matt to figure out learning strategies.

"He should do fine there. The school even frequently brings in speakers who are success stories, despite not doing well as teens," Ellen assured me.

Tom and I were intrigued by the school's teaching philosophy, so he called and asked them to send us brochures.

■ ■ ■

At our next visit with Dr. Welch, he suggested outside testing by Dr. Jane Greenstein. As an educational consultant and diagnostician, we were hoping she could tell us more about Matt's attention and organization problems and his failure to produce work in the classroom on time and in a focused manner. Matt reluctantly went to Dr. Greenstein's office for the evaluation in mid-December, and Tom and I met with her a few weeks after to discuss what she considered to be "significant" findings.

Dr. Greenstein assured us that Matt was smart and discussed his areas of strength and difficulties. Referring to her written report, she noted that Matt was particularly strong in verbal areas that required abstract reasoning and comprehension and the ability to grasp general knowledge. He also demonstrated "superior ability" in his alertness to visual details in his everyday environment.

He had great difficulty "resisting distractions, blocking out background interference, and staying on task in a vigilant manner." Another difficulty, although on a lesser scale, was his "active working memory," his ability to hold information at the ready while working through a problem. He also had sequencing problems; for example, he had a hard time putting a series of pictures, which illustrated the steps to send a letter, in the proper order. To me, this explained why he skipped steps in math, something I had always attributed to him being impatient with writing everything out.

Matt's reading comprehension was noteworthy in that he was able to correctly answer several of the last and most difficult questions on the subtest while making errors on easy earlier ones. I wondered if that meant he made mistakes on reading materials that he did not consider challenging enough to interest him.

In math, Matt almost totally avoided using pencil and paper. Dr. Greenstein noted that this behavior was often seen in students who were inattentive to academic detail, did not process the detail accurately, and had visual motor integration problems which made it difficult to write numbers legibly. "It is easier for them to see in their mind's eye than to see what is on the page," she explained.

Matt's deficits in attention, visual motor integration, visual processing, and ability to quickly and easily perform cognitive tasks were impacting his ability to produce academic work in a focused, timely manner and with ease, speed and accuracy. "These difficulties result in frustration, as he is not able to generate and execute assignments at a level commensurate to his conceptual abilities," the doctor noted.

After reviewing the report with Dr. Greenstein, Tom and I signed a consent form allowing her to discuss the test results and recommendations with anyone involved in Matt's education and development.

Her recommendations included:

Use of a computer for written work.

Use of a pocket organizer, such as a PalmPilot, with a collapsible keypad.

Short time periods for study and extended time for taking tests.

Buddy system to assist in following classroom directions.

Use of class notes provided by a student or teacher or a tape recorder for critical aspects of a class discussion.

A list of steps to be written up before starting a math problem.

Use of graph paper for writing math problems in order to keep the numbers in line.

■ ■ ■

To our surprise, Dr. Greenstein had not thought the Lab School would be the right place for Matt. In her view, Matt's issues were more due to emotional problems than learning disabilities. Even though she had spelled out several accommodations, Dr. Greenstein emphasized at the December meeting that she did not believe special education was appropriate.

Matt had also been vehemently opposed to the Lab School, even just for summer classes. "I just want to be *normal* at school. I don't want *special* help," he cried one evening.

Dr. Greenstein suggested we consider the New School of Northern Virginia, a private school located in Fairfax, which subscribed to a teaching philosophy that there were many ways to teach, learn, and present information. Although we believed Matt might do better in a program that offered greater flexibility in producing class assignments, the school was too far away from us. It would have been a logistical nightmare for us every day.

Dr. Greenstein had noted that Matt would benefit from tutoring to support his classwork and to help him develop skills and strategies for studying, time management, organization, and test preparation. Dr. Welch supported individual tutoring, but was opposed to using learning centers. "They have their own teaching agenda and do not incorporate homework from the student's school," he said. That meant Matt would have double the workload, so that idea was a non-starter.

■ ■ ■

With so many options spinning in our heads, many of them unsuitable and none of them perfect, it was no surprise that Matt was increasingly miserable at school and at home.

One evening, to break Matt from his funky mood, I asked him to accompany me while I took Lucky for a walk to the neighborhood deli. The prospect of leaving his homework for a while and getting on his scooter cheered him, but it was a heart-tugging moment for me to see Matt's silhouette as he pushed himself up the hill in the darkness.

How often does he feel like he is going at it alone?

■ ■ ■

I talked to Matt about praying and assured him he was never alone, but if he ever took my advice and prayed, he kept it to himself.

I believe that God gives all of us grace and loves us unconditionally. It's how we lead our lives, the choices we make, and whether or not we leave this world a better place that matter. I think both of our children lead lives of grace, whether they realize it or not.

I remember going to church one evening with Tom and wishing Matt had come and heard the homily. Fr. Kelly told us about his middle brother, an F student in high school. Their mother never gave up on him; she encouraged him to try community college. He eventually transferred to a four-year university, made it through, and was successful at his job. The theme of the sermon was to never give up on your family.

■ ■ ■

It was our Christmas tradition to spend winter break every year with my parents and family at my childhood home in western Pennsylvania. This year there was plenty of snow when we got there—perfect for sled riding.

When I dropped Emma and Matt off at the park, I was struck by the beauty of the sky in the distance, dark clouds with shafts of light shining through them. It was moments like these that I tried to appreciate—the lulls from the everyday world of deadlines, homework assignments, and appointments. As Matt and Emma raced down the hill on old wooden sleds, I think they treasured those moments, too.

But the hiatus didn't last very long. A few days after Christmas, we were home once again.

▪ CHAPTER 8 ▪

A Tough Transition
(2001)

Matt ended the year with two of his friends at Ski Liberty, his favorite place to snowboard. I thought it would be packed on New Year's Eve, but it was not crowded in the slightest.

Before getting on the slopes, each boy had to get his picture taken for an ID card. Matt looked so happy in his photo. I'm sure for those few brief hours, as he confidently balanced on his snowboard and maneuvered skillfully and effortlessly down the mountain with his friends, Matt felt as if he didn't have a care in the world.

His return to school after winter break, however, was a far cry from the way he'd smoothly sailed down the slopes at Ski Liberty.

Like many times before, his anxiety over school took its toll on him physically with asthma problems and stomachaches. His acid reflux worsened to the degree that a pediatric gastroenterologist recommended that he have another colonoscopy and endoscopy.

As with his previous procedures in seventh grade, Matt welcomed the thought of missing school. The day before his gastroenterological adventure, Matt cheerfully sipped hot chicken broth, drank green Gatorade, and ate clear lime Jell-O and Popsicles. He downed the prescribed semi-gelatinous liquid to clear out his innards that night, with a repeat performance in the morning. Tom and I were happy to see him be such a good sport once again about preparations, which most patients dread more than the actual procedure.

Old hands at this by now, Tom and I sat patiently in the waiting room of the hospital the next morning. While flipping through a magazine, I noticed that other doctors came out to talk to members of the family, or I heard them in the hallway, telling loved ones that everything was fine.

Instead of doing the same thing, Dr. Chao led us into a small room where photos of Matt's colon and esophagus were displayed on a table.

"Well, the good news is…" she began.

My heart jumped into my throat as I immediately began wondering what the bad news was. I tried hard to pay attention to what she was saying.

"The colon looks fine."

Dr. Chao pointed to a photo of the inside of Matt's intestinal tract, one segment at a time. It looked like the inside of a small watermelon after the seeds had been scooped out. Then she pointed to pictures of the esophagus. Most of them looked like the colon shots, only smaller in scope.

"My only concern is that there is some redness at the base of the esophagus…probably just a minor irritation. However," she paused, "we did a biopsy just to make sure there was no inflammation or damage."

The only word scarier in my mind than "cancer" was "biopsy," so news of the results loomed overhead like a raincloud until the next day.

The phone rang as I was about leave for work in the morning, and I quickly ran over to answer it. As I gingerly lifted the receiver, I wondered if my world was about to change dramatically.

"Hello, Mrs. Lazor?"

I recognized Dr. Chao's voice right away, but I could not tell by her tone whether she would be delivering good news or bad news. I held my breath, preparing for the worst. After all, so many other parts of Matt's life were spiraling downward. Why not his esophagus?

"Matt's biopsy report came back," she told me matter-of-factly.

I braced myself.

"The test results are normal. However," she continued.

"However," in my book, certainly wasn't as disturbing as news of a serious illness, but it made me wary nonetheless.

In this case, what was to come was manageable, thankfully. Matt's acid reflux was worse than she'd thought, but she said that it could be addressed easily by increasing the dosage of his medicine. Dark cloud now lifted, I could carry on normally with my work day.

When Emma came home from school that afternoon, she said she had worried about Matt all day. Once I told her the good news, she smiled and the relief spread across her face. Although Emma and Matt didn't often tell each other directly about their feelings, it was always touching when either of them showed how much they cared.

■ ■ ■

Sitting in the living room in early January, sipping chamomile tea with a classical music station on the radio on the last night before taking the Christmas tree down for another year, was one of those peaceful moments.

Matt had just finished his science display board, the one he had been painstakingly working on for several weeks. He had patiently cut out jagged-edged backgrounds from blue construction paper to give his tables, graphs, and written text a two-dimensional look. How was it that a child could be so patient and creative about a display board, yet fall asleep or tune out in English and math?

■ ■ ■

In mid-January, Tom and I dropped Matt off at Ski Liberty all by himself while we went to have lunch in Emmitsburg. He seemed a little anxious when we reunited and told us that a middle-aged man had hopped on the ski lift with him during one of his climbs. At the top, the man had peppered him with questions, asking if he was there with any of his friends or alone.

"He might have just been a friendly person, but I'm glad you stayed clear of him," I said.

Matt seemed relieved after he'd told us, and even asked if we could extend his ticket time an extra hour. It was a short enough distance between the ski lodge and snowboard park that Tom and I were able to spot Matt from the rest of the pack as he came gliding down the hill. We told him we would look out for him, something that I think made him feel better about his solo runs.

During his extra time on the slopes, we saw him fly over several ramps and do a 180, spinning half a revolution before landing on his feet. He looked so confident and happy on his board.

"That really relieved a lot of stress," Matt observed once he'd finished for the day.

Most kids his age would have simply said they'd had fun, but Matt wasn't the average kid. There were a lot of emotions he kept beneath the surface, but physical outlets helped. Activities like snowboarding and rock climbing not only required him to think quickly on his feet, they also gave him the chance to focus on things he was good at and loved to do.

■ ■ ■

The following week, it was back to reality. As with every Monday, I checked my voicemail messages mid-morning for Mr. Brent's weekly update. That was when the gray clouds moved in.

Mr. Brent reported that Matt had low Cs in science and geography, an abysmal 42% in math, and a failing mark in English.

"I'm afraid it looks like Matt will need to start the third grading period in special education math and English," he said.

I hung up the phone. Stunned.

Over the next several days, I grew tearful several times thinking about the undesirable options left for Matt in eighth grade. *How will it feel for a bright child to be placed in special education classes? What will that do to his emotional makeup, let alone his self-image? If he is convinced he won't do better in a special education classroom, is it better for him to stay in the regular classroom and repeat a grade? Maybe we should consider the Lab School.*

My head was spinning as I tried to make sense of it all. I grew so upset one evening that I took refuge for a while in the bedroom. There was a basket of laundry on the floor that needed to be put away. Somehow, the act of folding each piece of underwear and every pair of socks before placing them in their drawers helped me to calm down, even if I didn't have any answers to my questions.

■ ■ ■

The dreaded time had come; we needed to approve the revisions to Matt's academic plan that would place him into the special education classes. Tom and I walked into the IEP meeting in late January as if we were lining up before a firing squad.

Perhaps it was my imagination, but Ms. Naples seemed to be artificially cheerful as she waved hello to us before the meeting. In fact, everyone there made efforts to be pleasant. I was sure they realized how difficult this decision was for us.

Once everyone was seated, Mrs. Murphy welcomed us to the meeting and then gave the floor to Matt's English instructor, Mary Campbell, who offered a few revelations about him.

Tom and I had been under the impression Matt didn't participate in her class, because he'd told me more than once that he felt lost and intimidated by all the other students who did well.

However, Mrs. Campbell had a completely different story. According to her, Matt sometimes raised his hand several times during class so that he could be called on. Only, when he was, Matt would say something to make the rest of the class laugh.

We moved on to his math difficulties.

Matt had mentioned to Mr. Brent his weekend plans to build a "funbox," a structure with a flat top and side ramps used for practicing skateboard tricks. "If only he would apply the math he is using for building his ramp. In fact, it is too bad he is not in advanced math. They are working on slopes right now." Mr. Brent unmistakably saw Matt's potential and seemed to be as frustrated as we were about his lack of academic achievement.

I raised my concern that Matt would refuse to come to school once he learned he was being moved to two special education classes. Mrs. Karr suggested that Tom and I let them break it to him once he was in school.

After I left the meeting, I felt shell-shocked for the rest of the morning.

Knowing what was in store for him on Monday, Tom and I allowed his friend Tim to sleep over on Friday night. They both woke up at nine in the morning—surprisingly early—and it wasn't long before they started to work on the funbox. After taking a skating break with Tim and another buddy, Matt returned to continue on his box. Matt later told me he was "relentless" about getting this project done.

Matt and his other friend tested it out before dinner. It actually held up, although Matt made plans to reinforce it the next morning.

True to his word, Matt spent the first part of Sunday making his funbox more stable, only taking a break in the afternoon to go to a movie with his girlfriend, Amy, and her friends.

"Girlfriend" was a loose definition, since any time Matt and Amy spent together seemed to revolve around group outings, but I was still surprised that Matt didn't make himself more presentable for the occasion. It was obvious (at least to me) that he should have washed his hair and at least changed his sweatshirt. But Matt had been so immersed in his project that he'd barely had time to jump into the car before I drove him over to Amy's house. When he was interested in something, it was almost an obsession.

When we arrived, the girls warmly greeted Matt, who then slid into the backseat, followed by Amy and her friend.

"Hello, Mrs. Lazor," the girls said in unison.

The friendly chatting commenced as I drove them all to a nearby multiplex theater. It was nice—and reassuring—to see Matt spending time away from his box construction and with classmates who were obviously enjoying his company.

■ ■ ■

Normally, I liked the very beginning of a new quarter. When there were no grades yet, for a few fleeting days, Matt had a clean slate. This time, I dreaded it, because this one meant he would be in special education classes twice a day. Would his relationships change once word got out about his abrupt move from two of his classes?

As it turned out, the day of reckoning was delayed for two days. Matt woke up that Monday with a cold and an asthma flare-up. The two often went hand-in-hand, as his breathing problems could be triggered by a cold virus.

The next day, after getting up early to use his nebulizer, he wouldn't budge when I returned from dropping Emma off at school.

"You don't know how tired I am," he cried.

I let him rest until nearly nine o'clock, then futilely tried to get him to sit up to get dressed. I finally relented completely, since he wouldn't have been able to function at school this tired and upset. Plus, he was in no state of mind to hear the news about his change of classes.

Matt perked up after dinner and worked diligently on his vocabulary list, not suspecting it was a worksheet from his resource class. I did tell him that his English and math assignments had changed, and that he would have a lighter load that grading period. No complaints there.

The dreaded day arrived, and Tom and I both took off early from work so that we would be there when Matt came home. I had been nervous all day about how he would feel once they broke the news to him at school. I felt the all-too-familiar tug in my stomach when I heard the door open and Matt slam it shut.

He walked into the living room where Tom and I stood, as ready as we could be for his reaction.

"Why didn't you tell me about this ahead of time?" he said angrily, fighting back tears.

I decided to respond first. "Honey, we are sorry it had to be this way, but I was afraid if I told you about your move before school started, you wouldn't go."

I explained to him how Tom and I had been to a meeting at the school and they had explained the consequences he would face if he continued to fail English and math.

"Matt, I'm afraid you might have to repeat eighth grade if you stay in your regular classes."

Matt paused a moment, as if weighing his options, then his anger toward us subsided. Instead, he redirected it. He complained about the "obnoxious" kids in his new classes and appeared to be highly insulted that the math and English were so simple. At the same time, he showed no anxiety about being there; it seemed like an example of healthy venting.

And he had no homework.

What a remarkable difference we saw the first night. Instead of spending hours at the dining room table, Matt busied himself in the basement, putting the finishing touches on his funbox.

■ ■ ■

I had just returned from an evening walk with Lucky when I heard Emma's voice calling from the family room.

"I was looking for you," she said, giving me a warm hug. She had obviously picked up on how trying the past several days had been for me.

"I ran three miles with Lucky after school today. When we were on the bike path, I saw a forty-year-old man on a skateboard with monster wheels being pulled by his dog," she said, laughing at the thought of him.

She continued to play the cheerleading role after school the next day, too. She came home with words of wisdom, pointing out that it was actually that good the classes were easy for him.

"This way it will make him see that he isn't special ed material, and if he likes getting good grades in there, it might translate to the regular classroom," she said proudly.

It was clear that our daughter had been mulling over Matt's move a lot, trying to put a positive spin on it.

It wasn't until the weekend that we realized Emma's upbeat disposition was mostly a façade. On Friday evening, everything seemed to be just fine. Emma went out to a basketball game with friends and then took in a movie. It wasn't until the following morning that she gave us our wake-up call.

Emma was unusually subdued when she woke up and came downstairs.

"Is everything okay?" I asked, sensing something was wrong.

Emma started to cry.

She looked absolutely miserable as she sat at the kitchen table, eyes red and tears welling. It took a while, but she finally told us what she had kept inside herself during the last few weeks of January.

"Mom, I've been really worried about you. I even cried about this at school and was so upset that Anna bought me chocolates."

(Anna was her best friend and confidante, the first one she talked to whenever she had a problem she needed to share.)

All this time, Tom and I thought she was doing well and handling our family challenges concerning her brother. What pressure we had unknowingly put on her!

"Emma, I am so sorry that I upset you so much. It had been an extra-stressful time because I was worried how Matt would handle the move to special education. Thankfully, it seems to be working out better than I expected. He really seems less anxious now," I assured her. "You needn't worry about me anymore."

Emma looked me right in the eye as I spoke to her. She was very good at reading me and whether I was playing down my true feelings in order to protect her. Slowly, she wiped the tears from her eyes and smiled. It was finally clear to her that Tom and I loved her for who she was and not who she expected we wanted her to be.

■ ■ ■

It's so hard to find the right balance between high-maintenance and low-maintenance children, because, in the whole scheme of things, there is no such thing as a low-maintenance child.

Several years later, Emma told me that she'd felt resentment towards Matt for the attention and time he consumed, as well as Tom and me for giving it to him at her expense. I think it was particularly difficult for Emma to express her emotions when she felt angry or resentful because she felt guilty. She knew we were working hard to help him succeed.

While Tom and I went to every band concert and regatta, it didn't occur to us that she wanted more one-on-one time after school and on weekends, especially as she grew older and immersed in her schoolwork and activities with her friends.

Our daughter was both comforter and overachiever. One evening, while I was growing upset over Matt's recalcitrance to do homework, she ran to the store a few blocks from home and bought me Junior Mints. Another day, on our drive to school, she proudly told me that she'd scored a perfect thirteen on her IB math portfolio, the highest in the school.

At the end of the season that year, Tom and I watched Emma compete in a 200-meter relay in the warm, humid high school aquatic center. It was the first meet we'd attended; we'd respected Emma's wishes not to come to any others because she'd thought they were boring and she was only doing them to keep in shape for crew in the spring.

After the meet, Emma and one of her friends on the team went "clubbing" at a rival high school. I couldn't imagine dancing after swimming so many laps.

"Where do they get all that energy?" I asked another parent at the swim meet.

"They're young," she said with a smile.

As busy as Emma was with all of her challenging subjects, I was glad to see her able to balance academics with sports, band, and a social life, too. Our daughter had so many talents and abilities, and we were so proud of her, that we were somewhat blinded to the fact that she was a child, too, who needed as much attention as any other child.

One night, she came home from winter swim practice proudly announcing that she'd swam eighty laps at the high school pool. Looking back on this, I wonder if she swam so hard as much to vent her anger over Matt as to prepare herself for crew practice in the spring.

■ ■ ■

PAULA LAZOR

The next few weeks in Matt's special education classes went relatively smoothly. In his weekly Friday update near the end of February, Mr. Brent left a message about Matt's grades in special education math and English. It was good news; he had a B+ in math and a B- in English.

However, red flags were flying for his core classes in the regular classroom. He was teetering on the edge, with a low C in geography, and his grade had plunged on his latest quiz. When I asked him what had happened, he said he had fallen asleep during it. As for science, he was failing.

So...if he fails science for the year, can he still pass eighth grade? Will this mean summer school? I wondered sometimes, especially when he was extremely forgetful or lost assignments, if he was even ready for high school.

It did not take long for these questions to be answered. A few days later, Ms. Naples called and suggested we make arrangements to visit the Interlude program. It had been mentioned once in passing earlier in the year, but not in any detail—just a possible option down the line if he continued falling asleep.

At this point, Tom and I were open to at least checking it out. The way Matt's guidance counselor described it, Interlude would provide a lot of latitude for Matt to move on to high school and utilize the program only for the subjects he needed it most.

Tom and I had noticed in the past week that Matt's anxiety had started to return. While doing well in his special education classes seemed to initially make him less anxious at school, his continued struggles in geography and science were taking a toll. Then he began to fall asleep in math and English, too.

The evening after my talk with Ms. Naples, Matt was in one of his wired and tired moods. He had been okay when he'd arrived home, but he'd grown weepy after dinner when he'd needed to redo some of his math problems. I made him tea, hoping it might soothe him, and took it down to the basement den. I found him playing solitaire on his computer, and decided it was as good a time as any to broach the subject of Interlude. I asked him casually what he thought about it and about the possibility of switching to it for some of his classes.

"No way," he said. "It's for kids who think they are smart, but they are really dorky."

I told Tom later about Matt's reaction. "Poor Matt. He just doesn't seem to fit into any program."

"It can't hurt to check it out," Tom said. "Why not give the teacher a call in the morning?"

I waited until lunchtime the next day to call Jamie Borg, the Interlude teacher, and her cheerful voice and easygoing manner immediately put me at ease. I asked to set up a time when Tom and I could meet with her, and to my surprise, she was able to see us in a few short days.

As I hung up the phone, I once again felt a gnawing sensation in my stomach. *Here we go again. Another program. Will this one be any better? Or will it just offer him a new way to fail?*

▪ CHAPTER 9 ▪

Interlude
(2001)

T he first thing we noticed about the Interlude class was how quiet it
was. In fact, the entire time that Tom and I waited in the adjacent
room to meet the teacher, we didn't hear the students at all.

One young man in the program happened to walk past us into the
guidance office. He had neatly trimmed dark hair and wore a black t-shirt
and jeans. I also noticed a gold chain necklace that Matt probably would
have liked. He looked, well…normal.

"Hello, Mr. and Mrs. Lazor," Ms. Borg said cheerfully as she walked
into the small meeting room. There was no mistaking that she was a
woman who felt good about herself and enthusiastic about her job.

Once she sat down across from us, Ms. Borg folded her hands on the
table, leaned forward, and smiled.

"I'm sure you have plenty of questions about Interlude, so please feel free to cut in at any time while I explain how it works."

Ms. Borg noted that Matt's guidance counselor had told her about Matt's sleeping problem. She said that was not unusual behavior in her classroom when a student first started.

"There is no need to worry about that. I have a way to keep everyone awake," she said.

She didn't explain what that was; nonetheless, there was something about her voice and can-do spirit that made me feel I could trust her.

She then began to talk about the program: "The classes are very structured, and all the work is done throughout the day."

"What about homework?" I asked her.

"There isn't any. They are expected to finish it at school."

I was surprised and relieved to hear this, but both Tom and I were also puzzled. Since Ms. Borg seemed to welcome my inquisitiveness, I ventured another question: "What happens if Matt doesn't finish his homework at school?"

"There is a reward system. If enough points are earned, the student can join in activities on Friday afternoon. We usually watch a movie or take a trip to a nearby 7-Eleven."

Both Tom and I were a little skeptical that movies or Slurpees would be enough of an incentive for Matt to complete his assignments—especially if he couldn't stay awake. Ms. Borg must have picked up on our doubts.

"If, for whatever reason, Matt falls behind on his assignments, we will work with him to catch up," she assured us.

"And what happens if he doesn't?" I asked, already envisioning Matt coming home from school frustrated by all his unfinished assignments and afraid he would have to repeat eighth grade. No matter what, I felt that keeping Matt back a year would only make him more anxious and embarrassed about returning to school.

At this point, Ms. Borg must have realized that neither of us was convinced the Interlude approach would be more successful than any of the other programs we'd tried.

"I can understand your concerns about Matt," she said. Then she added the magical words, "No matter how Matt performs the remainder of the school year, we will not hold him back. Repeating eighth grade is no solution," she said. "Anything Matt does not complete in eighth grade, his teachers will work with him to complete in ninth grade."

For a moment, I was sure that I hadn't heard Ms. Borg correctly. I thought of all the hours Matt and I had spent at the dining room table every night, and all those moments when I'd guiltily completed his schoolwork out of fear that he would flunk eighth grade.

Seeing our looks of disbelief (as well as our unmistakable relief), Ms. Borg was quick to warn that she was not about to sugarcoat the program.

"I will warn you right now that Matt will most likely show some resistance to being there the first few days. And I wouldn't expect a miraculous improvement in his grades right away."

Tom and I exchanged glances.

"I think we will need a few minutes to talk this over," Tom told Ms. Borg. She nodded and left the room.

Tom and I agreed that we weren't happy with the idea of Matt being in a self-contained classroom for every course other than his electives. We were both concerned that he might feel like an outcast if he was not in regular classes with the other students.

Plus, how "different" were these other children? Would Interlude just reinforce the label that he *was* "emotionally disturbed?"

When Ms. Borg came back into the room, Tom and I looked once more at each other, and then he motioned for me to do the talking.

For an instant, I pressed my lips together tightly enough that no words could come out. Then I relaxed and said softly, "We've decided to try it."

Ms. Borg smiled and asked if we had any more questions.

"I think that takes care of it," Tom said.

The tone of his voice gave away how we really felt: unhappy but resigned. *What other choice is there?*

"I look forward to meeting Matt," Ms. Borg said pleasantly as she ushered us out of the room.

As we headed down the hallway, Tom and I happened to run into Mr. Brent. We told him about our decision to move Matt into the Interlude program.

He looked at us sympathetically. "I wish there were some way to motivate Matt. He's brighter than ninety percent of the kids in this school."

Mr. Brent shifted gears and told us that the homeroom teachers had distributed the packages of eighth-grade school pictures to students first thing that morning, and Matt had given him one of his. Mr. Brent gave us a sneak preview.

In the photograph, Matt flashed a winning smile; he looked so handsome in his dark blue shirt and yellow fleece vest. It reminded me of the New Year's Eve photo at Ski Liberty, taken after he and his favorite friend had spent the day gliding down the slopes on their snowboards and Matt had been totally in his element.

"You would never think he was having problems in school," Mr. Brent said, shaking his head in puzzlement.

When we returned home, Tom and I decided to break the news about Interlude to Matt the following day. Ms. Borg had told us at the meeting that she liked to start new students on Fridays, the activities day for those who'd completed all their schoolwork for the week.

Even with three more days before Matt moved to Interlude, I already felt relieved about ending the homework struggles. As usual, it was like pulling teeth that evening simply to get him to do a math worksheet and a single page of health definitions.

Shortly after, Matt had a scheduled appointment with Dr. Welch. Tom and I had decided that the drive to the doctor's office would be the best time to tell Matt about Interlude. Not only could he talk to Dr. Welch about it right away, but we also figured he wouldn't run out of a moving car.

Matt was sitting in the front passenger seat, adjusting the volume on the radio, when, about halfway to the appointment, I knew it was time to talk.

I turned to him as I spoke and used my calmest voice. "Remember how Dad and I mentioned that the teachers would be lessening the homework load for you this grading period?"

He finished fiddling with the radio and looked over at me; any cutbacks on homework got his immediate attention.

"You will be starting a new program on Friday that will make it possible for you not to have any homework at all.

That really piqued his interest. "What program is that?"

I hesitated a few seconds, and then slowly uttered, "Interlude."

I looked directly at Matt, expecting him to protest, and he looked back at me in disbelief. His eyes looked wounded, as though I had betrayed him.

"I don't want to go there," he told me firmly.

He looked out the window in dead silence for the rest of the drive. Once again, Matt hid his emotions, but how could he possibly have felt anything but abysmal?

About ten minutes later, I pulled into the parking lot of the medical building. Matt quickly got out of the car and headed into Dr. Welch's office without saying a word to me. He remained silent as he leafed through a few magazines that were kept on a side table in the waiting room.

When Dr. Welch opened the door to his office, Matt finally made eye contact with me again. He didn't look stunned anymore, nor did he seem angry. Instead, he looked resigned.

To my surprise, Matt appeared to rally during his appointment. When he walked back out of Dr. Welch's office, he seemed to be fine. Then again, Matt was a master at hiding his true feelings. I hoped he would open up, at least a little, to me on the car ride home.

Once on the road, I gingerly broached the subject of Interlude again and asked him what Dr. Welch had said about his new program.

"He didn't say much at all. We just played cards and he asked me if I wanted to talk about it."

"And what did you say?" I asked, trying to bury my reporter instincts to grill him.

Matt reached over to the radio to turn on some music, then he looked over at me and smiled. "I told him no."

Matt remained on an even keel during our pizza dinner, growing sad only when I asked him to do his homework. Then, like so many nights before, he pulled his school books out of his bag, took out the worksheets that had been stuffed inside his binder, and reluctantly began to work on them.

■ ■ ■

On the eve of Interlude, Matt had no homework assignments. While it was clear he wasn't thrilled about beginning the next day, he didn't fret about it either.

The following morning, I decided to drive Matt to school, just in case he had second thoughts about going. He didn't put up any resistance, but I was preoccupied at work all day worrying about how he would handle his new class environment, particularly his new classmates. I decided to go home early and work from there until Matt arrived.

Before school ended, I also decided to call Ms. Borg. She said Matt's first day had gone fine; he had fallen asleep in health class, but stayed awake in her program. The students had just returned from the 7-Eleven.

I was in the family room working on my computer when I heard the front door open. A few seconds later, I could hear Matt in the kitchen, opening a cabinet to look for a snack.

"So, how did it go?" I asked Matt as he walked into the room with a small bowl of pretzels.

"It went okay." Matt said.

He walked over to the television and turned it on.

"Do you want to talk about it at all?" I asked.

Matt looked over at me before sitting down to watch a program on the Discovery Channel.

"Not really."

And with that, he sat down on the sofa, munched on his snack, and quickly grew immersed in a show about rebuilding motorcycles.

Relatively speaking, this was a far better response than I had expected. While Tom and I certainly had a lot of doubts about the program, it was refreshing, when I asked about school, that Matt's response didn't include "sucky."

■ ■ ■

Wow. Weekends without homework. It really dawned on me that Saturday how much extra time I would have around the house. I no longer would have the headache of planning my weekends based on Matt's study times, or have Matt's assignments looming over me throughout the week.

With so much freedom ahead of me, I thoroughly enjoyed an hour-long walk with Lucky. It was such a luxury to sit on a bench facing the stream, watching the rushing water from a late winter snow melt and two ducks, their heads bobbing in the black water or plunged beneath the surface with their bottoms up.

■ ■ ■

The first few days of Interlude were uneventful, but Matt's first complaint arose midway through his first full week. He only brought it up after dinner and only briefly, but I could tell it upset him because he started to bite his nails when he talked about it.

A woman who worked at the Ritz-Carlton Hotel came to class and talked about compliments. Matt said he didn't mean to, but he fell asleep. Afterwards, Mr. Meanor, the teacher's aide, took him aside and told him he was rude for not paying attention.

When Matt finished all his work and asked to go on the Internet, Mr. Meanor would not allow him, adding, "Are you sure you are awake enough?"

It turned out that Ms. Borg hadn't been in school that day. I found it hard to believe that Mr. Meanor didn't know about Matt's sleep problem, and I made sure to raise the issue with Ms. Borg the next time we spoke to each other. One real positive about Interlude compared to the regular classroom was that I could reach Ms. Borg the same day if necessary.

■ ■ ■

While Matt's overall experience appeared better and he had been keeping up with his work, I wondered if that would change a week later, after he came down with bronchitis. Recollections flooded back about how overwhelmed he had become at the end of seventh grade when he'd fallen behind in his work. I shuddered at the thought of another hair-pulling incident.

With his cough worsening the next day, I made an appointment with Dr. Goldman. After the exam, to my dismay, Matt had strict orders to stay at home for at least a few days.

I called Ms. Borg about Matt's upcoming absences. The no-homework rule did not apply when Interlude students missed school, so Tom picked up Matt's assignments. He had a lot, but wasn't up to doing anything that required a functioning brain.

I was surprised (and relieved) to see he had pretty challenging work to do and quite a bit of it. I hadn't been sure how demanding the classwork was, but it seemed like his workload was fairly comparable to what he had been doing in the regular classroom.

When Matt was sick the following day, I called Ms. Borg to ask if we should continue to pick up his homework.

"Have him try to do what he has, and I will help him with the rest when he gets back," she said pleasantly.

Matt continued to be sick, so Tom and I took him to his allergist, Dr. Boltansky, who determined he had a sinus infection. Because of Matt's history of asthma, the doctor had him blow as hard as he could into a device, known as a peak flow meter, which measured lung capacity. A low peak flow reading would indicate that Matt needed to use an inhaler; a very low reading would indicate he needed to take prednisone, an anti-inflammatory medicine very effective for opening restricted airways.

Matt blew hard into the long, plastic device, and the measurement was well below normal. Given how clear his lungs had sounded when the allergist initially listened to them with his stethoscope, Dr. Boltansky took Tom and me aside and said quietly, "If Matt's peak flow measurement was really that low, his face would be blue."

Tom explained Matt's history of stomachaches and his claim of a "back injury" in seventh grade after he had missed several days of school and faced a backlog of homework.

Dr. Boltansky appeared somewhat amused by our son's school diversionary tactics. We found it more frustrating than funny.

On Friday afternoon, Matt's third day home from school, he rebounded. I gave him the okay to walk to the park with Lucky and me.

Since he felt one hundred percent better, we even allowed him to have a friend stay overnight. Sometimes when I look back on this period, I wonder why Tom and I didn't question his "illnesses" more often. We essentially rewarded him for "recovering" so conveniently.

■ ■ ■

A few weeks later, Swanson held a cabaret. Matt went but did not perform because he said he had a scratchy throat. Tom suspected it was because Matt had not practiced the choreography. It would have been nice to see him perform "Bye, Bye Love" with three classmates.

Throughout the evening, Matt mingled with several students, boys and girls alike. I noticed Matt would frequently say something that must have been funny, since the other students would begin to laugh easily with him. If Tom and I had any concerns about Matt's placement in Interlude affecting his social life, we were reassured that evening. You could see how happy he was to be among all his classmates away from the confines of a classroom.

I once asked Matt what he told his friends when they asked why he'd moved to Interlude.

"I just tell them I kept falling asleep in class, so they moved me to another program to help me stay awake."

I was glad to see him shrug this off so easily, at least on the outside.

■ ■ ■

Weeks in Interlude moved uneventfully along; Matt did his assignments and was rewarded each Friday afternoon with a variety of activities. However, as May began, Ms. Borg began reporting disconcerting news to us: Matt was beginning to fall asleep in class again and not completing his assignments. Ms. Borg wondered whether he was sleeping more to "prove" we were all wrong and that he didn't have control over his inability to stay awake.

Ironically, only a few weeks earlier, she had observed that Matt had started to come out of his shell in class and had everyone laughing. Until then, he'd generally limited his interaction with the other Interlude students, keeping himself at arms-length; instead, he had friends outside of the program, during lunch, physical education, and chorus classes.

Why had he become so disengaged in class again after showing such steady improvement?

One morning, after slowly getting dressed, Matt would not budge. I tried to make him move and brush his teeth; he only stiffened his body more. I decided to call Dr. Welch, and I was relieved he was in when he answered the phone.

The doctor said that, given Matt's ability to stay alert in school at lunchtime, it was possible he had anxiety about school, but not depression. "You can't turn depression on and off like a spigot."

I decided to offer Matt an ultimatum, rather than knocking my back out trying to physically move dead weight.

"Matt, you have two choices," I told him firmly as he laid in bed. "You can walk to school with Lucky and me, or I can call the school and have Ms. Borg come and get you in ten minutes."

Matt quickly got up.

"It worked like a charm," I told Ms. Borg later over the phone.

"You can use me next year in high school, too," she laughed.

■ ■ ■

That weekend, I had some time at last with Emma; I was the designated driver for her and her friend Katarina on their mission to buy prom gowns. It was such a welcome reprieve to simply listen to my daughter and her friend talk excitedly about the approaching dance.

Emma found a becoming floor-length strapless mint green gown. It was simple yet elegant, and unlike so many of the other selections, it left plenty to the imagination. I still remember how happy she was modeling it for me. My tall, slender daughter with her sparkling sky-blue eyes and brown hair cascading to her shoulders, looked so grown-up.

"You look beautiful!"

"Thanks, Mom!" she said, with a smile that made the price tag worth every penny.

■ ■ ■

The much-dreaded Standards of Learning tests began on Tuesday during the third week of May. Matt took his English SOL and said he slept through part of the testing period. By the time it ended, Matt had only written a single paragraph once again, while most of his classmates had written three or four.

Matt wasn't able to stay awake during his social studies SOL either. It took him two hours to finish the exam; everyone else in his class had finished in forty-five minutes. He was mortified.

■ ■ ■

Two days later, Ms. Borg called me at home: Matt couldn't stay awake at school at all that morning. He'd been sent back to Interlude from health class, and he'd stayed asleep most of the morning.

I made an appointment with the school's middle-aged, no-nonsense psychologist, Dr. Lane. It turned out to be an enlightening forty-five minutes.

He said he detected very little anxiety in Matt and thought his shutting down was passive-aggressiveness taken to the extreme. When he needed to exert effort, Dr. Lane noted, he did not seem to have the will to stay awake.

Years later, I looked back on Dr. Lane's end-of-year report in Matt's special education files. He'd said it was "…very frustrating to watch this pattern unfold. Matt's difficulties with self-regulation apparently have a very long history. He gives into a passive stance and his anger and boredom are being expressed through this ultimate passivity."

At the meeting, however, Dr. Lane used different terminology: "I think it is a subconscious, but nonetheless manipulative temper tantrum," he told me bluntly.

I didn't know quite what to think. "I have never heard his behavior explained quite this way before. What do you suggest we do?"

"Offer rewards to go to bed early. I think Matt is sleep-deprived; he should have at least nine hours of sleep to function normally. As it is," he explained, "Matt gets into a self-perpetuating pattern: he stays up late, sleeps during the day, and then has a hard time falling asleep at night."

I was not too impressed with this reward system recommendation, having heard it and tried it many times already. "If that is the problem, then why is he animated at lunch and during class electives?"

"He is motivated and wants to do those things," Dr. Lane said.

"So, what do you want us to do about his behavior?"

"Make it clear to Matt that his tantrums are not acceptable, and that he has to stay awake and complete his homework and go to bed, or he can't do things he likes to do. He has got to break this cycle in the next two years, or he will be setting himself up for a lifetime of battles," Dr. Lane warned.

So, once again, we were told to try tough love. It hadn't worked before, though—why would this time be any different?

■ ■ ■

Matt stayed awake all day. Then again, it *was* Friday. And the eve of his fourteenth birthday.

At his birthday celebration, everything went right. Matt spent the day with friends at an indoor skatepark, and then they all came over. After pizza and mocha mud pie, Tom and I were pleasantly surprised how well-behaved the boys were in the family room. They quietly watched a video they'd made of themselves while they were skating that morning, courtesy of one friend's camera, followed by a couple of real pros, including painful bloopers befitting a *Jackass* episode.

If only such normal days would continue in school.

■ ■ ■

A few days after his birthday, Matt was a dead weight again, moving in slow-motion while he got ready for yet another three hours of humiliation—another SOL.

I thought it was asinine that everyone, with the exception of extremely mentally challenged children, was required to take the high-stakes standardized test. As Matt dissolved in tears, I decided to voice my solution.

"Try your best, but if you find yourself shutting down, just fill in the damn bubbles any way you want. It's not a real measurement of what you know when you take that test half asleep," I said, the frustration rising in my voice.

If the state won't give exemptions, then beat them at their own game, I thought. *He might as well complete the test on his own terms.*

Not long after Matt made it to school, Ms. Borg called me.

"Matt took the test in record time," she said. "Thirteen minutes."

I stayed quiet until I could see where she was going.

"I have had kids hand in blank test sheets at the end of class, but I have *never* had a student get permission from a parent *not* to do the test. He simply handed it in *during* the test period." She paused a moment, then added, "He even filled in some of the bubbles to take the shape of his initials."

At that, I had to stifle a laugh, knowing Matt's imaginative wit could sometimes get the better of him.

"For the rest of bubbles," she said, "he spelled out an opinion about the test."

"And what was it?" I asked warily, knowing full well how much we both disliked the standardized exam.

Ms. Borg paused again before she told me, "SOLs suck."

While Ms. Borg seemed surprised, she did not sound angry. In fact, I thought I detected a trace of amusement in her voice.

■ ■ ■

I met with Dr. Lane again.

"Keep focusing on keeping Matt awake," he advised.

He was beginning to sound like a broken CD, and I found myself uncharacteristically questioning his judgment.

"I think we need to get to the root of his problem before he can snap out of his shutdowns," I told him, surprising myself.

I could tell Dr. Lane was unphased by my observation.

"An immature fourteen-year-old doesn't think in terms of 'whys,'" Dr. Lane retorted. He shook his head. "Matt is the first boy in about thirteen years that I would recommend go to a military school. I think its rigid structure and reward system would be the right environment for him."

It was my turn to shake my head. I was dead set against this notion, and I knew that Tom would be, too. "We are not sending him away."

Seeing my firmness on this issue (he probably called it stubbornness), Dr. Lane offered an alternative: "Your husband and you need to keep focusing on helping him to break his pattern of thinking, to rewire his brain from avoidance of situations to managing them."

"He's a complex young man," Dr. Lane opined with a sense of finality to his words.

I took his cue, thanked him for his time, and left his office.

When I spoke to Tom that evening, he readily agreed that military school was the wrong way to go. A teaching model that stressed uniformity would only reinforce the message that Matt received daily, namely that he was a square peg in a round hole. As for Dr. Lane's advice to help Matt "rewire his brain," we were completely dumbfounded. How could we possibly help Matt "break his pattern of thinking," when we didn't know what it was?

■ ■ ■

Shortly after my meeting with Dr. Lane, Matt had an asthma flareup.

Although I allowed him to come home, I also checked with the allergist's nurse. Since he had no fever and his chest was clear, she told me to give him a few puffs of his inhaler and send him back to school.

I marched him back just in time for lunch.

■ ■ ■

Finally, Matt's eighth grade graduation. A few of his friends came over after the quiet ceremony and ate a celebratory cake on the deck:

Despite the long and rocky road, Matt would start ninth grade in the fall. We had been warned about the Interlude program in high school from some teacher friends we knew. They'd called it a warehouse for students who were out of control or too withdrawn to function.

But for now, we tried to simply enjoy the day.

I breathed a sigh of relief. Once again, at least while Matt was out of school for the summer, we would have some weeks of normalcy.

▪ CHAPTER 10 ▪

College Media News Service
(2001)

It was only a few days into summer vacation, and Matt was already bored. Then, out of nowhere, he asked me if he could still work at the radio program I had mentioned to him earlier in the year.

I was surprised that Matt even remembered the internship that my friend Ellen had recommended when she'd found out about his problems at school. Then again, Ellen had also mentioned she would pay him one hundred dollars a week for his work. And that he could even bring a friend.

"Sure, he can start anytime he wants," Ellen told me when I asked her if the offer was still good.

We decided to wait until after the Fourth of July, since we would be visiting my family in Pennsylvania during the holiday.

Matt invited his friend, Mark, to work at the news service with him. They had been long-fast friends ever since Mark moved a few doors down from us when Matt was in fourth grade.

Their first internship day was July 10. It took me a long time to find Ellen's studio in Georgetown that morning. As I drove through the maze of streets, I stopped several times to ask for directions; befuddled pedestrians said they had never heard of the street before. Finally, a long-time resident pointed it out.

Mill Street turned out to be the rear alley of a parking lot behind an old brick apartment building. The news service was in one of two townhouses located on the small block.

The studio itself had a college dorm feel to it—newspapers scattered on a coffee table and several young men and women immersed in conversations about what they should cover that day for their web-based stories.

Once we arrived, I stayed long enough to introduce the boys to Ellen, who, busy as usual, was just about to dash out the door. She had to make a hastily arranged meeting and only had time to say hello before handing them over to the internship coordinator. She promised to talk to the boys about their assignments once she returned in the afternoon.

Even though she was barely five feet tall, Ellen's piercing dark eyes and tell-it-like-it-is manner left no doubt she was a force to be reckoned with in the media world. Yet she was also one of the most generous people I knew, always looking for ways to help the underdog and sparing no expense when it came to social causes she believed in.

Matt was someone she decided to take under her wing. She had no patience with the traditional school system, and when she saw potential in bright young students who were slipping through the cracks, she found ways to spark their creativity. Having the opportunity to work on interesting projects seemed like a formula that might work for Matt.

The first assignment for the two boys was an easy one: to accompany one of the college students to Capitol Hill to get their press credentials.

When Matt came home that evening, the first thing he said was how much he liked his new boss, especially after she disapproved of his green floral shirt and skateboard pants.

"You look like a fuckin' rag muffin," blunt-spoken Ellen had told him—an observation that had apparently won Matt over immediately. He promised her he would wear something more professional the next day. (As promised, after dinner, we shopped for clothes that were more presentable for the news service: khaki pants and five plaid cotton shirts.)

After telling Tom and me about his wardrobe malfunction, Matt proudly showed us his press pass. The expression on his face was reminiscent of the eighth-grade photograph, when he'd smiled as warmly at the camera as if he were on top of the world. Below his media credential, it read "Studio Producer – 2001."

That afternoon, Mark and Matt had shadowed a radio talk show intern at a campaign finance reform press conference featuring well-known Arizona Senator John McCain. What a contrast from Interlude and its classroom outings to the Seven-Eleven! He felt excited about returning to the studio the next day, not dread.

To my surprise, Matt's friend was lukewarm about going back the next morning, according to his mom. Unlike Matt, Mark did not feel comfortable surrounded by students so much older than him. He also wasn't keen about going out on reporting assignments.

Matt, on the other hand, loved the challenge of piecing information together, just like he loved to build things. We were impressed with how the radio internship helped him to work independently through complicated issues. A case in point was Matt's coverage of a Senate hearing on stem cell research. When he came home that evening, he noted that the moving testimony of all the diseases it could cure had led him to believe the scientific studies should continue.

His friend Mark's interest piqued, too, but for a different reason— the main speaker advocating for greater funding that day was a well-known actor, Ben Affleck. Matt and Mark had their picture taken with the celebrity after the hearing ended, and Matt told the Hollywood star that he liked him in *Good Will Hunting, Armageddon,* and his newest movie, *Pearl Harbor* (which Matt hadn't actually seen yet). He came away with an autographed copy of Affleck's testimony.

"How can I do this internship?" Emma wanted to know when she found out about Matt's celebrity encounter.

After a few days of attending press conferences and congressional hearings, Matt and Mark were given their first assignment. The internship coordinator sent them off to do man-on-the street interviews about skateboarding at Freedom Plaza, a promenade on Pennsylvania Avenue that had become a popular spot for skaters because of its wide-open space, granite steps, and low ledges. Keeping the skateboarders off the sidewalks had also become a major headache for D.C. police officers.

Matt and Mark interviewed pedestrians and a few foolhardy skaters who practiced kickflips between episodes scattering at the sight of an approaching cop. The boys asked the policeman and later a National Park Service officer why there weren't more skateparks in the D.C. area. Not surprisingly, their story put a positive spin on skating and explained why, instead of getting down on skaters for being on the streets, there should be more skateparks.

On one assignment, the boys interviewed Israeli and Palestinian children who visited Washington after attending Peace Camp in New England. Another story focused on a federal court ruling that Napster, a peer-to-peer file-sharing network, infringed on the intellectual property rights of musicians and recording companies by enabling access to free music downloads. Matt opposed the decision, no doubt swayed by the large number of songs he had downloaded for free.

Throughout the summer, Matt and Mark covered a variety of stories that would appeal to college students. Once they'd finished recording their interviews, the boys returned to the studio to edit their work and launch the audio pieces on the news service website.

I was impressed by the quality of Matt's work, and I asked him how he'd managed to put so much information in so few words. Did he have an editor help him write the script?

"What script?" Matt replied. "I didn't write anything down. I just did it."

How was it possible for Matt to put together well-crafted new reports when he couldn't stay awake to write a few paragraphs for his English schoolwork or his SOL? How could he focus for hours on producing work that interested him when he was unable to concentrate on much simpler work at school?

■ ■ ■

At an annual crab feast hosted by close family friends in early August, I talked about our challenges with Matt to one of the daughters. Jan was in her late thirties and had a special needs child. She worked closely with the school system to ensure they provided the necessary accommodations for her daughter, who had multiple learning disabilities.

"It's a lot different once your children get out of elementary school. If you want services in middle school and high school, you have to advocate for them, especially at IEP meetings," Jan stressed.

She added that it could even mean hiring a special education consultant, if necessary, who would speak the same language as the school counselors and teachers developing the plan. While I felt that our struggles with Matt were far less daunting than what Jan was tackling, I took her advice to heart.

■ ■ ■

A few evenings later, I was walking Lucky and ran into a neighbor I hadn't seen for a while. Val was a public school teacher, and we'd knew each other ever since our children had gone to grade school. Her son and daughter were not the same ages as Emma and Matt, though, so once they'd moved on to middle school, we'd simply lost touch.

I told Val about Matt's remarkable improvement over the summer and how awful Interlude had been for him.

"It's so frustrating because he wants to do well in school and go to college someday, like his sister, so much. Yet it all seems out of his grasp when he can't stay awake in the classroom."

"I have to admit, I am really surprised Matt hasn't given up yet, especially on college, after all he's gone through," Val said.

She thought for a moment and then mentioned a school in Fairfax a neighbor's son had attended. "It's called the New School of Northern Virginia," she said.

The school sounded familiar to me, and then I remembered why. Dr. Greenstein had mentioned it after she'd tested Matt in December. Tom and I had thought it would be too far away, so we hadn't seriously considered it.

"My neighbor's son is a smart kid, but he wasn't doing well at all in high school," Val told me. "His mom said he turned himself around once he got there. When he first met the head of the school, he mentioned how much he loved playing drums; the school tries to personalize learning, so he was able to do some of his assignments in relation to music."

Val noted that by the time the neighbor's son had completed high school, he was valedictorian of his class.

When I got home that evening, I mentioned the New School to Tom and how it appeared to work wonders. We looked up more information about the school on its website, and what appealed most was the school's respect for individual learning styles and its recognition of the many ways a child can be "gifted."

Given Matt's success working on his own assignments at the summer internship program, Tom and I hoped and believed Matt would do equally well in a college preparatory school that allowed students the flexibility to produce work the way they could convey it the best. We decided to make an appointment to see the school for ourselves and to bring Matt along with us.

■ ■ ■

In August, we met the headmaster, Dr. John Potter, in his office. Potter, with his snow-white hair and beard, explained the philosophy of the school, which was based on Howard Gardner's theory of multiple intelligences.

"Some of our students are visual learners. Others are kinesthetic, learning best by doing projects," he explained. As part of their graduation requirements, he said, students must submit a portfolio of their best schoolwork.

There was no mistaking that Matt could not learn the way Arlington Public School programs taught him.

Matt had not failed school. School had failed him. It simply did not reach him in the way he processed information and learned. We believed that the New School-style of teaching, however, might be able to reach him.

PAULA LAZOR

Matt did a great job explaining the work he was doing in the summer program, but I noticed that when only Dr. Potter and I were talking, Matt started to nod off. Once again, I felt a tight knot in my stomach. Matt had been so excited about starting the new school year at a different place. Why was this happening again?

I remained outwardly calm, but on the inside my heart was pounding. I frantically tried to dream up a diversionary tactic, then I found one. I nonchalantly suggested that Matt walk around the leafy grounds of the school while Tom and I filled out paperwork for admission into the program.

If Dr. Potter had noticed Matt's sleepiness, he never mentioned it, and once back in the car, Matt was fully alert and all smiles as he talked enthusiastically about the school.

Tom and I were reassured by his quick comeback. Even though the episode in Dr. Potter's office had been puzzling, we reminded ourselves that it had also been brief. So, hopeful about our prospects for the New School, I put it behind me, and so did Tom.

The following day, Matt had an appointment with Dr. Welch. The doctor readily agreed that it was time to try a different school, given how remarkably Matt had done at the radio studio.

■ ■ ■

As often happened during our long journey to find the right program for Matt, people would arrive in our lives just when we needed them the most. One afternoon in mid-August, I struck up a conversation with another neighbor at our community club pool.

Diane told me about the Applied Academic Career Education (AACE) program at Arlington Public School's Career Center. The program worked on a semester schedule and offered two required courses each session as well as hands-on electives, such as auto technology, audio and video production, and even a certified emergency technology program.

I was completely surprised by this. *Why didn't the school guidance office provide information about this program?*

I decided to call the AACE director to find out more about it. Did it start in ninth grade? If not, why not?

On Monday morning, I spent a lot of time on the phone with the Career Center to see if there was an alternative program for Matt. The best it could arrange was a patchwork solution: two electives at the Career Center, but all his academic work would remain in Interlude. This was too disjointed a solution, plus none of us wanted Matt to be housed in the high school Interlude program, particularly given the warning about it we received earlier.

■ ■ ■

Over Labor Day weekend, I had one other chance encounter. The mother of one of Emma's friends and I struck up a conversation at the community pool club, which seemed to have suddenly developed into a hub of special education information. She urged me to document all correspondence I had with the school system, including IEP requirements for Matt from Washington-Lee.

Little did I realize at the time how invaluable these written records would be in the years ahead.

▪ CHAPTER 11 ▪

The New School
(2001)

Matt's first day at the New School was September 10, but it did not start as smoothly as we had hoped. He was late.

Perhaps it was an ill omen, but Matt developed a serious infection in the cartilage of his right ear after having both of them pierced at the beach during our family vacation in mid-August. He had spent the weekend in the emergency room twice to treat the ear infection with prescribed antibiotics, but the condition worsened.

The ER doctor directed us to have Matt see a surgeon on Monday morning, right at the time he would have begun his first-period class on his first day of school. We drove to the surgeon's office, only to find out he would not be in until the afternoon.

Matt took two Advil to ease the pain of his throbbing red ear and we set off to the New School. Even though he had missed the morning classes, at least he would be there the second half of the day, sore ear and all. Tom arranged to pick Matt up from school for his afternoon appointment while I went downtown to work.

I still remember driving home from the Metro that evening in the heavy rain. Tom and Matt were not there, but shortly after my arrival, the phone rang. It was Tom.

Matt's antibiotics were not fighting the infection completely, so the surgeon had admitted him to Arlington Hospital shortly after seeing him. No one said it at the time, but given the location of his infection, the surgeon must have been concerned that it could spread. He scheduled a procedure the following afternoon to lance the cartilage, drain the infected fluid, and put him on a different, heavy-duty antibiotic.

■ ■ ■

Tuesday morning. September 11. I had turned on one of the cable networks in Matt's hospital room shortly before nine in the morning and glanced at the TV screen. My first thought was that the network was covering some window washers stuck on the side of a tall building somewhere.

"I wish the networks wouldn't draw attention to things that really aren't national news," I told Matt, tired of seeing aerial coverage of car chases or celebrity breakups cast as breaking stories.

Then I looked more carefully at the television screen.

"Oh my God," I uttered in disbelief.

The World Trade Center had a large black hole in the side where a plane had shot through it. Only a few moments later, as Matt and I were trying to figure out how many floors were below the crash scene, a news anchor reported excitedly about the horrific accident.

At first, we thought we were watching a replay of the initial crash. When we realized it was another airplane hitting the second building, we knew this was a terrorist attack. I ran to the nurse's station to tell them what had happened.

I ran back to the nurse's station again to relay the news after the third plane crashed into the Pentagon. One nurse looked at me with all the color drained from her face.

"We are the closest hospital to the Pentagon," she said.

Not long after the Pentagon crash, a fourth plane dove to the earth on farmland in Shanksville, Pennsylvania.

Tom joined us at the hospital shortly after the Pentagon attack, but Emma was not allowed to leave high school, and because all the phone circuits were busy, she could not reach us at the hospital. She later said that she and her classmates were riveted to CNN and actually watched people as they fell from the 110-story buildings.

At first, Matt was as mesmerized as the rest of his family over the unfolding drama. At one point, however, he said he had seen enough and asked to switch the station to Comedy Central.

It was so surreal and impossible to process. What could Matt have been feeling, trying to take this all in while awaiting surgery? His medical procedure was distinctly overshadowed by such incomprehensible and horrific acts of violence.

■ ■ ■

Matt was trapped in a hospital in disaster mode for the next four days; he was finally released on September 15. On Monday, one week after his belated start at the New School, Matt returned with his head and ear bandaged.

A few days later, we received a letter from Dr. Potter. He sent it to all the families, assuring them that the New School was a safe haven. The letter was prompted by the fears of several parents of Middle Eastern descent, who had suddenly withdrawn their children from the school immediately after the attacks.

The New School was a welcoming and inclusive community. I believe their fears were unfounded, but I also remember the news reports of individuals with Middle Eastern names being treated with suspicion by others for several months after 9/11. The thought of future attacks in our country still loomed large, particularly for those of us who lived in the targeted cities of New York City and Washington. Nonetheless, we tried our best to keep our regular routines at home and live each day as normally as possible.

This was difficult to do the first few weeks of Matt's arrival home. Twice a day, once before school and once in the evening, Matt was required to take an antibiotic so potent that it had to be administered intravenously, or else it could stunt his growth.

I was impressed how Matt managed to administer his medicine so skillfully. Before leaving the hospital, a portal had been inserted beneath the skin on his arm. He deftly injected the medicine through a rubber stop into the port. The antibiotic travelled through the portal to tubing, which carried it to a large vein leading to the heart.

If this procedure had been up to me to do, I probably would have passed out. Fortunately, Matt volunteered (with doctor approval) and was a quick learner. He even seemed fascinated by this hands-on approach to administer the medicine. As a fourteen-year-old, he probably thought it was a cool thing to do.

■ ■ ■

Despite his rocky start at school, the teachers' initial reports about Matt were encouraging. He participated in his classes and was particularly engaged in those involving class discussions.

A few days into the school year, I was surprised when he told me that he was disappointed so many of his classmates were older than him, since several of the courses were available at all grade levels. He had worked all summer long with college students and seemed to feel comfortable around older teenagers then, so I was a little stumped.

Then an idea popped into my head. Matt had mentioned when he registered for classes that the school had a lunch van for any students who wanted to buy a sandwich at a nearby shopping center. I suggested he try the van the following day as an opportunity to meet kids his age.

The next day was much better for Matt. He took my suggestion and hopped on the lunch van; it hadn't taken him long to strike up a few friendships. He came home that evening and told me how nice all the other students were in welcoming him aboard.

"I really liked everyone. Some of us went to a deli and bought sandwiches," Matt said happily.

I remember thinking what a difference the New School had on Matt's self-esteem. What a sharp contrast with Interlude. Compared to his confined quarters in eighth grade, where he had been identified as emotionally disturbed, Matt now had both independence and trust, at a school where he was treated equally and where there were no labels. He was once again a regular student, no longer "special."

■ ■ ■

Matt's first week back at school looked promising; he was doing his assignments and genuinely looked forward to his classes. However, he also missed two days.

The first time was because he'd whacked his ear on a wooden tray in the living room just as he'd finished his IV drip and was ready to head to school. It was so painful that he stayed home.

One morning four days later, Matt inadvertently bent his arm in such a way that it stopped the flow of his antibiotic from his IV drip. No one from home care could come to the house until early afternoon to replace the tubing.

Looking back years later, I can't help but wonder if these were accidents-on-purpose, especially since we discovered the following week that the days he'd attended school were not as smooth as he'd led us to believe.

On the evening of September 24, only two weeks into the school year, Matt was in a funk. When I asked what was wrong, he reluctantly admitted that he had begun sleeping off and on through many of his classes. That morning, he'd found out he had an exhibit due in his favorite but most missed class, Planet Manhattan, which ironically enough, focused on New York City.

Tom and I told him to talk to his teachers and advisers, and we assured him that it was still early in the grading period. We also reminded him that he'd had a tough start, given that his first week of school was spent in the hospital and he had to wake up each morning hooked up to an IV drip. There was also always the possibility that the sleep issue could be attributed to recuperation from what surely had been a traumatic event on September 11, or a side effect of his antibiotics. Thankfully, at least the antibiotic routine would end the following day.

We kept our fingers crossed for the rest of Matt's second week.

■ ■ ■

The phone call came as his third week of school began.

Matt called from the school office sounding very sleepy, almost in a stupor. He'd been asked to leave computer class because he'd fallen asleep. I gave approval for him to take a public bus home early.

That evening, he hardly did any homework; he half-listened, eyes closed, to a Planet Manhattan tape, falling asleep at the end of the recording.

Once again, he was very frustrated about shutting down in class and embarrassed that children were starting to notice his behavior and comment on it.

"One kid keeps asking me if I am going to fall asleep again," Matt said, tears welling. "One boy drew a flower on my finger while I was asleep," he said, showing me the pen and ink drawing on his index finger. Matt didn't know who did it, but it was a sore reminder of his bad day.

Matt was too upset by bedtime to fall asleep easily. When Lucky barked at midnight, I was surprised to see that Matt was still awake and was holding our lovable dog in his lap. At least he was no longer upset.

■ ■ ■

The following day I confided in a reporter friend who had been an understanding sounding board for me about Matt in the past. Keith often boosted my spirits and encouraged me to press on.

"I know Matt is having a rough time at school. Make sure he knows you love him, but also be frank with him about his future there if he doesn't wake up and smell the coffee."

If only it were that easy.

■ ■ ■

Back to school night at the New School was held on October 3. If sleep had become a major issue for Matt, his teachers did not let on about it. *Maybe Matt has built it up in his mind and it isn't as pronounced as he presents it to us.* Tom and I held on to that hope as we followed Matt's class schedule, moving from room to room to meet with the teachers and chat for a few minutes.

"I would have loved going to a school like this!" Tom exclaimed as we changed classes.

It was a collegial atmosphere. Matt could not have had a more perfect adviser, who also doubled as his math and computer technology teacher. In both classes, there was only one other student, and in both cases, they complemented each other.

Janis (all teachers and students were on a first-name basis with each other) said Matt was a natural at mathematics and did a lot of complicated steps in his head. His math classmate, however, struggled with the problems and wrote every step down. Of course, it was only natural that Matt would try to write as little as possible, which goes with the territory!

What puzzled us, however, was the stark contrast in mathematical abilities he displayed at the New School, given the nightmare it had been for him in middle school. Why the difference? Was it the one-on-one attention, or had they simply not advanced to the level of mathematics he had struggled with in the previous three years?

We could understand why Matt liked his world studies teacher, a burly, friendly, German-accented man with a droll sense of humor. He, too, gave favorable reports about Matt, noting how bright he was and how much he participated in class discussions.

When I'd reported Matt's sleep problem to Dr. Welch earlier that day, he'd concluded that Matt's sleeping state was not school avoidance and had to be physiologically based.

"Something neurological is triggering the shutdown. Why else would he fall asleep in a class he likes and feels comfortable attending?"

On the one hand, I was encouraged by the reports by Matt's teachers after the open house. Dr. Welch's comment remained in the back of my mind, though, too.

If the problem is neurological and not related to school, what will happen to Matt as the school year progresses?

■ ■ ■

I didn't have to wait long for the answer.

I had barely found a parking spot near the metro in the morning when I noticed a message on my pager from the New School. My heart sank as I got back into the car and drove the ten miles to pick him up.

Matt had fallen asleep again.

When I entered the school office, Matt got up from his chair, said a quick goodbye to the receptionist—without making eye contact—and followed me out the door.

He was very quiet in the car on the ride back home. At first, he simply looked out the window. When he did turn to me, he looked as befuddled as Tom and I were about this development. Finally, Matt fell asleep.

For the first time, when I pulled into the driveway and woke him up, Matt noted that he could make a distinction between his nap in the car and "shutting down" at school.

"When I fall asleep at school, I feel like I'm under anesthesia," Matt told me.

No doubt he was able to make that comparison, given how recently he'd had ear surgery.

■ ■ ■

Less than a week later, Matt was placed on stage two of the five-stage school disciplinary process. The school reported that he hadn't done any work, except for math, where he was behind. Neurological or not, the impact of Matt's sleep problem on his studies was snowballing.

We spoke with Dr. Potter throughout the course of the week. He suggested we consider a sleep study to see if the root of Matt's problem was a sleep disorder. We were able to set up an appointment at Children's Hospital in Washington, D.C., but the earliest they could take him at the sleep lab was in November.

Thankfully, the New School was willing to work with us to find alternative ways to help Matt catch up with his classwork. The plan: Matt would go to school in the morning and meet me in the afternoon at the Farragut West Metro stop near my office downtown.

The first day we attempted this, Matt was unsuccessful at staying awake at my office to work on his math and Planet Manhattan assignments. When I tried to nudge him into doing his homework (math he'd known easily when we'd gone over the problems orally), he got a deer-in-the-headlights look.

The following day, Matt met with Dr. Welch, who prescribed two anxiety medicines—the first to address the sleepiness issue, and the second one to treat the underlying stress Matt had about school and his school performance. Dr. Welch also offered him the wise counsel not to worry about falling behind, that grades weren't everything, and to focus on keeping up with his current assignments.

Janis emailed me in the evening and said that Matt only needed to read through chapter two of his math book and do a few examples from each section. She also gave him a Microsoft tutorial to download that was supposed to be entertaining.

Matt came into work with me again the next day and tried to do his assignments, but once more, grew too sleepy to do any homework.

We stopped for lunch at Reeves Bakery, my favorite restaurant for home-style cooking. I was a regular there, so, not surprisingly, the waitresses showered Matt with attention. On our way to the metro, we walked through Lafayette Park across from the White House. As luck would have it, a mounted policeman was standing guard on Pennsylvania Avenue and let Matt pet his horse, who (much to Matt's delight) tried to get into his knapsack for an apple! I felt thankful that through an otherwise frustrating day, Matt and I were able to find some light moments at lunch and the park.

And there was great news when we arrived home. Children's Hospital had been able to move up his sleep test to the following day. Hopefully, we would be able to get to the root of Matt's problem and take action sooner than later!

▪ CHAPTER 12 ▪

Narcolepsy and the New Game Plan

If alien abductions were common, Matt could have easily been mistaken for an extraterrestrial's captive. With tubes and electrodes tangled all around, he looked like an earthling being probed by higher intelligence from a faraway galaxy, at least to me, in the sleep lab of Children's Hospital the following evening.

The sleep lab was in a separate section of the hospital and, not surprisingly, was very quiet when we entered it. A friendly lab technician introduced himself and told Matt he would be preparing him for the test before leading him into a room that included a television and nightstand. It was set up for him to watch shows or read; prior to the testing period, patients were encouraged to go about their usual nightly routines.

Just before the lab's designated bedtime, the sleep technician attached sensors designed to measure brain waves, heart rate, breathing and oxygen level to Matt's scalp and chest. The wires were long enough for Matt to easily move around and turn over in bed. At the start of the test, the technician asked Matt to move his eyes, clench his teeth, and move his legs to make sure that the sensors were working.[2]

Fortunately, Matt had no objection to taking the sleep test; in fact, he'd seemed more than willing to try it. "I'll do anything to find a way to stop this," he'd said to Tom and me when we told him about his upcoming procedure. He still appeared to be fine with the in-lab study as all the devices were attached, probably because of the novelty of it. However, I couldn't help but wonder how accurate the results would be. *How could anyone possibly have a normal night's sleep while hooked up to monitors tracking every eye movement and brain wave?*

The technician assured me that while many patients did not sleep as well as they would at home, it typically did not affect the results. "In most cases, you don't need a full eight hours of sleep for the doctor to make a diagnosis."

When Tom and I returned to the hospital the next morning, Matt pleasantly greeted us. He was scheduled for the second part of his sleep study, a daytime "sleep latency" test that measured the amount of time it took him to fall asleep. The technician (this time, a cheerful young woman) explained how the procedure worked.

Matt was required to take four short naps scheduled about two hours apart. Because it normally takes about twelve minutes to fall asleep, a latency period of eight minutes or less would suggest a disorder of excessive daytime sleepiness.

During the first two tests, Matt would work on some math problems, and I would notify the technician if he fell asleep. The technician would then attach sensors to monitor Matt's brain waves and other vital signs. We would repeat the same procedure for the third and fourth studies, only during the last two tests, Matt would read books. Each test would take fifteen minutes, unless he fell asleep; if he fell asleep, the test would take an additional fifteen minutes.

---

2. For more information about how the sleep studies are conducted, please see The American Academy of Sleep Medicine, Sleep Education In-lab Sleep Study Testing Process, http://www.sleepeducation.org/essentials-in-sleep/in-lab-sleep-study/testing-process-results

Shortly before ten in the morning, I handed Matt his math book, paper, and pencil. He dutifully began to read the examples in chapter two, section one. He put the thick math book on his lap, placed a sheet of paper on top of it, and started to copy down one of his homework problems.

It didn't take long for Matt to demonstrate how quickly he could fall asleep. After only a few minutes, I noticed his head bobbing forward suddenly. He caught himself and began his task once again, but in less than five minutes, he'd conked out, his head resting up against the back of the chair.

As instructed beforehand, I left the room immediately to let the technician know. Unfortunately, when she came in, Matt woke up.

We repeated this procedure twice, and each time, Matt fell asleep well before the eight-minute mark. Thankfully, in these two test periods, the technician was able to apply the sensors without Matt awakening.

Next, he began reading an English assignment. I told him to keep trying, even if it meant reading some paragraphs over and over again. Sure enough, within five minutes, he was asleep again, even experiencing full body jerks. I could see why this really embarrassed him when it happened in class.

The first time, I ventured over to move his book and he woke up, so the next time he fell asleep, I decided to leave it on his lap. Matt's body had jerked completely for the fifth or sixth time (the last one waking him enough that he sat up and shifted his body before falling asleep completely again) by the time the technician hooked him up. He remained asleep for the prescribed time.

As part of the fourth and final test, I'd requested and the doctor had agreed to let Matt read a book that would hold his interest. Matt stayed awake for this test, reading something stimulating—in this case, *Ripley's Believe It or Not*.

Preliminary results showed that Matt had an unusual pattern of Rapid Eye Movement (REM) in one stage of sleep. Based on that information alone, Dr. Pearl felt confident beginning him on Provigil, a new medication used for treating narcolepsy.

．．．

While we waited for final test results, Tom and I thought we should send Matt to school, even if only for partial days, limited to classes that involved physical activities. New School was willing to allow Matt to withdraw from his speech class and "audit" Planet Manhattan if it looked like he would not be able to catch up or do a scaled-down exhibition; they also looked into adding a physical education class or two to his temporary schedule. In hopes that a hands-on approach to math might work for him, they sent Matt an Algebra CD-ROM to use at home.

We were so appreciative of the school's flexibility and willingness to help us make this work. Because they were on a quarter system and students signed up for new courses each grading period, Matt would be able to start with a clean slate for the next session in late November.

We began an unconventional form of education that allowed Matt to spend part of his school day at museums downtown. On his first day using Provigil, Matt went to the Air and Space and the Holocaust Memorial museums. Since it was so soon after September 11, tourists were spooked about visiting D.C., and the museums were sparsely attended.

Matt told us he'd ducked into a comic book store in Georgetown before heading home, where he'd run into a student from the New School. Surprised to see him, he'd asked Matt why he hadn't been coming to the Planet Manhattan class lately.

"What did you tell him?"

"I told him I'm trying new medicine to see if it can keep me from sleeping during the day," Matt said matter-of-factly.

While I was glad that he'd handled this chance encounter so smoothly (it certainly could have been an awkward one), it also made me wonder how he truly felt about being away from a school that he actually wanted to attend. It had to be frustrating for him. But was he also embarrassed? The last thing he needed was to feel like an outcast.

Matt told us he felt perkier that evening, yet he grew sleepy and was unable to stay awake when he tried to do math. When bedtime arrived, though, he was wide awake again. He didn't fall asleep until well after midnight, when I finally hit the covers.

■ ■ ■

While we waited for Matt's medicine to take effect over the next few weeks, Ellen agreed to let him work at the studio again in the afternoons. We hoped that his experience at the studio would boost his self-confidence once again, enough to get him back to school awake and alert later in October. Matt told us he really liked it and he seemed a lot happier with himself.

To get home the first day, he walked from the studio to Farragut West with a college intern to get his press pass fixed, then hopped the metro to Ballston, where he caught a bus home. This was one certain learning experience for Matt: he learned how to get around on public transportation, probably better than many adults in Washington.

To our surprise, the following Monday, Matt rode home on an electric scooter.

Part of his duties for the college media news service included doing reviews. Most interns asked for CDs to do music reviews, but Matt didn't limit his scope like that. He'd been doing research on mopeds (motorized scooters), so he'd contacted manufacturers and asked them to send scooters for him to review.

He was allowed to keep the electric scooter after reviewing it for the news program. His next review was on a gas-powered scooter that he donated to the studio. *How generous.* I had to admit, this kid was pretty enterprising when he put his mind to it.

Matt was in good spirits when we drove to his appointment with Dr. Welch that Wednesday. The mood did not last, however—Dr. Welch told Matt to forego the scooter until he finished some math.

The doctor broached the prospect of a residential therapeutic school if Matt continued to not perform. Tom and I were troubled by the thought, but tried not to show it in front of Matt. We thought Dr. Welch was playing hardball, provoking Matt to get him angry enough to crawl out of his academic hole. Matt, as usual, showed no emotion—but what was brewing inside of him?

■ ■ ■

Emma's homecoming weekend fell in mid-October, during those first fruitful days at the studio. It was such a blessing to have some normal lulls, to simply help out other high school parents set up snacks at the homecoming pre-game concession stand. There was such a small town feeling to it—excited teens competing in the float contest, exuberant cheerleaders screaming the team on to a 43-0 victory. I enjoyed watching Emma in the marching band during their half-time performance when she didn't notice—she was so happy, confident and grown up.

Although Emma had wondered about Matt's experience at the sleep lab, it hadn't appeared to weigh on her mind very much—and understandably so. She was on the verge of circuit overload at school. Ironically, she was so busy juggling homework, projects, school activities, and her social life that she hadn't found the time to look at colleges—the whole point of all her studying and SAT prep.

After we'd visited Dr. Welch, Emma gave me one of the parenting lectures she'd occasionally dredge up. She said she was not mad at me, but at Matt, because he didn't do any schoolwork. Rather than grow defensive or argue with her, I decided to take Lucky for a walk to let off some steam. When I walked back into the house and entered the kitchen to take off Lucky's leash, Emma was sitting at the table.

"Mom," Emma said, her voice quivering a bit, "I'm sorry. I don't mean to complain to you about Matt. I just get upset because I work so hard on my homework and stay up late to finish it. When I go to bed, Matt is usually still up, too. But he is playing games on his laptop. No wonder he can't stay awake during the day!"

The next morning, I removed Matt's laptop from his bedroom. "Staying up late to play on your laptop is not an option," I told him in exasperation. This wouldn't be the last time I had to remind Matt to go to bed at a decent hour.

The second quarter at the New School was only a few weeks away, but I didn't see any possible way he would be ready to go back. As soon as I tried to have Matt solve any math problems in the evening, he began to shut down.

One evening, Emma offered to help Matt with his math. She good-naturedly told him he might as well do his algebra right away, because she had finished all her homework and would follow him wherever he went until he got it done. I actually held out hope that this might work, that maybe all he needed was prodding from his sister. As much as he disliked algebra, he would dislike the prospect of Emma bugging him all evening even more. While they had their verbal tug-of-war, I headed off with Lucky for a walk.

I wish I could say that upon my return, Emma and Matt were seated at the dining room table, delving into algebraic equations. Instead, Emma had pursued Matt so much that he'd taken off on his bike. I spent the next several minutes looking for him, first with Lucky and a friendly black lab who'd befriended us, and then by car.

I finally saw him, riding his bike at the deli parking lot up the street. He'd just ducked into the neighborhood pizza shop for breadsticks when I pulled into a space.

So much for any breakthrough in mathematics.

■ ■ ■

With the new quarter beginning in only a few days, I met with Dr. Welch in mid-November to devise the game plan. We settled on mornings at the studio and a half-day in the afternoon at the New School and crossed our fingers.

On the first day, Matt worked at the studio in the morning as planned, but then took the wrong Fairfax bus once he arrived at the Vienna metro stop. Consequently, he didn't make it to his first afternoon class until forty-five minutes after it had started. Even in the short time he was there, though, he fell asleep.

The following period was a music class. It was even worse. The teacher started out by asking what he was doing there without registering first, then told him she would not tolerate any sleeping. He shut down almost immediately, and once again, he had to leave school and come home.

Before Matt arrived, Tom and I talked about a stopgap plan: Matt would go to the studio the following day, and we would regroup with Dr. Welch the day after. I also decided to call Paul James, an assistant superintendent at Washington-Lee, to get the ball rolling for a possible return. Then, of course, there was the other option: Dominion Hospital for intensive therapy. But Tom and I didn't want to discuss that at this point.

Matt came home crestfallen. "What do I do next?" he asked in sad bewilderment.

Tom and I told him our plan for the next two days, but we left out considerations of Washington-Lee and Dominion.

■ ■ ■

Dr. Welch agreed that Washington-Lee was the best option; I could meet with counselors there to work out the curriculum, and Matt could begin public school the following Monday.

Matt showed no emotion as we made these decisions. It was clear he had resigned himself to returning to a school he had never wanted to attend, and, even worse, returning to the Interlude program.

I called Dr. Potter and told him we were reluctantly withdrawing Matt from the New School. He was very understanding, and ended our conversation with an unexpected offer.

"I just want you and Tom to know that Matt is welcome to come back whenever you find a solution to his sleep problem."

I thanked him and said I hoped that day would arrive soon.

■ ■ ■

The following morning, I walked into the high school guidance office to enroll Matt. It seemed so surreal to be back; I felt dazed as I asked for a registration form.

To my surprise, I was able to meet with Dr. Pane, the head of the special education department, as well as one of the Interlude teachers, Ms. Novak, and one of the school therapists.

I introduced myself and explained why Matt was transferring. I told them we all liked the New School, but that Matt was struggling academically because of his sleep disorder. Unlike the public schools, I noted, the private school did not have a nurse clinic for taking naps, which his neurologist had advised.

Ms. Novak seemed to be unperturbed by our situation and got right down to looking for the most suitable classes available at W-L. There were plenty of hands-on classes at the Career Center, but the career and technical education courses—the classes that seemed to be perfect for Matt—were only available for eleventh and twelfth graders.

"Here we are," she said, looking quite pleased she had found a course so quickly. "This should be a good fit for Matt."

The course was theater tech, where students learned how to build sets and do lighting for plays. This could even turn into an after-school activity for Matt.

I was cautiously optimistic that the high school program might not be as awful as I'd feared; his teacher seemed to be sincerely concerned about his welfare.

■ ■ ■

That weekend, I took Matt to see *Harry Potter*, and we ran into one of his friends afterward.

"Is it true you are coming back to W-L?" he asked.

"It looks that way," Matt said, adding that he'd been asked to leave the New School.

When I asked him later why he'd put it that way, he replied, "Wasn't that more or less what the school did?"

On the eve of his return to public schools, Matt did a five-and-a-half hour clean-up in the utility room; he even reorganized the tool bench for Tom. While I was impressed at the time, I later wondered if he'd focused all his time and energy on this project to keep his mind off returning to Interlude. Starting high school was nerve-wracking enough for any student, but to add everything else that preceded Matt's new start—the ear infection, September 11, his failure to stay awake at the school where he'd so hoped to succeed, the abrupt end to his time at the studio where he had thrived—I wondered what had to be going on inside his head. It was a question that had no easy answer, as we'd soon find out.

▪ CHAPTER 13 ▪

W-L Interlude

Emma inherited her mother's habit of arriving a few minutes late, and the school's computer system had recorded her as absent several times. Since she had to go to the guidance office to clear up the problem, she was able to escort Matt into Washington-Lee on his first day and show him where to find his room. I breathed a sigh of relief and kept my fingers crossed that he'd make it through the school day.

At one-thirty that afternoon, Matt ended the suspense. He called me at work and asked permission to leave school early. My heart sank.

I responded, in the firmest voice I could muster, "Matt, you have to hang in there. This isn't the New School. W-L has a nurse clinic, and you can go there if you can't stay awake. Falling asleep in public schools isn't grounds for dismissal."

Matt protested, but to no avail. I told him he simply could not go home.

He called me again about ninety minutes later to tell me he'd left school during his computer class because he hadn't wanted to risk the embarrassment of falling asleep among other students.

I thought he was calling from home, but then he said he had taken the subway downtown to pick up a gas-powered scooter from the studio. He had gotten a flat tire, though, and was ready to hop on the subway again to get back to Arlington.

I was dumbfounded.

In less than a minute, the phone rang again. I assumed it was Matt—I was wrong. His Interlude teacher was on the line.

"Matt left school today without permission. He was supposed to be in computer class," Ms. Novak said, unmistakably annoyed.

To my surprise, she did not read me the riot act about his behavior.

"Normally, we would give a student in-school suspension, but since tomorrow is only his second day, I have decided to have him see his monitor, Mr. Moore, and a school administrator instead, so they may read him the rules about leaving school," she said firmly.

At this point, there was nothing more Tom or I could do until Matt got home. Since the scooter had a flat tire, Tom picked him up at the Metro station; I couldn't imagine the exact words they'd exchanged in the car, but when Matt arrived home, he looked miserable. Tom and I then worked together to make it clear to Matt that he should have gone to the clinic rather than taking off without telling anyone where he was going.

"It's only your first day at this school, and you are already in trouble," I told him.

As was so often the case with Matt, rather than face his problems, he'd chosen to cut and run.

■ ■ ■

The following morning, Matt met with his monitor and a school administrator. He promised them (as he'd promised Tom and me) that it would not happen again.

When Tom and I got home, Matt reported that he'd stayed awake for nearly the whole day. We asked him how he'd remained alert, and he told us that he'd gotten out his laptop and drawn pictures. Not ideal solutions, but at least he had been able to remain in the classroom.

Everything had gone well except for his final period math class. Mrs. Winters, the teacher, had even put him on the spot about falling asleep.

"She told me right in front of everybody that if I kept this up, I would be lucky if I got a GED," Matt complained, truly upset.

Tom and I looked at each other, searching for the right words of encouragement.

Tom ventured first. "Don't let one teacher get to you. You've got to have thicker skin."

Then it was my turn. "Think of the positive parts of the day. You stayed awake for six periods. Don't let one teacher ruin the fact that you started working on strategies to keep yourself alert in only the second day of school."

Emma, however, leaned more toward the blunt instrument method of teaching. She pointed out that her band teacher was "mean" to freshman students all the time.

"That's how you whip them into shape," she said, in her most authoritative voice.

Matt was unimpressed.

■ ■ ■

The following week, we had our first IEP meeting at Washington-Lee, but that was no cause for celebration. Mr. James, the assistant principal who also served as representative of the Local Educational Agency (LEA)[3]; Mrs. Winters, the math teacher with the "attitude;" one of his Interlude teachers, Monty Forest; and Pam Ricker, a general education teacher who specialized in theater and arts.

I liked Monty Forest the best. He appeared to be genuinely concerned about Matt's sleep condition and what could be done to keep Matt awake and engaged in the classroom.

---

3.   LEA reps must be qualified to provide or supervise special education and knowledgeable about the general education curriculum. They are also authorized to commit the available resources of the local educational agency.

During the ninety-minute meeting, Matt toyed with a rubber band to stay awake. Throughout the session, Mrs. Winters looked preoccupied; she did not offer any suggestions on how to keep Matt engaged in the classroom. Near the end, though, she did take away the rubber band.

■ ■ ■

Pam Ricker had been called away from the meeting early by drama duties, but before she'd left, she'd suggested Matt join the after-school tech crew for play productions. Considering his fifth-grade interest in audio-video equipment and his college media news service experience, editing audio pieces, I realized tech had the potential to positively engage Matt's abilities again, as well as get him involved outside the classroom.

That night, I was still thinking about extra-curriculars as I helped supervise a fundraising project by the school band. The students worked happily together to unload crates of citrus fruits from a delivery truck and carry them into the band room. *What a nice group of helpful kids. If Matt gets involved in an after-school activity, won't he feel like he's part of the school, rather than set apart from it?*

Emma suggested Matt try out for crew. She had been a rower for four years and thought the rigorous training and after-school commitment might help him connect to the school and make some new friends. Dr. Welch thought it was a good idea.

To our surprise, Matt seemed interested in joining the team; however, it soon became apparent that his heart was not into it. Instead of simply telling us, he missed practices and offered a variety of excuses. Though she'd initially been pleased to think Matt would take up the sport she loved, Emma was embarrassed and very upset when he kept being a no-show.

It all came to a head when Matt told us he'd decided to quit. "I simply don't like it very much. You don't get to spend very much time on the water," he said—none too believably, since he hadn't shown up at enough practices to draw that conclusion.

Emma was beside herself, and she let me know in no uncertain terms how she felt: "I don't respect Matt or even like him. He doesn't work for anything, while I work so hard for everything!" she vented.

■ ■ ■

We were disappointed, too, of course, that Matt had bailed out; it would have been such a healthy outlet for him. Instead, we found ourselves worried over other ways he was choosing to spend his time.

I had once raised my concern that Matt's Interlude placement would alienate him from his friends to Emma. She'd assured me that, for the most part, students did not pay attention to where their classmates spent the day; the Interlude program just wasn't on their radar.

Three days after the initial IEP meeting, Tom and I were reassured that Interlude had not jeopardized Matt's old friendships. He had a throng of boys over on Saturday afternoon to play with his Xbox, a group of good friends from middle school. While Matt was spending most of his day in a self-contained classroom, his social life outside of school could remain normal.

His Interlude classmates were a different story; Matt kept an arm's-length distance from all but one of the students. He told us that some of the boys in the class bullied the introverted students when the teachers left the room, and that nearly all of the students had probationary officers. Alarmed, I called Ms. Novak to find out if this was true.

"Matt is right, but don't worry. The probationary officers were assigned because the students were skipping school. None of them are committing any crimes. It's just for truancy."

Tom and I found this far from reassuring, especially after we heard reports from Ms. Novak that Matt and some of his classmates had been caught several times during lunch period heading to an off-limits part of the school grounds. We also had real misgivings about Paul, the classmate Matt had chosen to befriend.

Paul came by our house occasionally, and he usually looked unkempt; his long, dark hair always needed a good shampooing. I met Paul's mother once, when I picked up Matt from his friend's home. The inside of the house was dark and cluttered and reeked with the smell of cigarette smoke. There was something about the whole atmosphere that made me feel very uneasy.

Matt once invited Paul to join him and another friend for snowboarding at a nearby ski resort. Matt and his other friend were old hands at snowboarding, but Paul was a novice. Matt told me that he was planning to spend time showing him the basics.

When I saw him, though, Paul was not dressed to be on the slopes. He wore a thin jacket and jeans, rather than the heavy outerwear and snowboard pants Matt and his other friend sported. Matt admitted later that Paul had not been on the slopes very much. I wondered, in fact, if any of them had been, and it made me uncomfortable.

More than once, Matt came home with a faint smell of cigarette smoke clinging to his clothes. He would tell us it was from Paul's house, or from walking through the smoking area in the car garage at a local mall to meet up with friends. While I was suspicious of his explanations, I gave him the benefit of the doubt. I wonder to this day how Tom and I could have possibly believed him.

Fortunately, the friendship with Paul did not last too long. Still, we couldn't help but wonder how many other "Pauls" were out there, and how often Matt would engage in the wrong "extracurricular activities," especially when he was surrounded by a classroom full of truants.

■ ■ ■

Meanwhile, Matt continued to battle his sleep problem at school. He had occasional success sleeping soundly during the night, and invariably, Ms. Novak would tell us about the notable difference in his school performance. I couldn't help but think wistfully back to that brief period when we had tried Dr. Pearl's sleep cycle procedure—if only "Rockin' Round the Clock" had worked!

Dr. Pearl did come through for us again, in a letter from January 25, 2002, to the school's guidance office and Interlude teachers. It stressed how important it was for all adults working with Matt to recognize that he might have irresistible urges to sleep.

"Narcolepsy is a sleep disorder characterized by unwanted intrusions of sleep during the daytime when there is less motor activity. This is particularly likely to occur in a high school student while sitting in class, either at a quiet time or in a relatively darkened room, such as the environment during a lecture when slides or other media are being shown," Dr. Pearl explained. He strongly recommended that Matt be allowed to take brief naps, usually for about twenty minutes; he said they could be "very therapeutic."

He also made a key observation, given Matt's placement in the Interlude program: "It is not unusual for children and adolescents with narcolepsy to have significant co-associated disorders, including learning disabilities, attention deficit disorder, mood swings, and moodiness in general."

To their credit, in addition to the short naps at the nurse's clinic, Matt's Interlude teachers tried several strategies to keep him awake in the classroom. They allowed him to walk around the room, take water breaks, and read newspapers or magazines that interested him. At a mid-February IEP meeting, the school psychologist, Dr. Laffer, mentioned one of Matt's magazine requests. Tom and I expected it to be something like *Popular Mechanics* or *National Geographic*, but no—Matt had asked for the *Wall Street Journal*. I credited the interest to his reporting assignments at the studio, but I had to admit I was impressed. That was not typical reading material for a ninth grader.

Still, Matt's overall school performance was dismal. Ms. Novak noted that even on the days he was able to stay awake in class, he did not make any apparent effort to do his schoolwork. He had zero after zero in history and math.

The teachers were still trying to find alternatives and workarounds for him. One suggested that Matt try to do his work in increments. Ms. Novak asked him to complete and submit at least one assignment by the end of the week. After all the pep talk, though, Matt still came home that evening claiming he didn't have any schoolwork to do.

As the meeting ended and Matt returned to Interlude, Dr. Laffer took Tom and me aside. She told us she was very concerned about Matt's well-being, and requested permission to contact Dr. Welch. I readily signed the form permitting the release of medical information to her.

"I think he sees himself in a hopeless situation and wonders why he should bother if he'll just end up in ninth grade again next year," she said.

By the last few weeks of April, Matt's Interlude teachers had brought up concerns about how "problematic" his behavior was becoming. At times, he would participate in class and earn good grades on assignments—he would do what any student was expected to do. But that happened less and less frequently.

Occasionally, Matt would be on task, but even then, he would try to simply answer questions and complete assignments without reading the text. He frequently avoided class work by not telling the truth. The teachers reported that he continually engaged in off-task behaviors— drawing on his hands, taking apart his pen, playing games, or doing other non-school related activities.

Matt cooperatively attended his school therapy sessions. While he was usually pleasant with Dr. Laffer, she advised us that he was "unable or unwilling to acknowledge any learning or behavioral disorders other than the narcolepsy." He could talk about his "off-task" behaviors, but he attributed not doing classwork solely to falling asleep.

■ ■ ■

Matt's behavior at home was also becoming very odd, and it was so confusing at times. Some days, Matt seemed determined to make poor choices, but on others, he'd happily spend time with Tom and me. He wasn't even ashamed to be seen with us in public—something rare at his age.

I remember one mid-April evening in particular. It was one of those lovely days in early spring in Virginia; the daffodils, redbud trees, and tulips were in full bloom, and the azalea buds were on the verge of bursting with color. Tom and I were heading out to walk Lucky through a local park after dinner, and we asked Matt to join us. He said he would come if he could skateboard.

For those moments in the early evening light, everything seemed so normal again. Matt cheerful and happily clowned around, talking easily to two little twin girls who wanted to pet Lucky. As he skated down the winding path to the park's rose garden, I joked with Tom about how Matt was on a long and winding road right now.

And Tom piped in, "Yeah. And it's all downhill."

Matt continued on his way, and I turned to face Tom. "It might seem that way now, but he will get on the straight and narrow path," I said. I know I didn't sound like I really believed it.

■ ■ ■

The day before Emma's last band concert, Matt asked if he could get his hair cut. Any time I could get him to shorten his hair in those days, I was an avid supporter, but I'd never expected the look he'd sport when he come home from the neighborhood barber this time.

Matt had chosen to have all his hair trimmed except for two blonde locks, which he gelled to look like yellow horns.

I jokingly nicknamed him "Diablo" (wonder why the image of a devil would come to mind!). I couldn't help but think of Emma's seventh-grade concert, when we'd came home to find Matt curled up on the couch and clumps of his hair in the bathroom sink.

That wasn't the most drastic change Matt made to his appearance that year, however.

Late on a Sunday evening in April, when I went down to the basement to remind Matt it was time for bed, he asked if I remembered when a friend had pierced my ear. That had been years ago, when I was in college, so I was curious why he was suddenly interested. I noticed that he was sitting with his left hand up against his forehead, and then he turned to face me.

He had pierced his left eyebrow. I looked down more closely at him and saw he had threaded a safety pin through his skin.

Matt looked at the expression on my face. "It's a sterile pin," he said matter-of-factly. "It doesn't hurt."

"Take it out!" I screamed, horrified at the thought of another infection. Memories of his five-day stay in the hospital rushed back at me.

He sat there calmly while I grew increasingly upset, repeatedly asking him to take the safety pin out of his brow.

Emma came downstairs to see what the problem was as I ran upstairs to tell Tom. She was staring in disbelief at her brother as her father practically tripped down the stairs.

I had never heard Tom yell so loud before. He demanded Matt remove the safety pin, pronto, and he did.

I practically shoved him a bottle of rubbing alcohol and several cotton balls, insisting he cleanse the wound.

"I don't know what you are worried about. I got the pin from a first aid kit. It's for pinning someone's tongue to their lip if they have an epileptic seizure."

Of course, this was a ludicrous explanation, but that was the least of our worries.

Matt wasn't one bit apologetic; he finally admitted he'd done it without thinking (or caring) about how anyone else would feel.

Tom and I were completely baffled by his attitude that evening. He had a completely different personality; he was not the affectionate son we were used to seeing.

What's happening to Matt? Why did he do something painful to himself?

■ ■ ■

That Sunday, I confided in a friend at church who had known her share of family woes.

"Don't believe it when families say everything is fine. Everyone leads messy lives," she told me.

Though it wasn't an answer to our problems, it was a comfort to know other parents were facing teenage challenges—often the families you would least expect.

Despite the many times it felt like Matt had moved one step forward and two steps back, I made sure to appreciate the small moments that brightened my days: the pink sunset out our kitchen window one day as I washed dishes and prepared dinner; driving home from grocery shopping and being overwhelmed with gratitude that I had a husband who truly loved me. Among so many other things, Tom had spent considerable time finding a nice bed and breakfast in Williamsburg for us to stay when Emma visited William & Mary in early April. There were the surprise suggestions from Emma, including one Saturday morning invitation to have coffee and a bagel at a popular sandwich shop after she returned from a 6:30 crew practice.

As concerned as we were about Matt, Tom and I wanted to focus as much on Emma as we could during her last few months at home. She'd decided on a college closer to home than William & Mary, and we were happy with her decision—since it was only a few hours away, we knew we could easily make plenty of day trips.

In one of my walks with Lucky, I ran into a neighbor whose son was already in college; only her daughter, who was Matt's age, still lived at home.

"It will be a different pace with only one child at home," Judy told me.

"I've noticed the difference already when Emma was away on a band trip. There were hardly any phone calls and a lot less laundry to do," I said. "But, of course, I will miss her."

As I walked back home, I smiled at the thought that no matter how brief our conversations were, Emma and I always kissed each other on the cheek as we crossed paths in the house.

■ ■ ■

Despite their rocky relationship at times, Emma set everything aside to celebrate Matt's fifteenth birthday. She took him canoeing on the Potomac River around Roosevelt Island for two hours. They came back home all smiles, joking easily with each other.

For Emma's birthday a few weeks later, a group of friends took her out to dinner. Before the gathering, I joined Emma and her best friend Anna in our kitchen to talk about their upcoming college year. The talk turned briefly to Matt's current state of affairs, and to my surprise, Emma seemed more understanding about his behavior than she had been. Waxing philosophical, she noted how rebellious a few of her guy friends had been over the years, and how they'd eventually straightened out. (Although, in one case, it had required military school.)

Unfortunately, we were still in the incubation period with Matt; no dramatic transformation was anticipated anytime soon.

■ ■ ■

As June approached, I met with Matt's teachers and Dr. Laffer for more than an hour, trying to figure out a path for Matt for the rest of the year and into the fall.

"If Matt can prove he can do the work in algebra and history in the next three weeks, we will throw him to the wolves in the fall and have him try world history class in the regular classroom," Mr. James said.

Meanwhile, Matt was in in-school suspension again since he'd brought a soda to class the previous day and hadn't done any assignments, choosing to draw pictures instead. He also was in trouble for defacing a SOL test and refusing to see Dr. Laffer afterwards.

"He shows a lot of passive-aggressive behavior in school; he's polite, but unwilling to work in classes that he believes are beneath him," observed Dr. Laffer.

Matt's passive-aggressive behavior came to a head the last few weeks of school. In one incident, he was put on full-blown two-day suspension (not the in-school kind) for placing a television remote control in the classroom microwave. He claimed it wasn't a prank, that he'd just been sitting next to the microwave half asleep when an Interlude classmate, who had been using it to watch the Spice Channel while Ms. Novak was out of the room, told him to hide the device somewhere.

Tom and I told him that he didn't have to jump off every cliff just because someone told him to. He was grounded.

The only benefit to his suspension was that he would have ample time to do his world history project. I picked up the textbook when I went to the guidance office to sign his revised IEP the following day. For the first time, I had two different versions to sign: one if he was mainstreamed into a core history class, one if he was not. What next year looked like depended on this project.

It took him about two hours to settle down to work on it. He was sidetracked first by playing my father's harmonica, which had been given to him as a gift when he was a young child. I finally got him to at least start underlining the material he planned to outline on his laptop. He took a break after doing about half of his six-page section of the assigned chapter and pronounced he was going skating.

"No, you're not. You're grounded," I reminded him.

That led to many tears and much moping. He said he felt like he was being punished more than he deserved, since he insisted the microwave incident was an accident that he'd taken responsibility for. While I was on an afternoon conference call with my boss, Matt took off on his skateboard anyways, "to vent some steam," as he put it later. He did not return in time to see Dr. Welch, and I rescheduled the appointment for the following day.

Thankfully, Matt was much more focused on his second day of "house arrest," as he called it. He rigged up an ethernet connection which enabled us both to be online at the same time, and we worked together out on the deck all morning. It seemed like a golden opportunity to finish as much of his project as possible, so I told him if he completed the third section before Dr. Welch's appointment, I would allow him to skate when he got home. He finished before I left for work at 11:30, and, as promised, I let him take a skating break.

For a few brief days, I remember feeling relieved that Matt might be able to mainstream at least one of his classes in the fall, since he had completed his history assignment during his involuntary home confinement.

■ ■ ■

Like too many times before, though, I had barely finished sighing in relief when the next crisis occurred.

Matt claimed his laptop was gone.

I didn't know whether to be more upset about the disappearance of his computer or the fact that all his history work was on it.

Matt gave several versions of what had happened. First, he said a student had borrowed it for the weekend because he didn't have a computer and needed one to do his homework. When Matt still did not have his laptop with him after school on Monday, he said he had taken it to his theater class and it had disappeared while he was working on the set.

The following morning, the school resource officer asked Matt to fill out a form for the missing laptop and told him she would begin to make inquiries about anything suspicious occurring in the school theater. At this point, Matt must have panicked.

The following day, he came home and told us the student who he'd claimed had borrowed it over the weekend had actually taken it from Matt, and planned to sell it to pay for his girlfriend's abortion.

The day after that, he admitted to us and the school resource officer that he'd lied about the theft, but offered no explanation as to why he'd made the story up or what the true story was. The resource officer warned him about filing false police reports.

Matt came home the following day with his laptop in hand.

Understandably, we were all upset about yet another bizarre incident. We grounded him once again, but we were just as puzzled as the school about his inexplicable behavior.

■ ■ ■

I rang Ms. Novak again, a phone call I'd needed to place much too often. She told me she'd been able to get an apology out of Matt for wasting everyone's time with the laptop incident, but it had been a painful process.

She also said discussions were underway to consider another option for Matt in the fall if he continued not to function in Interlude.

Mr. Forest still favored the carrot-and-stick approach, saying he believed that Matt could do the work, but he simply hadn't tried. On the other hand, some of Matt's teachers thought he was severely disturbed. His impulsive antics at school and outlandish falsehoods when he was under the least amount of stress had made Tom and I wonder, too. Still, I was surprised by Ms. Novak's recommendation.

"We think it might be best to contract service Matt to a smaller school, one that specializes in providing more mental health services and more one-on-one work with students. The class sizes are small with only about forty students per school," she explained.

Tom and I started mulling it over that evening; we wondered if it could possibly be the best route for our son.

At least we had the summer to explore the options.

▪ CHAPTER 14 ▪

Twice-Exceptional
(2002)

Leafing through literature on alternative education programs in late June, I came across the article "Gifted but Learning Disabled: A Puzzling Paradox," by Susan Baum, a well-known authority on "twice-exceptional" students. I read with growing interest about the academic problems faced by the population of gifted children who also had learning disabilities. The education system provided programs for each population, but rarely a single program that served both.

Twice-exceptional children exhibited "remarkable talents or strengths in some areas and disabling weaknesses in others." Baum grouped them into three categories:

1. Identified gifted students who had subtle learning differences
2. Unidentified gifted students whose gifts and disabilities were masked by average achievement
3. Identified learning-disabled students who were also gifted

Students in the third category were first singled out by the tasks they weren't able to do, rather than by the talent they showed. They were "most at risk because of the implicit message that accompanied the LD categorization that there was something wrong with the student that [had to] be fixed. Little attention, if any, was paid to the student's strengths and interests, other than to use them to remediate weaknesses." They were passionate and had advanced knowledge about high-level interests outside the classroom, but they were more acutely aware of their difficulty learning. Over time, their positive feelings about accomplishments outside of school were overshadowed by their pessimistic feelings about their poor school performance. She added that research showed that this group of students was often rated by teachers as the most disruptive, and they used their creative abilities to avoid tasks.

It was as if she had attended IEP meetings with us or observed Matt in Interlude.

Baum was clear that all twice-exceptional children required environments that would nurture their gifts, attend to their learning disabilities, and provide emotional support to deal with their inconsistent abilities. Thankful for this information, I started searching for local programs.

To my dismay, there was only one school district, Montgomery County, Maryland, that offered twice-exceptional programs in elementary school. They only had half-day programs for middle school and high school (and even those were scarce).

How is it possible that these children are slipping through the cracks?

School districts voluntarily reporting their data identified 70,000 kindergarten through twelfth grade students as twice-gifted.[4] It's estimated the two to five percent of the gifted population was learning disabled and two to five percent of students with learning disabilities were gifted.

As this clicked, my mindset shifted.

Until then, all I had concluded about his special education and Interlude experiences were that they had been disasters. He'd ended ninth grade with a huge question mark after his name.

---

4.   Bracamonte, Micaela, *Twice-exceptional Students: Who Are They and What Do They Need?*, http://www.2enewsletter.com/article_2e_what_are_they.html

What possibly can be next? Should we—and Matt—be resigned to repeating ninth grade in Interlude again?

It was suddenly clear to me that Matt's "emotional disturbance" was the result of being placed in totally inappropriate programs. There was no doubt in my mind. Our son was twice-exceptional: highly able and learning disabled. I finally knew why Matt was failing miserably in school. It wasn't the child that was the problem—it was the program.

At the recommendation of a friend with expertise in learning disabilities, we contacted an education consultant, Ilene Schwartz. Ilene was a former teacher who'd left the profession to help parents with special-needs children determine what accommodations should be provided in the classroom.

She arrived at our home one evening in early July to meet Matt and discuss his learning experiences. She suggested we write a letter to the school outlining what we were seeking to accomplish and why we believed Matt's identification needed to be changed.

"Matt has been identified as emotionally disturbed when he actually has been displaying all the typical symptoms of a bright and bored teenager with a severe case of narcolepsy," Ilene told us with certainty.

■ ■ ■

Meanwhile, Mrs. Quentin called to inform us that Matt could begin the new school year in one regular classroom, but needed to take the rest of his core subjects in Interlude. My heart sank.

Dr. Welch supported the idea of moving Matt to regular classes for all his core subjects, making homework adjustments and utilizing a learning resource teacher as needed. Still, we would need documentation, including testing, for the school to consider the request. Remembering Matt's previous testing, we decided Dr. Greenstein was our best hope once again for determining where a twice-gifted child belonged in the new school year.

■ ■ ■

What a difference a day made!

Dr. Greenstein called us in the late afternoon after quickly reading Matt's test results. He had scored in the superior range for several portions of the exam, including general knowledge information and verbal reasoning abilities. His scores also indicated he would do well in higher level creative-constructive activities that were consistent with his hobbies.

The assessment showed difficulty with processing speed and working memory. These challenges were affecting Matt's ability to produce work quickly, easily, and efficiently, she explained, adding that his academic problems stemmed from his production and output, not his intellectual ability. With moderate educational accommodations, she assured us, Matt could succeed academically. Matt had the brain power, he just needed the tools to help him produce the horsepower!

"Matt does not belong in a program for emotionally disturbed children, or in a large regular classroom either."

Dr. Greenstein advised us to try the New School again, where Matt could benefit from small class sizes and the individualized attention of his teachers. She even offered to call Dr. Potter on his behalf.

Just the thought of Matt leaving Interlude and having a second chance at the New School filled me with nervous excitement. Tom and I wondered how Matt would react, though, going back to a school where his inability to stay awake had led to such an abrupt and embarrassing departure.

I broached the subject carefully with him, focusing first on his encouraging test results. I hoped that telling Matt about his superior ratings would buoy his spirits, so much so that he would be willing to put the past behind him and try the New School again. Then I told him about Dr. Greenstein's recommendation that we speak with Dr. Potter.

"If I do go back, W-L should pay for it," he said, with unmistakable anger in his voice.

I was surprised that Matt would bring up the cost of tuition. It never had occurred to me that he would think about how much we had spent the previous year to enroll him in the New School. I agreed in principle, but my practical side took over.

"Starting you on the right track is more important right now than some lengthy legal battle to get Arlington to pay for the cost of this.

Besides," I warned him, "if we try to settle that first, you'll be stuck in Interlude again."

Matt was clearly weighing the options. After a moment of thought, he looked up at us and smiled.

"I'm willing to try the New School again."

■ ■ ■

With Matt on board, we didn't waste any time. I left a voicemail message for Dr. Potter that evening and followed it up with an email. I spent a good part of the following morning leaving phone messages with Dr. Greenstein to approve contact with Dr. Potter and Dr. Welch.

Everything hinged on Dr. Potter approving Matt's re-admission. We were optimistic, given that the headmaster had told us the previous fall that Matt was welcome to come back if he resolved his sleep problem.

Less than a week after getting the test results, Dr. Potter welcomed Tom, Matt, and me into his office.

"It's good to see all of you again," he said pleasantly—and encouragingly. "So, Matt, I understand you would like to return to the New School. What didn't work out at your high school?"

Matt paused a moment and gave the question careful thought. "The program they put me in was a mismatch. My sleep problem got in the way of my learning at the New School last year, but I no longer have trouble keeping awake."

Dr. Potter sat attentively, listening to his answer, before he continued. "I'm glad to hear that. What is it about the New School that makes you want to return?"

I didn't know whether to be curious or anxious about his answer. *Will he say the right thing? What if he bad-mouths Interlude and makes it sound like he's simply trying to escape a class of troubled children? If he mentions the school labeled him emotionally disturbed, how will Dr. Potter react?* Matt could clinch the interview or strike a nail in his coffin, and I had no idea which it would be.

"I want to try again because I like the philosophy of the school and think I can make it work this time."

Dr. Potter smiled, then he stood up and reached over to shake Matt's hand. "Matt, I'm pleased to accept you into the program again."

As we were leaving, Matt looked back and spoke to Dr. Potter again. "I'm really glad to come back and I'll do whatever it takes to stay here," he said.

Gone was the boy who wanted nothing more than to escape school each day; Matt was determined to make a fresh start. He wasn't emotionally disturbed, he was just a bright child who had been boxed into the wrong program. Thankfully, the New School was giving him a second chance. Matt would start ninth grade again, but this time in a small, private school that would teach him in the ways he learned.

▪ CHAPTER 15 ▪

Best School Year Ever
(2002–2003)

Matt was in great spirits on the day that he registered for his first classes back at the New School. Students selected three or four core subjects and a few electives per quarter (unlike the fixed curriculum at Washington-Lee). Certain subjects, like math or foreign language, were taken for the entire year, but students could mix and match the rest of their classes. As long as their course credits ultimately totaled the requisite amount for graduation, students had the flexibility to explore a wide range of material during their four years of study.

The first module of the day required hands-on learning projects, perfect for Matt. We were initially disappointed that Planet Manhattan, a course that focused on the history and culture of New York City, had filled up. He'd really been enjoying the class the previous year, before he'd needed to drop it when he left the New School. To our delight, when Matt was about three-fourths of the way through picking classes, a student dropped the course. A slot opened, and Matt immediately signed up for it.

He also registered for Spanish, social studies, algebra 1, and soccer. The whole process went smoothly, especially considering that the upper classes got first dibs, so Matt, as a freshman, was limited to leftovers in some subjects.

■ ■ ■

Exactly one year to the day that Matt had first started at the New School, he was back. Unlike his first time, though, there were no phone calls asking to come home because he couldn't stay awake—he was excited to be there. As we had hoped, his enthusiasm for the school had not waned.

As September continued, we were happy to see how well Matt adapted to his environment and how collegial Matt's teachers were with him. When he had trouble understanding the advanced course material on Marxism in his social studies class, for example, the teacher gave him extra time to finish the assigned essay. What a change from his Washington-Lee days, when the workload of late assignments had just kept growing to the point that he'd felt too overwhelmed to even try.

■ ■ ■

At the end of September, we received a phone call from Emma, her voice bubbling over with excitement.

"Guess what! I made it! I'm going!" she exclaimed.

"Going where?" I asked, delighted by her happiness, but also clueless about the reason.

"I'm going to the Head of the Charles Regatta!" she said breathlessly. "I made first boat in the novice crew."

First held in 1965 in Cambridge, Massachusetts, the Head of the Charles Regatta was the world's largest two-day rowing event. It attracted more than 9,000 rowers each year. As I was later informed by one of my friends, an avid rower, it was a really, really prestigious race. All I cared about at the time, however, was hearing Emma's excitement at sharing such wonderful news with her family.

I couldn't help but pinch myself. Both of our children were at good places in their lives at the exact same time. What could possibly be better than that?

■ ■ ■

By mid-October, Matt was fully immersed in his Planet Manhattan project. He'd chosen to write a report and to do a display board about Astoria, a Greek section of New York City.

I drove him to a Greek import grocery store, also named Astoria, not far from our home. It sold a mix of Greek and Arab foods and displayed several Arab magazines on a rack. We found a selection of Greek food staples, such as packaged pita bread, Kalamata olives, and jars of olive oil. The friendly shop owner cut us a deal on Greek newspapers, which were usually only provided on order.

Afterwards, we drove to a nearby office supply store for a display board. We also stopped at Home Deport for speaker supplies, part of his incentive for getting the work done.

Watching Matt work on the project, I noticed a big improvement in his ability to stay on task for longer periods without becoming overwhelmed or frustrated. He paced himself, allowing time for breaks to make enlarged copies of the Astoria map or walk Lucky in the fallen leaves at a nearby park. It was so encouraging to see Matt complete his report and display board on time.

■ ■ ■

In mid-November, we held our first conference call with Dr. Potter. "Matt is making progress and is on track," Dr. Potter said.
What wonderful news to hear!
Then he added, "But his grades are all over the map."
Matt had an A in his Planet Manhattan class and an A in phys. ed. Then came the all too familiar part. Matt was struggling in social science

with a D. He was doing so poorly because he had only completed one of four essays, Dr. Potter noted. He was also floundering in algebra, but it was still possible for him to pass if he continued to do his homework and worked with a tutor.

In early December, Tom and I met with a few of Matt's teachers. His Planet Manhattan teacher told us that Matt had a "brilliant mind" and was a leading class participant who made very sharp observations. His algebra teacher added that he'd substituted for the Planet Manhattan class one day and that Matt's contributions to the class discussion about the movie *Letter from Sarajevo* really shined. He was an avid listener and could absorb information like a sponge when it was a visual presentation, whether in front of the class or on film.

On the other hand, his math teacher was frenetically concerned about Matt passing algebra. I assured him that our main goal for Matt was to understand the basic concepts before we grew concerned about grades. If he needed to repeat algebra again the next school year, so be it. At least Matt was getting a homework system established so he earned partial credit for homework.

■ ■ ■

Throughout his first year back at the New School, Matt continued to excel in courses that required him to learn by doing. In his Japanese studies class, he worked on a project about zaibatsu, the powerful, family-controlled pre-World War II financial and industrial conglomerates in Japan. As part of the display, Matt included photos that were loaded on a computer disk, at a time when the use of computer-based images was not nearly as commonplace as it would become only a few years later. Matt took the disk to a nearby Staples and patiently instructed the clerk on how to enlarge his images; the clerk complimented him on his knowledge of computers.

During breaks from typing the bibliography and cutting and double-taping his text onto blue construction paper, Matt set up a voice activation system on his computer. That included reading several lines, so that the computer could distinguish and recognize his sound patterns. I presumed that he planned to use this feature as a note-taking device; however, given his natural-born curiosity, Matt simply might have been tinkering for tinkering's sake!

In his final quarter, Matt signed up for a drama techniques class with three of his best friends, and one of their assignments was to write skits. Matt finished a very good character history in about fifteen minutes, and I was very impressed that he did the writing so well and so quickly.

"What internet site did you copy it from?" Tom kidded him good-naturedly.

I knew it was a Matt original—not only because he was answering specific questions his teacher had asked, but by the humor in it.

At the same time, I noticed Matt was spending more of his after-school time on activities that centered around his mechanical abilities. It was not unusual to find him taking apart and putting together his motor scooter or soldering metal to repair parts of broken equipment.

Whether in or out of school, there was no mistaking the change in our son. Compared to his previous year in Washington-Lee's Interlude program, Matt had grown tremendously, both academically and personally.

■ ■ ■

I will never forget Matt's final day of ninth grade at the New School. To celebrate, I suggested we have lunch near the school. When we stopped at a sandwich shop, there were two older New School students inside already, eating at the front window counter.

"Hi, Matt," they said, smiling at him.

While we were waiting in line for our sandwiches, a girl who had just completed her junior year walked by to go to the restroom.

Without skipping a beat, Matt drily said, "I kept the seat up for you." She laughed.

When we sat down in our booth, I mentioned how nice it was to see some of the other students from his school.

"That's one of the things I like about it. We aren't separated by age. Everybody has the chance to get to know everybody else," Matt said.

I could see that Matt got along easily with older classmates. How nice it was to see him so comfortable with everyone! What a contrast to the first time he'd attended!

As we headed home, Matt said something I'd never expected to hear from him: "This has been my best school year ever."

I will never forget how happy he sounded.

At bedtime, when I came in to say goodnight, Matt thanked me again for sending him back to the New School.

▪ CHAPTER 16 ▪

Advocacy First Step: Narcolepsy
(2002)

Most parents who've had to battle to find the right school for their child breathe a sigh of relief and move on after they have won. There is nothing wrong with that, but Tom and I felt differently. We knew no children should have to go through experiences like Matt's just to have their neurological issues taken seriously and taken into consideration in their educations. We wanted to see what we could do to ensure no one did.

With that in mind, a few weeks before Matt started at the New School, I hand-delivered a copy of Dr. Greenstein's report to an assistant principal at W-L, who assured me it would be included in Matt's school record. Remembering the advice to document everything, I'd also written a letter to the special education chairman. I'd included a brochure about narcolepsy and requested that copies of it be distributed to school nurses and faculty at all grade levels, to ensure they were aware of the sleep disorder symptoms in children.

Mission accomplished, I headed back down the hallway, trying to contain my glee at the thought that this would be my last walk through the building.

■ ■ ■

About halfway to the door, I ran into a familiar face. It was Linda Henderson, who was president of the PTA that year and very knowledgeable about navigating the school system. When I told her about Matt's battle with narcolepsy and his pending switch to the New School as there was no suitable program for him in the public school, she advised me to raise my concerns at a school board meeting.

"How would I do that?" I asked, puzzled by her suggestion.

She explained that thirty minutes were set aside at each meeting for any member of the public who wished to raise issues about the education system that were not scheduled on the board's agenda. Each speaker had three minutes to address their concern.

"Talk personally *first* to a few of the school board members and give them a heads up that you plan to be a non-agenda item at the October or November school board meeting—preferably the October meeting, in time for the next budget cycle," Linda advised.

As it happened, I knew two of the members: one was a neighbor and the other attended our church. I felt like the gods were smiling down on me. Following Linda's advice, I made sure to let both members know about my possible school board appearance.

■ ■ ■

I told Tom and Matt about my plans to speak before the board after dinner, as I dished out some ice cream. I figured it was a good time, since I had a captive audience.

They ate their desserts and listened closely as I laid out all the issues that needed to be discussed. Saying it aloud, though, I realized I faced a major dilemma: It wasn't enough to simply raise public awareness about narcolepsy. There needed to be a way to *humanize* it. And what better way than to tell Matt's story?

But how can I possibly do all this in such a short period of time?

Then it dawned on me—I had the solution right in front of me.

"There's just one major hurdle," I told Tom and Matt, slowly winding them up and gauging their reactions.

"What is it, Mom?" Matt asked.

Ever since he'd learned he was going back to the New School, I had noticed him take a greater interest in anything school-related.

"I can't figure out how to boil down everything that needs to be said in three minutes." I still had their attention, but I wasn't sure how they would react to what I had to say next. For a second, I held my breath.

"If both of you would join me, we would have nine minutes to make our case! Nine minutes should be enough time, barely."

Then I looked over at Matt. "And, Matt, if you are willing to, you could talk about your sleep problem, how much better you are now, and how you think the New School will be the right fit for you."

There was dead silence.

I thought of a sweetener.

"If you agree to help me out, I will write what you need to say. All you will have to do is read it."

Tom and Matt looked at each other. Then they both smiled.

"Sure, we'll do it," Tom said.

■ ■ ■

For the next week, I stayed up late to work on the presentation, trying as best as I could to divide the speech into three equal parts. Once the first draft was finished, we rehearsed our parts several times and I revised them several more times to meet the nine-minute limit.

The day of the school board meeting arrived. Tom, Matt, and I were running on pure adrenaline as we approached the meeting room. In the front, there was a sign-in sheet for members of the public who wanted to bring school-related issues before the five-member board; all three of us signed our names and walked into the room.

Looking around, I estimated that it could easily seat 150 people and that more than one hundred places were already taken. Before sitting down, I stepped up to the stenographer to hand her copies of our remarks, and I asked her to distribute them to the school board members.

Shortly afterwards, the board members entered and sat behind a long desk on a raised platform in the front of the room. Below them on the right side was a podium for speakers. There was a camera set up about fifty feet to the left of the podium; the local cable channel would be covering the meeting live, but the gadget was far enough away to keep us from getting too nervous about it.

Unbeknownst to my family and me, it was awards night; several teachers were recognized for their years of service. While we certainly appreciated their time and commitment, I only half-listened to the ceremony; I was too pre-occupied with my upcoming remarks and rehearsing them in my mind.

We waited nearly an hour, but finally, it was time for non-agenda items. Tom, Matt and I were the first up to bat.

Tom walked up to the platform with his prepared remarks in hand. He dreaded doing briefings at his job, and I knew it was a challenge for him to speak before a large group of people.

He cleared his throat and began:

"I am here this evening with my wife, Paula, and our son, Matt, to briefly discuss the sleep disorder, narcolepsy, how it affected our son's life in school before it was correctly diagnosed, and how he is successfully managing his medical condition in school now that he is on the proper combination of medicine and a strict sleep schedule.

"Matt began showing signs of excessive daytime sleepiness, or EDS, at the start of eighth grade at Swanson Middle School. Except for a brief period of time when his neurologist adjusted his sleep pattern to nine hours a day, Matt had difficulty remaining awake and alert in nearly all his classes.

"What was particularly puzzling was how alert and animated Matt would be between classes and in the cafeteria at lunchtime, because as soon as he returned to a large classroom setting, he would fall asleep within minutes. The only exceptions were his classes that involved hands-on learning, such as the percussion section of the school concert band.

"Unfortunately, because he was falling asleep in his other classes, the guidance office pulled him out of band in the first month of eighth grade, since it was the only period of the day that offered a study skills class. The guidance office thought this class would benefit Matt—but for the most part, he slept through study skills, too.

"The school guidance counselors, teachers, and school psychologist were mystified by Matt's behavior. The guidance staff and school therapist had a wide array of theories as to why Matt was shutting down in his classes; we heard that our son had everything from an extreme form of school avoidance to a passive-aggressive form of temper tantrums.

"When we transferred Matt to a small, private school at the beginning of last year and he was still struggling with excessive sleepiness, the headmaster suggested a sleep study. We had Matt tested at Children's Hospital in October 2001. The lab conducted both nighttime and daytime sleep tests. The results? Matt was diagnosed with the sleep disorder narcolepsy.

"Narcolepsy is NOT a psychological or mental disorder. Narcolepsy is a neurological condition. Failure to identify narcolepsy and mislabeling it as a behavioral or emotional disorder instead can ultimately *lead* to such problems—particularly if a child is led to believe that his sleepiness is a voluntary or willful act that he can somehow control if he just tries hard enough to stay awake. Children with undiagnosed narcolepsy understandably have difficulties learning, including issues with concentration [and] memory impairment…

"We are here today to urge all teachers, school counselors, and nurse clinics to learn about the symptoms of narcolepsy so that they can recognize the signs of the sleep disorder in children…

"Children with narcolepsy left untreated face many learning challenges. However, children who are properly identified and treated can lead very successful lives in and outside of school."

Just as Tom finished speaking, the warning bell rang. They weren't kidding about the three-minute limit.

As Tom returned to his seat with a look of relief on his face, I looked around the room at the other faces. It was apparent he had caught the audience's attention. They waited with interest as the school board president invited the next speaker—Matt.

■ ■ ■

Matt went to the podium, looked up at the board members, then, after introducing himself, he began to read from his paper in a loud, clear voice.

"I am a ninth-grade student at the New School of Northern Virginia in Fairfax County. I transferred to the New School this year because the ninth-grade program at Washington-Lee wasn't right for me.

"When I began to fall asleep in eighth grade at Swanson Middle School, everyone was puzzled about my behavior, including me. I tried as hard as I could to stay awake in my classes, but nothing worked. After a while the teachers and guidance counselors grew very frustrated about my situation.

"Because my grades were failing, they pulled me out of band, which was about the only thing I liked at school, and they transferred me to study skills class. When that didn't work, they tried the math and English classes for special education students. That was *really* the wrong fit for me. Finally, in February of eighth grade, I was transferred to the Interlude program.

"The Interlude program at Swanson worked temporarily for me, thanks mostly to its enthusiastic teacher, Jamie Borg. However, after a few months in Interlude, I began to grow sleepy again and I struggled to keep awake the last few weeks of school. Somehow, I managed to graduate from Swanson.

"The summer after I finished school at Swanson, I had the chance to work as a talk radio news intern. The experience was great for me. I interviewed people in Washington, edited the tapes, and learned how to launch the audio pieces on the web-based college media news service. I discovered I had strengths that had never been tested before.

"Because of my successful internship, we decided to try the New School last year. I was very excited about going to a different school. The classes were small, and many of them involved class discussions and hands-on style learning. What mattered most to me were the small size and the amount of attention the teachers paid to each of us.

"Unfortunately, as happy as I was to be there, I started falling asleep in all my classes again, and eventually had to withdraw from the program because I was unable to keep up with the class work.

"Fortunately, the New School headmaster, John Potter, suggested a sleep study. We did that last October and finally got to the root of the problem, but it took several months before I was alert enough in class to do any work.

"My parents transferred me to Washington-Lee last November. Quite frankly, I don't think the school really knew what to do with me, so they put me back in the Interlude program. That was a disaster for me...I did my best to tune out what was going on, and for the most part, the Interlude students left me alone. But it was not an environment suitable for learning.

"Even though I was tested this summer to identify my strengths and weaknesses and the test results showed that I should be in a regular classroom, W-L still planned to put me in Interlude for nearly all my classes this fall. Fortunately, my parents were able to send me back to the New School for a second chance. This time, I am on the proper medicine and getting enough sleep. I am now awake, alert, and doing my work at the New School."

I looked at the school board members as he spoke; it was clear his words had caught their attention, because several of them were taking notes during his presentation. And as Matt's story unfolded, it was clear that he had a very attentive audience in the rest of the room, too. Perhaps one or more of them suffered from narcolepsy or another sleep disorder that had gone undiagnosed. If our presentation helped just a single person, it was worth it.

■ ■ ■

Then it was my turn to speak.

Since Tom had explained the sleep disorder and Matt had described the personal toll on him, I had time to devote some of my presentation on the need for smaller classes that have a stimulating environment like the ones at the New School.

After finishing my remarks and returning to my seat, I look around the room. This time, too, it looked like we had struck a chord.

■ ■ ■

"Your testimony was riveting," Linda Henderson told me as we stood momentarily in the hallway to catch our breath after we had left the room.

Alvin Crawley, the assistant principal for student services, followed us into the hallway and offered to help us in any way he could. He said he had been tipped off ahead of time about our plans to speak. Before the meeting, I had emailed a copy of our testimony to all school board members, so they wouldn't feel blindsided by our presentation. I guess the word had gotten around.

On our way home, we stopped for dessert at one of Matt's favorite sandwich shops. As we sat down at the table, Tom turned to Matt and said we wanted to congratulate him on his bravery. It had taken a lot of self-confidence to talk passionately about things that matter in front of a large group of people. Not only had Tom and I become public advocates, so had our son.

The growing sense of confidence our son displayed that day could be seen throughout his first full year at the New School. He participated enthusiastically in classroom discussions and worked diligently on school projects. Meanwhile, I became more involved in setting the record straight about Matt's placement the previous year at Washington-Lee and what could be done to wipe the slate clean.

▪ CHAPTER 17 ▪

A Matter of Principle
(2002–2003)

We were buoyed by the positive reaction our appearance before the school board on narcolepsy awareness had garnered; even more so after we learned that the school planned to add information on the sleep disorder to its guidebook for teachers and counselors. But one issue that had arisen out Matt's experience in public school still troubled us—the "emotionally disturbed" classification in his special education record. If only as a matter of principle, we wanted that label removed.

Washington-Lee set up an eligibility review and IEP session for us. The meeting was cordial and went smoothly. Not surprisingly, the staff proposed an IEP that we would have refused to approve had we decided to return Matt to public school. They suggested keeping Matt in Interlude for all but one of his main subjects. Even if they had offered to place him in regular classes, each of those had at least twenty pupils enrolled, much too large to suit Matt's needs.

The staff granted our request to send a school psychologist to the New School to determine if Matt's current learning disability identification should be modified. Matt's New School teachers were asked to fill out reports on him, and we met with a public school social worker for a "social history update." I described Matt as enthusiastic, bright, funny, sensitive, sweet, and sociable; a boy who had many friends and maintained friendships for long periods of time, whose favorite pastimes included indoor rock climbing, BMX biking and building things.

The New School was working wonders for Matt. I was cautiously optimistic that his classification as "emotionally disturbed" would be dropped on October 25, at the next eligibility meeting.

■ ■ ■

Unfortunately, the October meeting was a joke. It was as if the material I had sent everyone on narcolepsy had never been written or read. Despite Dr. Pearl's January letter about Matt's sleep disorder and Dr. Welch's call to the school nurse about how well Matt was doing, all the members of the committee (even those who said openly they did not know Matt and felt the classification could go either way) supported the standing emotional disorder classification.

Looking closely at the school document that defined the terms, it listed "inappropriate behavior under normal circumstances." When I asked the committee members to provide examples of that, they referred to observations of Matt's behavior the previous spring, both in the nurse's clinic and therapy sessions with Dr. Laffer.

I turned to Dr. Laffer directly. "How is it possible for an emotionally disturbed child to be doing so well now, in his new school setting? He isn't afraid to try new things now, in a small, nurturing learning environment." I pointed out the New School's method of teaching also seemed to be lessening his chronic problems with attention, alertness, and anxiety, which were among the "weaknesses" spelled out in the eligibility findings.

At the conclusion of the meeting, I contested the eligibility committee's decision on the record; my statement was included in the final minutes. I wrote:

I believe that Matt is eligible for special education services due to learning disabilities and other health impairments. Tom and I believe

Matt's underlying health impairment is narcolepsy and that he is not emotionally disturbed.

You could feel the tension in the air.

Mr. Forest spoke up, as much to diffuse the situation as to offer a suggestion. He calmly noted that the issue could be revisited in a few months, once Matt had been at the New School a little longer.

So, basically, the verdict was still out. According to Dr. Pane, the next step was to see Mrs. Quinten, who chaired the Special Education Review Committee (SERC), about a future eligibility review. A few weeks later, Dr. Crawley set up a three-way conference call with Mrs. Quinten, who confirmed that her panel would review all the data and anything new I could gather. She advised that the school psychologist would go to the New School to conduct testing and observe Matt's classes for the day. If the SERC review concluded that a change in his identification was in order, we would set up another IEP meeting to see what the county could offer.

With great difficulty, I kept my emotions in check and reminded myself to count to one hundred and choose my battles. This one obviously had a way to go.

■ ■ ■

In mid-October, Dr. Welch had told us that if Matt continued doing so well, we could consider scaling back his therapy to monthly appointments, and on November 7, Matt achieved this milestone. The doctor marveled at the change in Matt and how much he had improved in his alertness, focus, and sense of self-esteem since August.

"This is clearly the result of Matt no longer being in the Washington-Lee Interlude program and instead being enrolled at the New School," he said.

I asked Dr. Welch if he would write a letter that I could submit to the SERC while they assessed Matt's progress. Although there were mixed reviews about Matt's academic performance for the first quarter, there was no mistaking the significant progress observed by Dr. Welch.

At Matt's first monthly session on December 5, the doctor handed me the letter. He'd written that Matt's emotional state had been dramatically improved:

It is now clear that much of Matt's behavioral difficulty was a secondary phenomenon related to his frustration of school failure and his response to his educational environment...

Matt is now functioning well both at home and in school. His mood is bright and his outlook is positive. At this time, a designation of Emotional Disability is not indicated. His narcolepsy is successfully treated, his school performance is improved, behavioral issues are no longer present, and his anxiety is well managed.

Tom and I were elated to read Dr. Welch's letter; it thoroughly challenged the classification and vindicated our position. We felt confident that this assessment would help to tip the scales in our favor when the time came for the committee to reevaluate.

Now we only had to wait for Matt's teachers' reports and the findings of the school psychologist.

■ ■ ■

To its credit, the school system followed through with reevaluating Matt. The school psychologist was to draw her findings from class observations made by six of Matt's teachers and projective tests she'd conduct over the course of one day to determine Matt's ability to view and assess situations, his coping skills and thought processes. Tom and I waited anxiously (if not impatiently) for the evaluation. We knew that the findings would carry a lot of weight in the SERC decision.

It took much longer to receive the report than we'd expected, but at the beginning of April, I warily opened the manila envelope with the evaluation tucked inside.

According to the report, as we'd hoped and expected, the New School teachers' observations generally concluded that Matt's overall behavior fell "within the range that is typical of his peer group." However, both Tom and I were disturbed by the rest of the findings. We didn't even recognize our son in the assessment of some of the results from the psychologist's single day of tests.

A few of the observations seemed believable, like his tendency to "submerge his emotions and feelings" and his struggle with self-esteem. The second observation, in particular, seemed excusable though; it was bound to take some time to rebuild his self-esteem after Interlude had beaten it out of him.

Others made no sense to us. According to the evaluation, Matt appeared to have immature coping mechanisms "where he hopes for magical solutions that take away the problem." She projected that he might "easily become overwhelmed when confronted with everyday life stresses…and keep his stress reduced by avoiding challenges," and lead "a fairly undemanding life in order to keep stresses to a minimum." She claimed he was "not likely to seek out new/challenging activities [and] advanced academic classes and [instead] prefer to take an easier class." However, Matt was already taking challenging courses, and he was not feeling overwhelmed by school or day-to-day activities.

Still other findings seemed to be truly off-base. We were particularly bothered by the observation that Matt might have "maladaptive coping mechanisms" and "prefer to deny a situation, blame others, withdraw/avoid and also fall asleep." How could a trained psychology professional conclude that Matt was willfully falling asleep?

Matt had several long-time friends, yet the report noted that he "may have difficulty with sustained relationships." The psychologist posited that "when confronting failure, Matt is at risk for developing an anti-social stance," including "an unwillingness to work with adult figures in his life." I shook my head at this observation, which ran completely contrary to his relationships with adults. In fact, in the psychologist's own assessment of Matt's behavior, he was described as "cooperative." She'd noted that he "responded to test demands, yielding valid protocol" and that "it was a pleasure to work with him."

After reading the full report and all the negative assessments, Tom and I found its recommendation equally puzzling. The doctor had concluded that "in spite of [his] emotional difficulties, Matt appears to be performing schoolwork and exhibiting adequate behavior in a small classroom."

■ ■ ■

I poured out my feelings about the report to Tom. "We've never received any calls or teacher notes about him not getting along with others. How is it possible to draw so many conclusions about Matt's emotional state based on tests he took in a single day?"

Tom had the best description of the evaluation: "This is a bunch of crap."

I wish he had not let Matt see it. Descriptions like "maladaptive coping mechanisms" and "low self-esteem" were not what he needed to read. Matt was understandably upset, and he underlined all the portions he thought were untrue.

Tom repeated the same words to Matt that he had shared with me— the report was cow manure, no buts about it. It seemed to reassure him, and fortunately, after some healthy venting, Matt did not brood about it.

The next time we saw Dr. Welch, I showed him the school psychologist's assessment. He rolled his eyes and shook his head.

"I don't think projective testing and extrapolating how a person will behave based on the results is very accurate."

The only part that he thought was worth pursuing was the distractibility issue, in case a switch in medicine was in order. I was glad Matt had heard his review of the report.

Bolstered by Dr. Welch's opinion, I decided to call Matt's New School adviser, Carol Clark, the next day. She was as surprised by the test findings as we were. I asked her to write a letter to the SERC committee, and she readily agreed.

A few days later, Mrs. Clark provided me with a copy, addressed to the SERC chair and copied to committee members. She'd written:

> Based on my observations of Matt outside the classroom and on my discussions with his teachers and fellow students, who observe him in the classroom milieu, he has healthy and normal interactions with all of his classmates.
>
> Matt has a normal range of friendships with other children in this school. The other students see him as friendly and

humorous. In social interactions he is never avoidant, but always looks others in the eye when speaking to them and makes a point to say "hello" when passing someone he knows. Unlike many ninth graders, he also is friends with upper-class students, who like him quite well. He is kind and polite to both teachers and other students.

One of Matt's teachers gave me a small example of his usual behavior: During a class in which there was some free time, Matt chose to approach another student and ask him to watch the program on Matt's computer. They became interested in taking the program further and together they were able to download a multimedia presentation and watch it together. This is typical of his ability to approach and interact with others.

During weekly faculty meetings at the New School, any children with problems are discussed. Although Matt's narcolepsy has been mentioned in connection with his performance, no faculty member has mentioned that it interferes with his social interactions.

In short, I find Matt…to be an emotionally healthy and interactive ninth grader.

After Tom and I read the letter, we made sure to share it with Matt. He went through it slowly, as if digesting every morsel, and then broke into a wide grin.

■　■　■

A few days after we received the evaluation, Mrs. Quinten notified us that the SERC meeting was scheduled for April 22.

With supportive letters from Dr. Welch and Mrs. Clark, Tom and I entered the room on the day of the meeting cautiously optimistic that Matt's classification would be changed. We were hoping for the best, but prepared for the worst.

The room was packed. There were six committee members seated around the table: the supervisor of special programs; the director of pupil services; the special education representative; the vocational coordinator for special education; the school health physician; and a social worker. Others in attendance were the school psychologist who had conducted Matt's test; the special education coordinator, Dr. Pane; and Mr. Forest. Tom and I felt outnumbered five times over.

The SERC chair welcomed us pleasantly and introduced everyone in attendance. Reading from the committee document, she said, "Matt has a history of distractibility. However, his cognitive skills fall in the average to superior range. Matt exhibits overall adequate behavior at school, with frequent inattention to tasks and slow work completion. Matt's grades at the New School are Bs, with difficulty noted in mathematics. Matt's previously diagnosed ADHD continues to impact him in the academic setting."

She went over the summary of findings, including Matt's strengths and weaknesses. It seemed somehow surreal to hear them boiled down in so few words.

"Strengths: cognitive skills, classroom performance and grades are good at this time, with the exception of mathematics. Weaknesses: Processing speed, academic fluency, maladaptive coping mechanisms were positively indicated on the Roberts test."

I caught my breath as I realized the chair was about to hand down the verdict.

She spoke calmly and slowly. "The committee recommends continued special education eligibility at this time due to Matt's other health impairment of ADHD, which continues to impact his educational performance. In addition, Matt's diagnosis of narcolepsy may also be impacting his educational performance."

"Based on the review of the assessment information, the eligibility committee determined that a disability does exist, but the nature of the disability has been changed from Emotional Disturbance/Other Health Impairment to Other Health Impairment."

Tom and I squeezed each other's hands.

The label had been dropped!

After waiting what seemed like years for this meeting, the session itself was brief. In my mind, it was a blur—we could hardly wait to tell Matt the good news.

"The psychologist even apologized at the meeting for making the report too negative and not emphasizing the positive traits. She said it was just her writing style," I told Matt.

He, of course, was happy with the outcome.

The SERC decision made our day. We realized our cause of joy was so different than those most parents anticipate and experience—but with the public school system, we would take a victory wherever we could get it.

■ CHAPTER 18 ■

A Squeaky Wheel for the Twice-Gifted
(2003–2004)

Tom and I were elated when we got Matt's emotional disturbance label removed, and we felt vindicated in our choice to remove him from the W-L Interlude program. We felt more strongly than ever that keeping him there would have been incredibly detrimental to his well-being. As Matt began his second year at the New School and settled happily into being a tenth grader, it was clear that moving him to this small private school had not been a luxury, but a necessity.

But one huge issue continued to bother us.

Tom and I were lucky to be in the position to afford a private school education—what about the other children pigeonholed into the wrong programs whose families didn't have that financial flexibility? There was no program for twice-gifted children in the public-school system; without it, we knew there would always be students suffering through the same emotional, intellectual, and even physical pain our son had endured for years.

■ ■ ■

Throughout our first full year back at the New School, I remained in contact with Ilene Schwartz. She kept noticing similar struggles among some of the students she assisted for IEP meetings. Not all the parents had children who fit in the gifted and learning-disabled category, but there were some common threads—namely the need for smaller class sizes and more individualized approaches to learning.

Ilene also mentioned an attorney she knew because their paths had often intersected in parent advocacy work. She gave me his name: Harold Dean. Tom and I contacted him shortly afterwards and set up a meeting at his home office in Arlington for mid-September.

When we met, Mr. Dean greeted us warmly. He was genuinely understanding about the academic challenges children with learning disabilities face. He told us he had a son who was bright, but also struggled in school. His son had not been successful in public schools, but was doing well in a small private school that met his individual learning needs.

He, too, had noticed how many other families he worked with faced similar problems to Matt with the traditional school system. They had each placed one of their children in a private school because public school was not working out for them.

Over the course of our conversation, I mentioned Matt's struggles with narcolepsy and how he had been placed in Interlude. I also told him about our school board presentation on narcolepsy a year earlier.

Mr. Dean paused for a moment after I mentioned the school board appearance.

"What would you think about appearing before the school board again? This time it would be to set up a twice-exceptional program. I think I could get a few families together to join you. If you make your case as a group, I think it would make a greater impression on the board, and also add pressure for them to do something."

Tom and I looked at each other and shook our heads in agreement.

"We'll do it," I said.

■ ■ ■

Harold rounded up two more couples and a single parent who had placed their bright children in private schools because the smaller, more personalized programs they needed weren't offered in the public school system.

The parents all had compelling cases. One family had a son who battled bipolar illness. Had he stayed at his public high school, he would have had a social promotion, but would have been short-changed academically. Another family turned to private schools after the IEP process at their son's high school proved inadequate, particularly ineptness at dealing with bullies and the victims of bullies. The mother of another student moved from public to private school so her son would be academically challenged and receive the support he needed to do well.

We all met to plot strategy at Mr. Dean's house one week before the meeting, and then in early October, our group spoke before the school board.

In our allotted three-minute periods, each of us emphasized that we supported public schools and would gladly return our children to them if the system offered the right programs.

When it was my turn to speak, I explained why the New School was the best choice for Matt. As I spoke, I made sure to take turns looking at each school board member. I thought it was important to make a connection with each of them, no matter how brief my statement.

"We believe Matt needs to be in small classes where teachers respect and are able to work with a student's individual learning style, and where students have the flexibility to choose the format that information will be presented in to match the way they learn.

"Matt has found such a school at the New School of Northern Virginia. The New School's teaching philosophy is based on Harvard professor Howard Gardner's theory of multiple intelligences. The school recognizes the seven intelligences in their students and encourages them to utilize all of them, rather than focus or limit their expressions to primarily verbal and mathematical means.

"Unfortunately, the county is not devoting sufficient resources for 'twice-exceptional children'—children who are gifted, but have learning disabilities or learning styles that require individualized attention by the teacher. These children are bright. They want to graduate from high school. They want to go to college and they can make amazing contributions to society, both now and in the future. But they must be given the right tools in the proper program.

"If these children are educated in the appropriate academic program, they will succeed in school and in life. We ask you to give them that chance."

The school board members politely listened to our presentations. Afterwards, the school board chairman thanked all of us for bringing the "very complicated issue" to their attention and said staff would continue to work on the issues we raised.

My heart sank. This seemed to be nothing more than a brush off, like saying "Let's do lunch" without really meaning it.

Then, to my delight, one of the school board members, David Foster, intervened. He recommended referring our group's remarks to the Gifted and the Special Education Advisory Committees.

That in itself was a notable victory. The lack of communication between the gifted and special education communities was a major hurdle for correctly placing twice-gifted students. In too many cases, smart children with learning disabilities received special education services, but not the challenging academic courses that were appropriate for them.

The board chairman responded that because Dr. Crawley was currently engaged in the issue, he believed the assistant superintendent should decide how to follow up. It sounded like another stalling tactic to me.

Fortunately, there was another heaven-sent intervention, this time by school board member Libby Garvey. Rather than leave the task open-ended, she asked the assistant superintendent to submit a report on the issues raised that evening and to complete it shortly.

Barely two weeks later, we received word from Dr. Crawley that he wanted to meet with parents in early November about establishing a program for twice-exceptional children!

Things were certainly falling into place.

■ ■ ■

On October 28, I attended a very informative and productive Special Education Advisory Council (SEAC) meeting. I could not have asked for a more sympathetic and friendly audience of parents. They were very receptive to establishing the twice-exceptional program, and appeared to be interested in beginning it with the ninth grade.

Years later, I still remember how stunned I was at the November meeting when several parents gathered with Dr. Crawley and representatives from the special education and gifted programs. The first part of the meeting focused on a draft guidebook for teachers on identifying disabilities. Acknowledging the issues that Tom and I raised on sleep disorders in 2002, and the mental health concerns raised at the September 2003 school board meeting, the guidebook would incorporate sections on narcolepsy, bipolar disorder, and executive functioning skills.

But the most memorable part of the meeting occurred when Dr. Crawley put two blank sheets of paper on a chalkboard and wrote a preliminary outline for a twice-exceptional children program. The program would offer blocks of core classes and an elective, with an established maximum class size of ten students taught by two teachers with a resources aide. Dr. Crawley had a budget proposal for it, too.

The first class would start in 2005 with the incoming ninth graders.

I sat there, trying to process all the information, wondering if I was dreaming it. I was absolutely astounded that the twice-gifted program would be established so soon.

■ ■ ■

A few months later, in early January, I ran into a former neighbor whose children had gone to grade school with Emma and Matt. She said that she had been flipping channels on TV in the fall and saw Tom and me making presentations before the school board.

"How did that go?" she asked.

I told her that, to my surprise, Dr. Crawley had proposed a twice-exceptional program for the next school year.

"Your parent group must have made a difference," she said.

I paused for a moment and thought again about our parent group's persistence before the school board and follow-up meetings. Finally, I responded.

"They must have known that we weren't going away."

■ ■ ■

At a SEAC meeting on May 24, 2004, Dr. Madden, director of the Office of Special Education, announced it had requested the establishment a twice-exceptional program, beginning with identifying students who could benefit from participating in the 2005-2006 school year.

A twice-exceptional program began at Wakefield High School in the fall of 2005. By its inception, the model had changed from Dr. Crawley's original plan, but the goals were the same. Under the new program, Bonnie Nelson, the twice-gifted teacher, taught ten students and provided support for several other students who were not enrolled. In addition to consulting on academic support, she was able to provide emotional and behavioral support for the students as needed, since she was also certified as a counselor. Although it started too late to help Matt, it has been wonderful to know that other bright children with learning disabilities can benefit from it.

The many hours I spent reading books and articles about twice-exceptional children and how closely their academic struggles mirrored Matt's; the mixed emotions I felt upon realizing that Matt's "learning disability" was mislabeled; all the IEP meetings basing accommodations on his perceived weaknesses and how to remedy them, rather than finding ways to build on his strengths—the positive outcomes made it all well worth the effort.

Though I did not realize it at the time, publicly making a case for the twice-gifted program paved the way for more educational advocacy work that could (and has) benefited an even greater number of students. My experience working behind the scenes with other parents, teachers, and school officials, as well as the background research I did in preparation for those meetings, has served as groundwork for many of my endeavors, from writing this book to hosting a radio show on hands-on, project-based learning.

▪ CHAPTER 19 ▪

Now What?
(Fall 2003–Summer 2004)

As much as Matt was looking forward to starting tenth grade at the New School, Matt surprised Tom and me over the summer when he mentioned a growing interest in vocational training. Given that he had loved building projects since he'd been a toddler, it made sense that working with his hands would be attractive to him, but this was the first time he'd mentioned switching academic tracks to turn those skills into a career.

"And what type of jobs are you thinking of?"

Matt mentioned welding and machining, but added that there were other avenues worth considering, too. Of course, none of these courses were offered at the New School.

As summer drew to a close, though, Matt put technical school on the back burner. He was looking forward to starting tenth grade at the New School.

▪ ▪ ▪

Shortly after Labor Day, it was time to meet with Dr. Potter again; the headmaster conducted meetings with all incoming students prior to the start of each school year.

It was a relaxed session. Dr. Potter reviewed Matt's progress in school and discussed the future; he noted Matt's improvements, and then asked him how he thought the last year of school had gone.

"I hate to use the word 'transition,' but that's how I saw it," Matt replied. "I think I could be on time more often and try harder in my classes. For one thing, I need to ask my teachers about assignments or board work that I didn't copy down."

I was pleased with how confident Matt sounded. It was a far cry from his low self-esteem in Interlude at Washington-Lee and the struggles he had faced his last two years at Swanson.

In mid-September, Matt began his second year at the New School, happy to be reunited with friends, and settled promisingly into tenth grade.

■ ■ ■

I remained involved with the public school system, lobbying for a twice-gifted program with Harold and the other parents.

During the course of my research, I recalled hearing of the Applied Academic Career Education (AACE) program, which paired academics with hands-on courses at the Career Center for eleventh and twelfth graders. When I mentioned the program to Harold, he suggested that Ilene and I join him to meet with the head of AACE.

The three of us stepped out of our cars and into the Career Center's parking lot on a sunny day near the end of October, and as a group, we burst into laughter. It looked like we had all received the memo: we were each wearing a black top and beige khakis, as if in uniform.

We walked together to the entrance of the school, a non-descript gray building that shared its space with a public library, and Dr. Myer greeted us warmly in the large lobby. As he led us to his office, he pointed out several of the classes taking place in the classrooms along the hallway, ranging from commercial art and computer technology to culinary arts and physical therapy. He noted that there was also a state-of-the-art television and radio studio, a garage for auto technology, and an animal science lab.

Once we were seated in Dr. Myer's office, he enthusiastically launched into the history of the program. Before the AACE program was established, he explained, a group of teachers toured the countryside to develop a program for hands-on learners.

To my surprise, they'd even met Harold Gardner at a seminar, and AACE had adopted five of the seven principles of his multiple intelligence theory, along with the same project-based curriculum and philosophy as the New School. Besides the array of electives offered at the Career Center, the core subjects in AACE ran in block schedules, only two per semester—a definite plus for students like Matt, who worked best when they did not have to focus on several classes at a time.

As the meeting wrapped up and Dr. Myer saw us to the door, he said proudly, "Yes, the Career Center is the 'best kept secret' in Arlington."

Once out of earshot, Harold, Ilene and I looked at each other, completely puzzled. *Why is this school under the radar? Why don't more counselors and teachers seem to know about it?*

■ ■ ■

After that interview, I couldn't stop thinking about AACE and Matt's desire to pursue vocational training. As wonderful as some portions of the New School program had been for Matt, it was not a perfect fit, and it was a college prep school—a path Matt wasn't interested in taking. I decided to make further inquiries to determine what might be the best program for his last two years of secondary school.

I thought it was very important for Matt to tour the Career Center—it would make no sense to jump through hoops to get him there if he didn't want to go—so we went together in early November. After signing in at the entrance, we were given visitor stickers and directed to Dr. Myer's office. He greeted us at the door and we left for a quick tour.

Matt's eyes brightened when we entered the animal science lab, particularly when he walked by the iguana, boa constrictor, goat, donkey, and birds. Students in the program could prepare for a variety of careers, ranging from veterinarian and wildlife biologist to park ranger and pet groomer. He asked a few good questions about the green wall used for filming various backgrounds in the TV studio and about the equipment in the emergency medical technology lab, and when we briefly peeked into the AACE English class, Matt recognized one of Sam's friends in the classroom. I was happy that he'd seen a familiar face.

As he led us through the classrooms and labs, Dr. Myer indicated there was some flexibility in AACE program prerequisites, but Algebra 1 was non-negotiable. He stressed that AACE was not a special education program. It was not designed for students who had pronounced focusing issues or learning disabilities, but then again, New School was not a special education school. Matt was capable of doing the work—he just needed help remembering to complete assignments and hand them in.

The half hour sped by, and soon enough, Matt and I were thanking Dr. Myer again for squeezing us in.

Even before Matt said anything, I could see from the look on his face that he badly wanted to attend.

"This is your ticket out, Matt," I told him as we headed back to the parking lot. But I also warned him that it would take more than enthusiasm to get into the program. "Nothing will be handed to you. It's important that you work hard at the New School this year."

■ ■ ■

The first quarter at the New School ended in mid-November, and Matt looked neither proud nor disappointed as he handed over his report card.

He had passed Algebra 1—barely, with a D, made possible by his teacher's "second chance" policy of letting any student correct mistakes on failed tests to earn a C.

"He's a bright student but has difficulty focusing in class," his math teacher had noted, suggesting a homework tutor.

Much to my disappointment, he was failing English.

"Too little, too late," Vivian had written, referring to a book report he'd written on Tolkien.

Fortunately, it was a two-quarter course; he could still pass if he stayed on top of his assignments in the next quarter. The teacher even offered him a lunch meeting once a week to make sure he was caught up with his homework, screenplay, discussion papers, and personal journal.

Matt seemed to be receptive to enlisting additional help—or, more accurately, he did not protest, although he wanted to review his math nightly with me first, before we made a final decision about hiring a tutor.

I emailed AACE about the courses Matt needed to be considered for the program next year, and confirmed that a lot hinged on his ability to improve his English and algebra grades.

As the weeks slipped by, though, Matt's schoolwork continued to be inconsistent. He was truly a mixed bag—sometimes irresponsible, while willing to work on his assignments without much prodding at others. While he remained engaged in the classes that were centered around lively group discussions or project-based assignments, he still did poorly in courses that required analytical reading or research. Success in Algebra 1, in particular, eluded him.

At least one direction in his life seemed clear. His heart was set on taking courses at the Career Center the next school year. And that would mean returning to public school.

■ ■ ■

In late May, Matt went to the APS Vocational Assessment Center for a comprehensive evaluation of his interests and abilities in order to develop an appropriate vocational plan.

The test results showed that Matt's greatest vocational strengths were in the areas of trade-related reading and writing, trade-related math, spatial aptitude, form and clerical perception, listening and following oral directions, motor coordination, and color discrimination.

The conclusions about his learning styles were the same as they'd been from other tests he had taken over the years. He was strongest in auditory-visual-kinesthetic learning, preferring the visual mode above auditory. The assessment showed he best remembered information relayed through all the modes: "hearing, seeing, manipulating material (touching), and also experience."

On the reporting portion of the exam, Matt's responses indicated a preference for expressing himself through oral means: "He probably feels comfortable talking with peers and adults, and he may know more than the written tests show."

During the interview portion of the evaluation, Matt had said his greatest strength was his ability to build things, like electric go-carts: "Matt's dream career is to be a car designer/engineer. He would also consider becoming a metal fabricator because he loves to machine and weld metal."

While the assessment certainly reaffirmed Matt's interest in vocational classes, enrolling him at the Career Center for the 2004-2005 school year would turn out to be far more complicated than we'd envisioned. To begin, Matt and I needed to go back to Washington-Lee and set up a new IEP.

■ ■ ■

I still remember how awkward I felt as we walked through the front entrance; these were hallways I'd never expected to pass through again. To my further chagrin, Mr. James came out of his office just as we passed by. I was embarrassed to see him again, thinking of all the hours we had spent hammering out IEPs, only for me to reject them. It was an uncomfortable few minutes as the three of us marched into the meeting room in the school library together. There was a special education teacher and a general education teacher already sitting at the table, and Matt did not know either of them, which only added to how disconnected we felt from the high school.

When I'd contacted Dr. Pane earlier in the year about the credit requirements to enroll as an eleventh grader in the Career Center program, she'd warned me that Matt would face difficulties qualifying by the end of tenth grade, since the New School used a quarter system, not semesters.

"I'm telling you now so there won't be any surprises in June," she'd said, somewhat irritably.

Reviewing the education plan now, to my dismay, it turned out that some of the credits Matt had earned at the New School were not transferrable to the public school. Unless he could earn two credits in English during summer school, he would have to repeat tenth grade! And since AACE was only offered to eleventh and twelfth graders, Matt would not even be able to enroll in the Career Center program.

There was also a striking change to his graduation date. Matt was no longer listed as a candidate for a standard diploma; instead, he would be eligible for a "modified standard diploma," which only required him to pass his eighth-grade English and math SOLs. It also listed a projected graduation date of June 24, 2007—under this plan, Matt wouldn't finish high school until he was twenty years old!

There was only one positive aspect to the IEP—because Matt's emotional disturbance classification had been dropped, he would no longer be placed in the Interlude program. However, he would find himself back in small, structured special education classes for all but one of his core subjects.

I was completely dumbfounded by Matt's choices; how he could possibly take any of them when they were all so wrong? It wasn't supposed to be this way! After all of our advocacy work, it looked like we were back to square one.

■ ■ ■

After the Fourth of July, Matt began summer school. It started at 7:30 in the morning, and each class was ninety minutes long with only a ten-minute break in-between.

Shortly after nine on his first morning, my office phone rang.

It was Matt.

"Mom, I can't stay awake in class."

Once again, my heart sank to my feet. I asked (well, pleaded, really) for him to try to stay through the second class.

"You don't understand. It won't do any good. I can't stay awake."

Matt told me that he'd already left. He'd gone to the attendance office and no one had been there. Instead of waiting around, he'd left with his friend Jesse.

That evening, we begged Matt to attend the next day.

"Please, Matt. Don't give up. It was only your first day of class."

The conversation brought back memories of Matt's first year at the New School, when he couldn't stay awake and we'd ultimately needed to withdraw him. In that case, though, once he'd been prescribed sleep medication, he had been able to go back and stay awake.

The key must have been the way the New School's ninety-minute courses were designed, with plenty of class discussion and a hands-on project to complete by the end of the quarter. In sharp contrast, Matt's summer school courses began ninety minutes earlier, and he had to remain seated in a stuffy classroom the entire time, no doubt surrounded by students who did not want to be there either. It was not a stimulating learning environment, to say the least.

Matt reluctantly agreed to go one more day. I already knew it would only be for appearance's sake, so that it would look like he tried, and sure enough, he called from the bathroom during the first break—he couldn't stay awake.

I felt a mixture of anger and frustration that Matt had given up so quickly, but I knew how tortuous it had been for him in eighth grade to fight sleeping all day. I wished I could think of something, some new strategy to help him keep his eyes open. I was completely out of answers.

When I got home from work that evening, Matt was sitting in the family room. Dismay must have been written all over my face, because he took one look at me before standing up and reaching towards me.

"Don't worry, Mom," Matt said, hugging me. "It will be okay."

As lost as I was, I still felt that Matt would find his path, somehow. But I also believed in my heart that it wouldn't be any of the conventional ways.

■ ■ ■

I vented my frustration to a friend who worked with at-risk students in the Arlington School district, and her response led me down an entirely new path:

"If Matt can't go to any of the Career Center classes, why don't you look at the county's GED program?"

A GED? After all our lobbying in school for developing alternative programs, will it actually come down to Matt quitting school?

I first broached the subject with Tom, and we decided it was time to talk to Matt.

Of all places, the conversation happened in our car on a hot, muggy evening in mid-summer. Tom was driving and I was sitting on the passenger side when Matt started to complain about how nothing was working out for him in school.

"What's the point of going? Even if I pass all my classes, I still have to stay awake for my SOLs. I could end up going to school for three more years and still not have a diploma!"

Tom and I looked at each other, and then, somehow, the words came.

"Dad and I have been talking this over, and it doesn't have to be this way." I paused a moment before taking a giant leap of faith. "Matt, I can see you a year from now with a GED, going to community college for some technical training, working part-time. It's your choice, but these are achievable goals."

There was dead silence in the back of the car. Then we heard Matt's voice again—but this time, he wasn't complaining. I could almost *see* the wheels turning.

"So, if I get my GED and a part-time job in the fall," he paused thoughtfully and dramatically, "would you and Dad go in half-way with me on a car, so I could drive to community college?"

Tom and I exchanged glances.

I had expected Matt to rebel at the prospect of earning a GED. Instead, he sounded almost hopeful. This wasn't a miracle, but it was a start.

When we returned home, Matt was on the computer all evening. When he left the room at one point, I walked over to the brightly lit screen, curious to see what was keeping him so immersed—he had been looking up different trades, including auto technician and welder, to see how much they paid.

■ ■ ■

The very next day, I called the GED office, and the program coordinator, Jerri Rodriguez, cheerfully answered. I outlined Matt's situation and how the GED program seemed to be the best route for him, given his options at W-L.

She explained that to enroll in the program, Matt would first have to pass pre-tests in five subject areas. The first pre-test would be held the following Monday.

"Will he be able to be there?" she asked.

Although I wondered how well he could possibly do on exams covering content he likely hadn't studied, I responded without a moment's hesitation.

"Yes," I said. "It's worth a shot."

I had butterflies in my stomach on the day of the first exam, an English essay pre-test, but that didn't last long. Matt arrived early, but the proctor never showed up.

"I walked around the building for fifteen minutes before coming home," he said. "I'm supposed to come back next Monday."

My heart sank—this seemed very foreboding.

The next Monday, though, the proctor was there when he arrived.

It took a few days for Jerri Rodriguez to call with the result—but Matt had passed his first pretest! In fact, in short order, taking two pre-tests at a time, Matt nailed all five exams. I quickly scheduled an appointment with Mrs. Rodriguez to discuss where we would go from there.

The office was located on the third floor of the Clarendon Education Center, which housed several alternative education programs at the time, including one for young mothers completing their high school diplomas and another for students learning to speak English. I waited at an appointment desk until the GED coordinator came into the reception area to greet me. She shook my hand and smiled broadly.

Once settled in her office, she began.

"I'm happy to let you know that Matt is a good candidate for our program, the Individual Student Alternative Education Plan, or ISAEP. It is designed specifically for students between the ages of sixteen and eighteen who are behind by at least one grade level."

This immediately caught my interest; I wondered why I had never heard of it before.

"While students prepare for their GED, they are required to work at least one hundred hours. While they are here in the morning, they can use our job bank to look for work."

I looked at her, puzzled. Matt had a friend earning a GED in the evening, and I had assumed that Matt, too, would be attending night school.

"I didn't know the program was during the day," I told her.

"Oh yes. In the morning, the students use computers to search for jobs, find apprenticeships, or enroll in job training programs."

"Job training programs?"

I wondered if I had heard her correctly as an idea dawned on me, like one thin ray of light shining through a dark cloud.

I looked Mrs. Rodriguez directly in the eyes, said a quick prayer, and asked, "Does that mean Matt could go to the Career Center?"

She paused for a moment to think (it was obvious no one had ever asked that question before), but her response nearly knocked the wind out of me:

"Well, I don't see why not."

After years of trying to break Matt into the Career Center, Mrs. Rodriquez, in a matter of seconds, had just opened the door.

The GED coordinator reached behind her desk and picked up a handbook on the Career Center. She handed it to me, suggesting I look at the course offerings once I got home. My next step was to call the Career Center to find out what classes were available.

"If Matt takes at least one course at the center, it should be more than enough hours in job training to meet the requirements of the program," she said.

Just as I had felt about the AACE program, I believed that ISAEP could be his ticket out. Later that evening, I even excitedly sent emails to Harold and Ilene: "Matt would get the best of both worlds, Career Center classes and a GED diploma, without taking a single damn SOL!"

When I told Matt about the Career Center/GED option, he seemed very receptive, and a few days later, we drove over to the Career Center to pick out his two morning courses. For his first class, Matt chose commercial art, but he was the most excited about his second class: auto technology.

■ ■ ■

Almost from the moment we'd started discussing the GED option in July, I noticed a change in Matt. It wasn't dramatic, but he seemed to be showing a maturity that I hadn't seen before.

It came across in little ways, like helping me shop at Target for the back-to-school supply drive organized by our church. He helped pick out a backpack and school supplies for poor children, and we dropped off our donation stuffed with binders and paper—but only after Matt organized them. It was hard to believe this was the same son whose middle school backpack looked like it had been caught in a tornado.

On the day he completed the last series of pre-tests, I picked him up from the education center, which was across the street from an organic grocery chain store and one block away from a coffee shop. He asked to stop at each of them to fill out job applications before we lunched at a nearby Mexican restaurant.

As we downed our burritos, Matt thoughtfully discussed his future education and career options—an apprenticeship, perhaps, in plumbing or as an electrician; a NOVA associate degree in business, in case he wanted to run his own someday. He insisted that the county should pay for a taxi from the Career Center to the Education Center each way if they weren't able to provide direct bus transportation; what a far cry from middle school, when he wouldn't advocate for himself!

■ ■ ■

I think Emma, home from school for summer break, picked up on the difference, too. Just the day before my birthday, I cooked dinner together with both my children—what a lovely memory. I made meatballs and Emma whipped up a homemade gazpacho while Matt concocted a spaghetti sauce using fresh tomatoes, dipping them in boiling water for thirty seconds so he could peel off the skin. Emma read in the hammock until we all joined her on the deck to eat. The next morning, as Emma prepared crepe batter and Matt cut up the strawberries for my birthday breakfast, I heard them laughing and razzing each other. Later in the day, they baked my birthday cake, and while Tom and I went out on a dinner-theatre date, they ate at the Mexican restaurant where Emma was waitressing. It was a gift simply to see her treating Matt as an equal. It hadn't been so long before that Matt had complained about her "parenting" him, and she'd lamented about him not working hard enough at school.

One week before Emma headed back to college, we spent time at a cottage in the Poconos. For many years, we had taken beach vacations, and I'd worried how a week without the ocean and the Rehoboth boardwalk overflowing with teenagers would go.

It went even better than I had expected. By mid-week, Matt and Emma had found their own rhythms. Matt boated and fished. One evening, he cleaned and pan-fried two of the blue gills he'd caught on the embers of a campfire, a "second course" to the dinner of chicken and garlic-buttered pasta I had made. Emma worked patiently on a watercolor painting or read quietly on the cabin deck overlooking the lake. She had been battling a cold and so retired early each night, but we enjoyed taking walks, exploring the woods, and picking blueberries one morning at a local farm together. It was special to have some mother-daughter time.

We all spent time together hiking, including a particularly memorable trek through Promised Land State Park, a quiet, peaceful setting, with sun-dappled hillsides, and ferns blanketing the earth beneath a canopy of evergreens.

A few weeks after returning home, I hung a collection of photos from our lake vacation. My favorites were of Emma rowing on the lake and Matt proudly holding his string of blue gills. There was also one of the four of us posed in front of Bushkill Falls—a dramatic backdrop for a photograph, and also a fitting one for a family that had been through more than its fair share of whitewater rapids.

■ ■ ■

On August 30, Matt and I met Mrs. Rodriguez at the Education Center to fill out the paperwork necessary to enroll him in ISAEP. I had to sign a withdrawal consent form, which, with Mr. James' signature, would officially remove Matt from enrollment at Washington-Lee.

The form stated that withdrawal was contrary to what the Arlington Public Schools believed to be in the best interest of the student. I signed the form, but I also included my own note at the bottom:

> I have withdrawn Matt from Washington-Lee High School because I believe that enrollment in ISAEP offers him the best opportunity for a successful career.

▪ CHAPTER 20 ▪

ISAEP
(Fall 2004)

S eptember 7, the first day of school—but unlike the last time Matt had been in the Arlington Public School System, now he was happy to go. This time, he wasn't lugging along a backpack filled with notebooks and binders that would soon be stuffed with assignments he would not do.

I don't remember our conversation on the way to the Career Center, but I'm sure I felt a mixture of excitement and anxiety. *Will Matt succeed now, when other public school programs had failed so miserably?* If Matt was at all nervous, he didn't show it. When we pulled into the parking lot, he gave me a peck on the cheek and slipped out the car door. With a quick wave, he was gone.

His first period commercial art class started at 8:30, followed by a ninety-minute gap before his auto tech class began at 11:00. We had not worked out yet what he would do between classes, so for the first day, he simply went next door to the library. As for transportation to the

Education Center, he had already arranged a ride with a friend who was also taking a morning class at the Career Center, and could drop Matt off on the way back to Washington-Lee.

Everything seemed well planned and accounted for, but when the phone rang a half hour before Matt's afternoon class ended, I braced myself.

Here we go again. Another call to tell me he had fallen asleep in class.

"Hi, Mom," he said. "My teacher wants to talk to you."

I couldn't tell from the tone of his voice whether this was good or bad news. Given Matt's track record, I prepared myself for the worst.

Sheila Mack got on the line, and once again, I held my breath. As she began to talk, though, I felt a bit reassured. Her voice sounded very pleasant.

"Matt would like to know if he can leave school a little early."

I was puzzled as to why he would ask her this. *Is he having a hard time staying awake?*

Before I could respond, Mrs. Mack continued, "Your son is a conscientious and good student. He didn't take any breaks and worked straight through. It's fine with me if he leaves school early, but, of course, it's up to you."

Hearing this (understandably) amazed me. What a change from previous phone calls from Washington-Lee teachers and from Dr. Potter! Matt hadn't asked permission to leave early—he'd always just left.

The next day ran even smoother than the first. Matt caught a ride to his first period class at the Career Center with a friend; he also got permission from the Career Center director to work in the school's animal husbandry room during the time gap between his first and second class.

The difference in Matt's attitude toward school and classes took a 180-degree turn. He was out the door on time every day and was in good spirits when he came home. His auto technology class was a particularly perfect match for him. It combined time in the classroom (learning the basics about auto repair) with putting that knowledge to work (fixing cars in the school's garage).

■ ■ ■

Matt's momentum was incredible, and he began branching out in several directions. He was hired as a bagger at the popular organic grocery chain directly across the street from the Education Center, so he was able to simply walk over to his job after school in only a few minutes. On Matt's first day as a volunteer for the Career Center's Animal Science Program, he washed a Labrador retriever—a far cry from his previous extracurricular activities, like smoking in the high school parking lot. He also enrolled in a Sunday metal sculpting class at the Art League in Old Town Alexandria; he had no interest in sculpture, but he wanted to learn how to weld, and this was the class to teach it.

Normally, Matt would come outside to meet me after class, but one Sunday he asked me to come inside to meet his instructor. When I walked into the studio, there were about half-dozen adults there working on art pieces. Matt had just finished work on his anvil for the day and removed his uniform. When he did arc welding, he had to wear special heat-resistant clothing; to make the metal pliable enough to bend, the temperature had to get up to 10,000 Fahrenheit.

He smiled broadly when he saw me enter the room. "I'd like you to meet my teacher, Mr. Jones," Matt said, taking me over to a nice-looking, pleasant man who looked to be in his mid-thirties.

"So, you're Matt's mom!" Mr. Jones exclaimed. "I'm so happy to meet you."

He showed me around the studio; once we were no longer within earshot of Matt, Mr. Jones spoke quietly to me.

"Matt tells me that he wants to be an auto mechanic," he said. "I think that is a noble profession, but I think you should encourage him to look beyond auto technology. I don't often say this, but I think that Matt is a genius in metalworking. I would encourage you to buy Matt an electronics kit, so he can familiarize himself with circuitry in a hands-on way. I think he will be an inventor someday."

I was struck by his sincerity and mentioned his remarks to Matt later.

"I don't think I will ever be an inventor," Matt responded, matter-of-factly. "But I do think I will adapt pieces of equipment that already exist to make them work better someday."

His alertness and enthusiasm about learning new things contrasted sharply from his time in special education and Interlude. Gone were the days of sitting for hours in classes that were not a challenge to him, or where the lessons were taught in ways that he simply didn't learn.

I mentioned that Matt did not need to take SOLs to finish his ISAEP to a member of our church, who agreed with me that the money the government spent on standardized testing would be better used educating children how to think, question, and analyze, and how to apply that knowledge in courses that link academics with future careers.

"If we did that," I remember telling him, "I honestly believe we would have far less children dropping out of school than there are now under No Child Left Behind."

It was becoming so much clearer to me. Schools were forced to administer countless tests, requiring teachers to teach to the test rather than engage students in ways that matched their learning styles. If more alternative programs were developed, including those for hands-on learners whose kinesthetic intelligence was being overlooked, the education system could prepare these children for skilled jobs. It wouldn't be limited to trades training; career and technical education would benefit students across-the-board, from those in honors classes to students in general education programs.

■ ■ ■

Bolstered by this epiphany, I walked into the September 24 IEP meeting at Washington-Lee with Tom and Matt deeply satisfied. Like the previous session, this meeting was held in the high school library, and I couldn't help but remember June, the last time I had sat at this table, at a loss of what to do with a son who was floundering and whose future in school seemed so bleak and hopeless.

What a difference! This time, the conference room was filled with a sea of fresh faces that did not have pre-conceived notions about Matt. This time, instead of an Interlude teacher, there were two general education teachers, including Jerri Rodriquez. There was also a new IEP manager, Greg Butler, and a representative from the Career Center. This time, Matt had a plan that linked his education with skilled job training at the facility he had wanted to attend for the past two years. And this time, Matt would finish public school in June 2005, two years earlier than under his prior special education plan.

Mr. Butler amiably discussed the highlights of the IEP. The plan showed one measurable and certainly achievable goal: Matt would maintain his organizational skills to successfully complete the requirements of ISAEP and obtain his GED. Interestingly, all the accommodations listed in his IEP were no longer necessary once he was in the right program. Enrolled in ISAEP, Matt no longer needed "gentle reminders or cues" to help him refocus. He no longer needed "breaks during class time to maintain alertness" or "extended time" for oral presentations or schoolwork and accommodations for notetaking.

Then Mr. Butler came to the section on the standardized tests that were no longer required because of Matt's enrollment in ISAEP.

Virginia State Assessment: *Not Applicable.*

Virginia Alternate Assessment: *Not Applicable.*

And then the crème de la crème…

Virginia's Standards of Learning Assessment (SOL): ***Not Applicable.***

I remember making every effort to contain my glee when I saw that Matt could move on with his life without taking a single SOL.

Then it was time for the final action on our part. On the last page of the IEP document, there was a section that read "Parent/Adult Student Consent: Indicate your response by checking the appropriate space and sign below." Below it were two checkboxes and two choices: to approve or disapprove the IEP.

I checked the first box: "I give permission to implement this IEP and the placement decision."

After nearly five years, we finally had an IEP we could agree with, so I signed it.

But not without a final word.

There was a section where a parent or guardian had the opportunity to comment on "the other options considered and the reasons for their objection."

I made sure to comment. I wrote:

Matt's placement at W-L was for self-contained special education, a fundamentals class on food management, and no access to the Career Center's auto technology or other… electives for at least one year. The only way Matt could attend the Career Center in 2004-2005 was to enroll in the Interlude program, an inappropriate placement. In addition, the standardized testing format of the eighth grade English and math SOLs triggers Matt's sleep disorder. Even if he were to stay at W-L for two or three more years and earn all credits necessary for a standard modified diploma, he might not earn one if unable to stay awake and pass the eighth grade English and math SOLs. ISAEP, coupled with Career Center electives, was not only the best placement, it was the only acceptable and appropriate program for Matt. For the record, [we were advised that] the Career Center could not accommodate Matt academically at…AACE because of his IEP.

■ ■ ■

The next evening, I popped into the monthly Special Education Advisory Council meeting to make the case for ISAEP and the importance of increasing awareness of the program's existence among counselors, teachers, and parents. Although I knew most of the parents at the meeting were facing greater health or intellectual challenges than Matt, I thought it was important to get ISAEP on the record; I never knew who it might help someday.

My remarks were well-received, and driving home that evening, I began to wonder why so few parents knew about ISAEP. It was particularly surprising among the SEAC parents, who were strong advocates for their children. *Wouldn't some of the children, who, like my son, are struggling to complete high school and at risk of dropping out, benefit from this alternative education program?* I raised the question with Tom, who was equally puzzled.

When I searched online, it took me a long time to find ISAEP—and I knew what I was looking for! How would someone find it if they didn't know what it was called? It was under *adult* education programs on the APS website—how on earth would anyone find it if they were looking for programs available to students under the age of eighteen?

By the time I was done hunting down and sifting through the available materials, I knew we needed to go before the school board, once again, as a non-agenda item, to call attention to ISAEP.

■ ■ ■

The next school board meeting was October 7. We signed in ahead of time and were among the parents to speak that evening. As in the past, we submitted our prepared remarks to all members of the board in advance of our three-minute addresses.

Tom went up first and noted that Matt was currently enrolled in an alternative education program called ISAEP. He made sure to say the full name of the program as well as the acronym—we could safely presume that most of the audience, including the members of the school board, had never heard of it. He covered a brief history of our involvement, including how Matt had enrolled in ISAEP because we felt the program offered to him at W-L was not appropriate and because he was not eligible for the Applied Academic Career Education program at the Career Center. (Tom made sure to spell out the AACE acronym, too, because most people probably hadn't heard about that program either.) He then explained briefly how ISAEP worked, stressing the link between the academic work and technical education requirement.

Then I was up to bat.

I knew that as soon as Tom mentioned a GED program, it would undoubtedly raise eyebrows. *Did it look like we were coming before the school board to encourage some students to drop out of high school?* I framed my words carefully, emphasizing that ISAEP gave students the unique opportunity to acquire in-demand job skills after they'd completed their secondary educations—but first, they had to know about it.

I pointed out that ISAEP was not listed as a diploma option for students on the APS website, though it should have been. School guidance counselors needed to be guided to address it as one of the possible high school diploma alternatives when they reviewed each student's academic progress and future courses of study, particularly for students at risk of dropping out. For the small segment of the school population eligible, I said, ISAEP could offer students a pathway to a successful career.

When I returned to my seat, Tom squeezed my hand and smiled. We had no idea if speaking up would change anything, but at least we'd put the information out there.

■ ■ ■

Within a few days of the school board meeting, the Career Center held its annual open house, and I stopped by the auto technology program. The instructor, Mike McGhee, met us in the large garage space. Several cars were parked around, and one was perched on a lift. Some were donated, while others still had owners who were taking smart advantage of free repairs.

Mr. McGhee spoke highly of Matt, noting that he had earned a 100% on his first test, which had made him eligible to be an ambassador for his class and a guide for the open house that evening. Matt had bowed out of the offer, but he'd been very pleased about his high grade.

In the school lobby, I spotted Mrs. Thomas. She smiled warmly and told me Matt was a pleasure to have at the school and that he was fitting right in. What a difference from his past stint at W-L, when Matt had stood out for all the wrong reasons!

I was also pleased by her observation after I mentioned Matt was in ISAEP: "We don't think of any of our students in terms of the programs they're in or the labels attached to them. To us, they are all simply students who come here to learn."

Not long after, I spoke with Matt's GED teacher at the Education Center. She spoke about the open-mindedness of the Career Center and also said something I will never forget: "On the first day of class, I always tell each student how smart they are for choosing this program. For some of them, it probably is the first time anyone has told them they are good at anything."

■ ■ ■

As happy as we were that ISAEP was working for Matt, I still wondered if he would have done fine in AACE if it had accepted him directly. How many other students with IEPs might have benefited from the Career Center program if they'd had access to it?

I raised this issue with Mr. Dean, the lawyer who had been so helpful in our previous advocacy work. There was no doubt in his mind.

"Refusing children with IEPs into the AACE program was discriminatory," he said.

He offered to write a letter putting the school board on notice that Arlington Public Schools was in violation of Section 504 of the Rehabilitation Act of 1973, which protected individuals with disabilities from exclusion from federally funded programs. We sent it to the board chairman, Libby Garvey, shortly afterwards.

On a sunny Saturday in early November, I was chatting with a neighbor while she had a yard sale. Tom left the house to run errands, calling over to me as he was just about to hop in the car.

"Be sure to check the mail when you come home. We got a letter from the school board," he said.

I ended my neighborly chat quickly and jogged into the house. The letter was on the kitchen table; Tom had left it there, unopened.

I looked at the return address and realized that Tom must have only glanced at the envelope, because the letter was not from the school board. It was from the Office of the Superintendent of Arlington Public Schools.

I opened the envelope gingerly, curious about what might be inside. The letter, dated November 4, 2004, was addressed to both of us:

Libby Garvey, School Board Chair, forwarded your letter to me requesting specific actions related to the ISAEP and AACE programs. Your letter also requested that the School Board take specific actions to ensure full access to these programs for students with disabilities and that their parents are made aware of such programs. I am treating your concerns as an item for follow-up, not an individual negotiation, since there are specific procedural safeguards for special education when there is a disagreement regarding placement services.

I am pleased to learn that your son, Matt, has been successful in the Individualized Student Alternative Education Program and is expected to graduate this winter. The ISAEP is a state-sponsored initiative for students ages sixteen to eighteen who have decided to pursue a General Education Diploma in lieu of an Arlington Public Schools diploma. The ISAEP is operated in conjunction with the regular GED program. Both programs are housed within the Office of the Career, Technical and Adult Education located at the Clarendon Education Center.

Arlington Public Schools provides a wide range of offerings to all its students and specialized programs and supports for students with disabilities. One of our goals is to ensure that students eligible to participate in programs have access to such programs, including AACE.

Staff has informed me that plans are underway to provide special education support to eligible students with disabilities in these specific programs next year. Staff will take the steps necessary to inform parents and students of the availability of these options in addition to information about a wide array of courses and certification programs at the Career Center. The expansion of special education supports to these programs does not require School Board policy. The School Board has existing policies related to compliance with special education regulations and Section 504.

Finally, the Director of Career, Adult and Technical Education has agreed to provide website information on the ISAEP day program. This information should be available by mid-

November. Feel free to peruse the site at that time. Additional copies of the ISAEP brochure will be given to counseling staff and administrators in all high schools. Information on all three programs will be placed in the Special Ties Newsletter disseminated to all parents of students with disabilities.

I hope that this letter responds to your concerns, and that you are confident that specific steps will be taken to ensure access to these programs. Best wishes to Matt in his future endeavors.

Sincerely,

Robert Smith
Superintendent

I was astounded—it was even personally signed by Superintendent Robert Smith.

When Tom came home from the drug store, I showed him the letter. He read it, then looked at me in disbelief.

"He agreed to nearly everything we had asked for!"

We couldn't have been more excited; even if all these changes had come too late to benefit Matt, they would help to clear the way for other students to access programs that should have been available to him all along.

■ ■ ■

Thanksgiving arrived, and my family had much to be thankful for. Tom and I marveled that both of our children were on the right track, genuinely happy and self-secure.

The weather forecast predicted a sudden drop in temperature by midday. Knowing it would soon be blustery and cold, I took Lucky out early in the morning while it was still in the mid-fifties. We had only walked a few blocks when the wind picked up and the cloudy sky above us turned a foreboding charcoal gray.

For a few seconds, it reminded me of the weather when I'd taken seventh-grade Matt bouldering in Glencarlyn Park because he'd been too afraid to return to school. Just like on that November day five years earlier, the dry brown maple and oak leaves were swirling as if caught in a vortex, but now, I simply took in the power of nature. I didn't feel threatened by it.

A minute later, Lucky and I were caught in a sudden downpour; luckily, I was wearing a heavy cotton sweatshirt and denim jeans and could run the short distance with Lucky at my side. After racing through the front door and laughing as I dried off a very wet schnauzer, I slipped into some dry duds and tiptoed up the stairs to awaken Emma.

She groggily got up and gave me a weak smile as I handed over a steaming hot cup of coffee to perk her up. Then we got down to business in the kitchen. Emma mixed the pumpkin pie filling while I made a cranberry Jell-O salad. (Matt and Tom helped mostly by staying out of the way.)

Gathered around the dining room table in the late afternoon, we passed around the heaping side dishes of mashed potatoes, whipped sweet potatoes, and classic green bean and mushroom casserole, along with the rich gravy, stuffing, dinner rolls, cranberry salad and, of course, the thick slices of turkey.

I said the blessing, thanking God for our time together as a family. "Bless this meal and bless this conversation and bless the time ahead, especially for our children Emma and Matt."

We topped off the evening watching *Shrek 2*, a family movie in which the main characters, ogres Shrek and his wife Fiona, must overcome many obstacles to keep their marriage intact.

Our family, of course, did not battle wicked fairy godmothers or a devious Prince Charming, but there had been times when we'd all wondered if there would ever be a happy ending with Matt.

■ ■ ■

Shortly after Thanksgiving, Matt took his first GED test. A few days later, he received his results: he had easily passed. Within the next few weeks, Matt completed and passed all his GED exams, preparing at his own pace and focusing on one subject at a time. As projected, he completed his ISAEP in December.

Buoyed by Matt's success in ISAEP, I decided to go before the school board for yet another three-minute non-agenda item presentation. I was the only person who'd signed up to speak this time, but Tom sat by my side while I waited for the school board clerk to call my name.

Usually, before the presentations, the school board chairman outlined the procedures. She reminded the listening audience that the school board members had office hours every Monday evening from five to seven. I had not known that, and I immediately tucked that nugget of information away, just in case I needed to pay a visit someday. Then Libby Garvey looked at me and smiled.

"There is no need to explain the procedures at length. You know the drill," she said.

Speaking before the board that night actually had a two-fold purpose. Yes, I wanted to call attention to ISAEP again, but I also wanted to make sure that all the changes that Dr. Smith had outlined in his November 4 letter were on the public record. I also made one request that had not been addressed in Dr. Smith's letter: that the Career Center's Applied Academic and Career Education program be made available to students beginning in the ninth grade.

■ ■ ■

On December 28, a letter addressed to Matt arrived in the mail. Tom and I waited beside him as he opened it.

Matt pulled out two documents. The first was his GED transcript—he had scored in the top twenty percent! The second document, though, was the one we had all been waiting for, a creamy white certificate with the gold seal of the Commonwealth of Virginia at the top of it and his name inscribed below. Matt had been awarded his GED, dated November 22, 2004.

Tom suggested going out to dinner that evening to celebrate together, and we chose our favorite family restaurant, Romano's Macaroni Grille. What a wonderful way to end 2004!

While Tom, Matt, and Emma ordered soda, I made sure to order the house Chianti.

When the waiter brought our drinks, Tom looked around at the three of us. We all raised our glasses in unison as Tom exclaimed:

"A toast to Emma and Matt and their academic success!"

▪ CHAPTER 21 ▪

Beyond the Box

With his ISAEP completed and a diploma under his belt, Matt continued his auto technology class through the end of the school year. In fact, he did so well that Mr. McGhee moved him to Auto Tech 2 for the second half of the year, effectively allowing him to finish a two-year course in half the time. He'd been promoted to cashier at the grocery store and began working full-time. He was very pleased with the wage increase, especially since his fall plans hinged on purchasing a car so he could take auto tech courses at the local community college—plans that would all change suddenly in the early spring.

In March, a tech school recruiter met with Matt's class, looking for prospective students. Matt came home with a brochure about Universal Technical Institute (UTI) in Exton, Pennsylvania, about thirty miles outside of Philadelphia. The tech school had several locations and offered five different training programs; the Exton branch specialized in automotive training. He was very excited about it, and UTI was holding an open house on March 5—*could we go?*

Tom and I found the UTI website to do a little digging of our own. What struck us the most was its commitment to hands-on instruction methods and its underlying teaching principle that "people learn in different ways and at different speeds."

"UTI understands the learning process and has created an environment that caters to various styles. Our classrooms are interactive and stimulating. You'll 'think' with your hands as well as your mind as we give you the tools—metal and mental—to solve challenging technical problems."

The school bases itself on the multiple intelligences of its students, just like AACE and the New School, only streamlined for a specific skill—automotive repair! They've limited the class size in order to provide individualized attention to students! I nearly pinched myself to make sure I wasn't imagining anything.

The tech school had industry relationships with many top automotive names, including Audi, BMW, Mercedes-Benz, and Volkswagen. Eligible graduates also had the opportunity to enroll in tuition-paid, manufacturer-specific advanced training (MSAT) programs.

What's not to like?

Well, there was the price of tuition, which, at $22,000, would cause sticker shock for most applicants. However, the school was very hands-on about helping students obtain financial assistance.

Tom and I, of course, jumped at the chance. We marked our calendars for March 5, and waited eagerly.

On the day of the open house, Tom, Matt, and I left early for the 180-mile trip; we made such good time that we were able to stop for coffee and bagels along the way. My mind raced as I considered the hypothetical possible outcomes that could result from our journey.

The parking lot at UTI was jammed when we arrived, and we were immediately impressed by the size of the sleek new facility. A registration table was set up in the spacious lobby, and signs directed visitors and prospective students to the auditorium.

By the time we took our seats, there seemed to be about two hundred people in the room. I looked around at the rows of faces. Many of the prospective students looked to be young men about Matt's age, sitting with their parents, but there were a few older people, too, and even a few women. For the most part, everyone was casually dressed, which made sense—anyone who eventually enrolled in the program would spend their days in work clothes and heavy, steel-toed work boots.

The school director, a cheerful middle-aged man, gave a brief video presentation about the school and its mission before herding potential applicants into the placement exam. They were tested on their existing knowledge about automotive systems, and it was important—high scores opened eligibility for scholarships.

Tom and I decided to check out some of the classes while Matt took his test. Several of the classrooms had interior windows into the hallway, making it easy to walk around and observe students as they repaired engines or used diagnostic tools to determine sources of mechanical problems.

After about half an hour, we returned to our spot outside the examination room and waited for applicants to start trickling out. The first few walked out of the room about an hour after the exam began, and one-by-one, more applicants emerged, until there was a fairly steady stream of test-takers.

But still no Matt.

I glanced at my watch and began to feel uneasy. Within earshot, a young man who had just left the room complained to one of his parents that the test had covered areas he had never even heard of.

Finally, Matt stepped out of the room and walked toward us, looking a bit shell-shocked. He had been among the last to finish.

I asked him how the exam went, making every effort not to look too concerned. On the inside, however, I was afraid to hear his answer, and I tried to beat back memories of how his sleep problem had disrupted so many long tests in stuffy rooms over the years.

"It was hard. There were questions about NASCAR cars and trucks that I had never studied before. But at least I got it done." Matt paused to read my mind before he said, "Mom, you do realize that I can't fail this exam, right? It's only to determine if I get a scholarship."

He was right. It was funny that I still had nagging doubts about his future, even though he had proven how successful he could be by completing both his ISAEP and his auto tech courses at an accelerated pace.

We headed to the auditorium again for brief presentations about housing and employment services. UTI did not provide student housing, but Matt's recruiter had assured us that the school was very good about helping incoming students with housing arrangements before they started the program.

We were in luck—two of the prospective students lived less than twenty minutes from our home in Virginia. Matt's recruiter made sure we all met, though the other two boys, Donald and Mark, had known each other in high school.

The plans came together quickly. Donald's parents were seasoned movers, as his father's job had required frequent relocation over the years. Renting and loading a truck was second nature to them, and they even offered to find the apartment from the list of three-bedrooms that the tech school had provided. I exchanged email addresses and phone numbers with the other mothers, and we scheduled a lunch, so we could meet up and decide who would bring what for the boys' apartment.

If I had any misgivings about Matt living more than one hundred miles away from us in an apartment building with two other eighteen-year-old boys, I'm sure I tried not to show it. Tom and I were certainly relieved that the two families seemed very nice, and I reasoned that it couldn't possibly get any better than this.

■ ■ ■

The days began to fly by.

In May, Emma graduated from college. Months earlier, she had made an unusual gift request: camping equipment. She was determined to hike the Appalachian Trail, and to prepare, she practiced carrying a large backpack holding all thirty pounds of her gifted equipment for several days. Just as she had during years of rowing, she practiced diligently, determined to reach the finish line.

Tom and I were impressed with her self-reliance and independence, but we were a little wary, too. It was one of those moments when we had to take deep breaths and, like every parent raising children, remember the adage, "First you give them roots, then you give them wings." There was no mistaking it—Emma had sprouted hers.

In early July, Emma and two of her friends from high school headed out on 'the AT' (as it was frequently called by seasoned hikers). They had planned a three-week trek, starting in southern Virginia and crossing the state line at Harper's Ferry into West Virginia. After two weeks, though, her friends had to bow out.

Emma came home with her friends, but only to reassure us it would be safe for her to go back alone; she had her heart set on finishing out the last week. "We all look out for each other. Everyone has a trail name and uses it to sign in at various points along the way," she told us.

A few days later, we set off to the spot where she and her friends had stopped their hike, checking in at a visitor center before walking her to the beginning of the trail. A gray-haired woman leafing through pamphlets of nearby attractions looked over at us.

"Is she going out there all by herself?" she asked me.

I mustered a weak smile and said yes. She shook her head disapprovingly and went back to perusing her travel brochures.

I could feel a numbness slowing seeping through me, from head to toe, but Emma must have overhead the brief conversation. She came over to cheerfully tell me it was time to go, as if the sound of her voice would make me feel better.

We walked to the hiking path together and hugged goodbye. Her backpack was considerably lighter; she'd learned over two weeks on the trail what her necessities were, and what she could do without. Sporting a blue bandana on her head, a t-shirt, a short denim skirt, and a huge smile, she turned to go on alone.

I called out and asked to take her picture; she humored me, then smiled once more and quickly headed down the trail.

I turned around, too, back in the direction of my car. In the distance, a young couple was heading toward me, and as we were about to cross paths, the young, slender, slightly sunburned woman spoke to me.

"Is that your daughter?"

When I said it was, she smiled and said kindly, "Don't worry. We'll look out for her."

I'm sure the relief that swept over me must have shown on my face when I thanked them. It was a good omen.

One week later, Emma returned as planned, exhausted but happy. She had spent three weeks in the Blue Ridge Mountains, and over the course of those twenty-one days, she had hiked 300 miles.

■ ■ ■

About one month before heading to Pennsylvania, Matt worked his last day at the grocery store.

When I wondered aloud why Matt hadn't chosen to work a few weeks longer, I was surprised when Emma staunchly defended him: "He's worked like a dog and deserves some time off." In retrospect, though, it was right in character. Throughout the rocky years, she had often offered different perspectives and solutions to Matt's dilemmas—like her calendar ruse to dispel his fear of Armageddon, or reassuring us that his middle school life was not as bad as it appeared to be.

She baked him a yellow cake with dark chocolate icing to celebrate his grocery store retirement, and I think Matt was genuinely pleased and surprised to find it when he came back later from a hot day of rock climbing. Soaked with sweat, Matt grabbed a few generous slices of Emma's creation as soon as he walked into the kitchen and spotted it.

A few moments later, Matt was running out the door again. He had only come home to grab some money to buy hot dogs, buns, and bottles of water for a picnic and more climbing at Great Falls—the very place he had learned to love the sport, eons before.

After a long break, Matt had taken up climbing again in the early summer, much to everyone's delight. It was incredible for Tom and me to see him so happy again, spending more time on the activity that had once been his greatest passion in life. His friends were glad too—he spent many hours teaching them to scale the cliffs. Meeting and seeing them throughout the summer, I found Matt's notable maturity in their presences very reassuring. In the blink of an eye, Matt would be leaving for UTI, and for the first time, I honestly felt he would be just fine.

■ ■ ■

Moving day.

Donald's dad arrived with the truck at the stroke of eight. We only had a few furniture pieces, a couple more boxes, and Matt's old television set to add to the load; we'd been able to fit the rest in our car and Matt's Mazda.

We were quickly on our way, but the truck beat us to the boys' new apartment complex. It was already parked in front of their place when we pulled in, teeming with helpers. Emma had returned to her college town to search for a job with a non-profit organization a few days prior, but with help of the other boys' siblings, Tom and I had Matt settled in by mid-afternoon. Mark's mom had brought a lot of staples, so we didn't even need to do the grocery run we'd originally planned.

The boys were all understandably excited about their new-found independence. Mark and Donald quickly got to the task at hand and began to set up the flat screen TV that Mark's grandmother had donated to him. Tom and I looked at each other and realized that, with the other families already gone and our duties done, it was time to leave the boys to their own devices. I think Matt was a little surprised, but we felt like we would be in the way just hanging around, so we decided to head home early.

After a hug and kiss goodbye, Tom and I headed out. As we got into the car, I continually reminded myself that Emma had moved away on her own three years earlier, and everything about that had turned out just fine. I crossed my fingers that this would, too.

We arrived back home in the early evening. The house seemed so strangely quiet, and I suddenly realized that Tom and I were now full-fledged empty nesters.

■ ■ ■

Of course, I found an excuse to call Matt later that evening—we had discovered that he had forgotten to pack his work boots. School wouldn't be starting for a few weeks, so rather than mail them, we offered to deliver them in person the weekend before. What a good reason to go back!

Two weeks later, with the work boots packed neatly in a shoebox on the backseat floor of our car, Tom and I made the drive for the second time to Matt's apartment. He greeted us at the door.

He looked very handsome—hair neatly trimmed, wearing a Billabong shirt (with a collar!) and his brown climbing shorts. The apartment, however, looked like the maid service hadn't arrived yet. I was particularly puzzled as to why there was candy scattered all over the nice dining room set. There wasn't. The boys had placed a cardboard box on the table for target practice—the 'candy' was actually colorful plastic BBs.

Noticing my expression as I took in the whole disaster area, Matt grinned. With a mischievous look on his face, he explained, "I had time to either clean the place or get my hair cut."

It was a pretty fall day, and the leaves were just beginning to wear hints of color. As much to enjoy the weather as escape the madness of the apartment, we took Matt out to lunch at an Irish pub in West Chester, passing the town's university campus on the way.

Sitting with us in the outdoor dining area in his sporty new outfit, Matt could have easily been mistaken for a university student. And why not? Tech school was postsecondary education, too.

After lunch, Matt lightheartedly told us that we were taking him to a movie next. And so we did, happy that our son wanted to spend the extra time with us.

There was a downside to our fun detour, though; those few additional hours put Tom and me right in the middle of a bad thunder squall as we drove home. There were a few minutes of truly terrifying, nearly impossible driving conditions. Fortunately, we safely rode out the storm, and the weather the rest of the way home was fine—not an unfamiliar metaphor for us!

■ ■ ■

I held my breath, dreading the possibility of the familiar phone call on Matt's first day of class at UTI, but it went smoothly, as did the next day and the next. It seemed like the curriculum was designed especially for him. Students met six hours a day, five days a week, and studied each component of a car in three-week sessions. There was no juggling several courses at a time and a student's grade each session was based on a combination of classroom instruction and lab work. Before I knew it, it was late November, and not a single crisis had arisen.

At the Sunday Mass before Thanksgiving, our assistant pastor, Fr. Kevin, gave a homily that focused once again on the theme of never giving up during family struggles. Following the sermon, there was a time set aside for petitions, which gave the congregation an opportunity to offer prayers. Many of the prayers focused on loved ones facing health challenges, but there were also prayers of thanksgiving.

I didn't often offer prayers publicly, but with all going so well with Matt, I felt led to pray in thanksgiving that he'd found his way, after several rough and tumble years.

When the church quickly responded "Amen," I interrupted, saying I hadn't finished yet. This drew a few chuckles.

I continued: "And for all families struggling with their children, that God give them the strength to never give up and to remember that God is with them always and they are never alone. "

■ ■ ■

The Career Center had also held its back-to-school open house in November, and alongside parents whose children were currently attending the school, I was invited to speak about Matt's experience in the program. I was honored and thrilled to have the opportunity to share our story.

When I walked into the Career Center lobby, there were about sixty parents and their high school-age children, all seated in fold-up chairs and facing a long platform. A table stood behind a center podium, with a half-dozen seats saved for the speakers.

I'd purposefully arrived fifteen minutes early, because I had wanted a chance to thank Mr. McGhee for seeing Matt's potential years ago. I spotted him standing along a wall with several other teachers, and he spotted me heading towards him.

Although we had met a few times before, I'd thought I would need to introduce myself again. There was no need to say anything, as he spoke first.

"I'm so glad to hear Matt is doing so well at UTI. The school recruiter keeps in touch with me and said that Matt has perfect attendance and is a straight A student," Mr. McGhee said.

"Matt told us he hadn't missed a day of school, but never mentioned his grades other than to say classes were coming along fine," I said, stunned that the news was even better than I'd known. "We owe a lot to you. Our son had been struggling for years in school. Special education was not the right place for him. It made such a difference in his life to find something that he really liked and was good at doing."

Mr. McGhee smiled. "I treat all my students equally. It doesn't matter to me what program they've come from. I figure any student in my class is there because they want to learn."

No sooner did we finish our conversation then I heard the announcement that the program was about to begin. I joined the five other parents on stage.

The Career Center principal, Dr. Caputo, spoke first and enthusiastically about all the programs available at the school. He explained what made the classes so unique: "Students come here to study a wide range of subjects: culinary arts, auto technology, TV and radio production, and information technology, to name a few. They can also take animal husbandry, which is a great opportunity for anyone interested in becoming a veterinarian, or they can earn a certificate as an emergency medical technician, an invaluable experience for anyone planning to pursue the field of medicine."

I noticed a few parents in the audience looked surprised when they heard that the center offered courses related to the math, science, and medical professions. It reaffirmed my belief that too many people still mistook the Career Center solely for a trade school, rather than a preparatory institution for professions that required college degrees.

After Dr. Caputo finished his talk, he turned the program over to the parents whose children had enrolled in Career Center programs. When it was my turn, I said I was honored to speak—and that the Career Center had transformed Matt's future. I explained how we'd accessed the programs through ISAEP, and what a lifesaver the combination of academics and job training had been for him: "Matt enrolled in the Career Center's auto technology program. His training in Auto Tech 1 and 2 laid the groundwork for his acceptance at a well-respected auto technology school."

I also noted that we had hoped to enroll Matt in Career Center classes much earlier in his high school experience, and hoped that, in the future, Arlington Public Schools would establish vocational education and the AACE program beginning with the ninth grade. "For some children," I added, "waiting an additional two years might be too late."

■ ■ ■

On September 15, 2006, Matt graduated from UTI.

I had been waiting a long time to write those words. I was so proud to watch him and over sixty of his classmates enter the room in their caps and gowns.

The program started with a slideshow of the last few weeks of school to the tune of "These are the Times of Your Lives." Each student's name flashed on the screen as he or she walked up on the stage.

As Matt received his diploma, his eyes met ours for a minute, and he grinned as broadly as he had the day he'd first climbed that high precipice overlooking the Potomac River.

Tom, Matt, and I left the ceremony and returned back to our home in Virginia together. We had more treats for Matt—Emma surprised him by coming home to celebrate with us.

After a brief hug as soon as he stepped out of the car, she asked him to follow her into the kitchen. Tom and I followed them closely all the way to the breakfast nook, to make sure we didn't miss a thing.

On the kitchen table, a chocolate Bundt cake was festooned with a dozen lit candles. Matt bent over to extinguish the flames, but paused for a second and then began to laugh. Emma had designed it to look like a Firestone tire, including a very ornate hubcap. Once again, Emma's empathy, caring nature, and attention to detail had culminated in exactly the right cake for the occasion.

Later that night, as I was washing dishes at the kitchen sink, Tom came over and gave me a warm hug.

"I think we've done alright," he said softly.

We were (and are) so proud of our children—both on their unique right paths and graduates from the best schools in their fields.

Yes, we had indeed done alright.

■ ■ ■

Emma came to my rescue countless times when I felt overwhelmed by Matt's school struggles. She shielded me from some of the emotional toll it took with things as simple as calling for a girls' day out or writing me a wonderful Mother's Day card, helping to bolster my spirits when it was needed the most. Although I didn't know it at the time, that was hands-on training for her future. Her compassion for others, her leadership qualities, and her problem-solving abilities have made her a key player in organizations that save lives and help the most vulnerable members of society.

It has now been twenty years since Matt started middle school, and that cluttered backpack that rivaled Pandora's box has been replaced by a 750-pound tool box.

While at UTI, Matt applied and was accepted at a Manufacturer-Specific, Advanced Training academy, an intensive four-month program. The MSAT would pay his tuition if he was hired afterwards and worked for at least one year at a dealership that sold the car models he was trained to repair. He graduated in February 2007 with a technician job waiting for him at a dealership in Northern Virginia.

After three years at the dealership, Matt began working with a German auto group, expanding his technical skills. He eventually moved to service centers out west, and along the way, he earned all his ASE certifications and the title of master auto technician. After several years of work experience, Matt became co-owner of an auto repair shop in Colorado, and the business is thriving.

Until recently, I had never seen the contents of that large, multi-drawer tool box, but the last time that Tom and I flew out to visit Matt, we stopped by his shop and I asked if he'd show it to me.

He opened the top drawer, displaying tools worth thousands of dollars, which he'd faithfully paid for in monthly installments.

"The first drawer is the largest," he explained, identifying a variety of sockets, extensions, and ratchets. "The sockets are organized by drive—1/4", 3/8", and 1/2"—as well as depth, deep or shallow. The black sockets are used with power tools, and the chrome ones are used with hand tools."

I looked into another drawer that contained nothing but pliers of all imaginable sizes. Yet another one was for power drills, and another contained at least fifty screwdrivers. On and on, Matt named all the pieces of equipment, including ones I couldn't even begin to identify, let alone know how to use.

But what was particularly significant to me? All the tools were in their proper placeholders.

■　■　■

On a hot day under blue skies in Utah, Tom and I followed the back roads behind Matt's vehicle as he led us to a spot he claimed was "perfect" for bouldering. Eventually, he pulled onto a gravel road that led to several boulders, each marked with chalk at the spots where other climbers had maneuvered their bodies as they had inched their way to the tops.

Matt and his girlfriend Katie hopped out of his dusty, black truck. Katie, a slim, athletic young woman who had swept her thick blonde hair into a ponytail to keep it out of the way, opened the back door to let out his two large dogs—a quiet, gentle German shepherd and a rambunctious mixed breed who thought she was still a pup—while Matt hoisted a gray fold-over crash pad from the backseat. It was an essential piece of equipment for climbing without harness and rope.

At twenty-seven, Matt had graduated to bouldering, one of the most difficult forms of climbing. As a mother, I didn't know whether to be proud of him or fear for his life.

Our son eyed several of the boulders to see which one would be both challenging enough for him and suitable for his girlfriend, a determined but novice climber. He studied one of the boulders carefully, a red rock formation with a climbing area approximately twelve feet tall. There were several footholds and small ledges visible with chalk marks around them.

"This one should be good for both of us," he concluded, turning to Katie with a smile.

Katie moved the crash pad below the area Matt would climb. If he reached a point where he could no longer hold on, he could let go and jump to the ground. If he slipped and fell backwards, Katie would act as a spotter, helping him break or at least soften the fall.

Tom and I were standing about ten feet away when Matt began his climb. He stretched his long, muscular arms above his head and grabbed onto a small ledge. He then lifted himself about five feet off the ground, his biceps bulging underneath his blue t-shirt.

Next, Matt pulled his legs onto the side of the boulder, bracing them in a spread-eagle position before moving his left hand over to a pocket of the boulder directly left of him, his right hand inching to where his left hand had just been. Muscles straining, Matt moved his legs against the rock wall in a squat position.

After studying the best route for a brief moment, Matt swung his right arm above him, grabbed the top of the rock, and quickly moved his left hand to another part of the boulder for support and balance.

At six-feet-two-inches, weighing 170 pounds, none of these had been easy tasks, but then came the hardest part. While holding onto the top of the boulder with his right hand, Matt set his left free, pausing just a second before swinging it overhead, too. With both hands now gripping the top, he pulled himself up, using every muscle fiber to get there.

Matt swung his left leg onto the top of the rock, followed by his right. He pushed himself up to a seated position and dangled both legs over the rim of the boulder, grinning broadly at us. His face lit up exactly like it had when he was eleven-years-old, scaling cliffs over the Potomac River.

There had been many footholds and crevices to navigate in the decades since that golden autumn day, but because of the skills he'd learned over the years, Matt could now make his way up a boulder, relying on his strength and intellect to reach the top of his climb.

▪ EPILOGUE ▪

While writing my book, I began to host a radio program, *Education Innovations*, exploring the multiple ways that students learn by doing. My original plan for the show was to primarily feature hands-on learning programs at the Arlington Career Center and throughout the Arlington Public Schools (APS) system. Guests on the first shows, when we began airing in June of 2016, included principals, instructors, students, and parent advocates for career and technical education (CTE).

However, after a few months, I broadened the reach of my show beyond the boundaries of Arlington, Virginia. I interviewed guests from national career and technical education organizations, universities, think tanks, and higher education institutes. Topics expanded to include Science Technology Engineering and Math (STEM) education, Outdoor Classrooms that create learning environments by connecting young students with the natural world around them, and Makerspaces that are designed to encourage student innovation and creative problem-solving through hands-on projects.

A common message emerged from those interviews: the most successful teaching methodology, the one that engaged students and set them on pathways to college and careers was hands-on learning.

It was a lesson my family had already learned through years of trial and error. Parts of the twice-gifted approach to learning and the multiple intelligence-based program at the New School worked for Matt, but ultimately, they were not the right fit. They did not offer pathways to a technical career, and did not hold that practical motivation. Matt only truly succeeded once he could make the connection between his education and a future vocation and learn by doing in his auto technology courses. The CTE program enabled him to do one thing at a time, at his own pace and in a stimulating environment, just as Dr. Pearl had recommended long before.

Matt owes much of his success in life to his participation in CTE, but we had to create our own nontraditional route to be able to access to it. Fortunately, there are more options now at the Arlington Career Center than when Matt finished ISAEP in 2004. Students as early as ninth grade can enroll in some of the classes, and, in conjunction with Northern Virginia Community College (NOVA), the school now offers more than twenty dual-enrolled courses, in which students can earn both high school and college credits simultaneously. These classes are taught by NOVA adjunct faculty, align to NOVA college credit courses, and the credits are transferable to most major universities.

In 2016, Arlington Public Schools made a giant positive leap in its approach to education by establishing Arlington Tech (AT), a high school program built on project-based learning (PBL), at the Career Center. AT is a rigorous STEM-focused program that incorporates CTE courses into its curriculum.

When I had the opportunity to interview the ACC principal, Margaret Chung, and AT coordinator, Catherine Steinmetz[5,] they stressed that the two programs have more in common than what distinguishes them. They explained how hands-on learning was the basic foundation

---

5.   Paula Lazor, *Education Innovations*, March 2018, https://www.wera.fm/listen/demand.

at the Career Center and Arlington Tech, and how students engage and learn when it is relevant to the world around them—that students were active, not passive, learners.

In project-based learning, Mrs. Steinmetz noted, the teacher acts more as a facilitator and a support, not necessarily the dispenser of information. "Project-based learning allows students to work on a task, and as they work through the task and projects, they inquire into what resources they need and what skills they need to develop." The activities are structured so that, in the process of doing them, students develop the four main competencies, or "4Cs": Critical Thinking; Collaboration; Creativity; and Communication.

To illustrate the 4Cs, Mrs. Chung described a project in which students had to engineer a small, drivable toy car for young children who could not walk. The students had to examine the existing vehicle, interview each child to understand his or her individual disabilities, and determine what modifications were necessary. They worked as a team, honing advocacy skills as each student made a case for why they were best suited for a specific role, assigned tasks, and rebuilt these vehicles to their needs. The successfully completed project didn't just result in good class grades—this accomplishment went beyond the classroom, providing children with disabilities the means and joy of mobility.

For AT students, PBL is not always a physical project; sometimes teachers pose open-ended questions, and the students must collaborate to find possible answers. For example, social studies and world history students recently examined the issue of ethics in child labor. The students narrowed down the question to whether the United Nations should address it as part of the Universal Declaration of Human Rights before analyzing the impact on the economy and on the children and drafting a proposal as it would have been presented to the UN. Mrs. Steinmetz observed that, through evaluation and analysis, they had not simply learned about historic and current child labor—they had constructed a project from that knowledge.

Another AT project that reached far beyond the boundaries of the classroom took place in the 2016-2017 school year, when the students participated in a collaborative project with the NASA (NOAA) Goddard Space Center. The challenge was to produce two to three-minute educational videos debunking popular misconceptions about atmospheric science.

Three AT classes were involved in the six-month project, each working within a two-month timetable. During phase one, chemistry students produced a science briefing book and visuals for English students; in phase two, English students developed storyboards and scripts for the TV students; and in phase three, TV production students created videos for NASA.

One of the films addressed misconceptions about the ozone layer. It was recorded in the school's TV production studio, and began with a news anchor reporting inaccurate information. Several times throughout the broadcast, a TV producer ran onto the set to correct what the anchor had misstated, until he finally got it right. The video was laced with humor, but it was also an informative piece that captured the imagination of the student participants.

There was a lengthy review process for the student videos, but theirs met the criteria. They were accepted and launched on the NASA website; they were also posted on the APS website, so they could reach an even broader audience.

Thousands of educators in the U.S. and abroad use the PBL[6] method of teaching. The Buck Institute of Education (BIE) established the Gold Standard PBL, at the heart of which are the Student Learning Goals and Essential Project Design Elements:

Student Learning Goals

Key Knowledge and Understanding

- Students learn how to apply knowledge to the real world and use it to solve complex problems and create high quality products.

Key Success Skill

- Otherwise known as "21ˢᵗ Century Skills" or "College and Career Readiness Skills," they are the ability to think clearly, solve problems, work with others and own one's own work.

---

6.   John Larmer and John R. Mergendoller, *Gold Standard PBL: Essential Project Design Elements*, http://www.bie.org/blog/gold_standard_pbl_essential_project_design_elements.

Essential Project Design Elements

Challenging Problem or Question
- The heart of a project—a problem to investigate and solve, or a question to explore. It could be concrete or abstract.

Sustained Inquiry
- To seek information or investigate—it's a more active, in-depth process than just "looking something up" in a book or online. A Gold Standard Project takes time and the process repeats itself until a satisfactory solution or answer is developed.

Authenticity
- The concept has to do with how "real-world" learning or the task is.

Student Voice and Choice
- Having a say in a project creates a sense of ownership in students; they care more about the project and work harder.

Reflection
- Throughout the project, students—and the teacher—reflect on what they're learning, how they're learning, and why they're learning.

Critique and Revision
- Students should be taught how to give and receive constructive feedback that will improve project processes and products.

Public Product
- The "product" can be a tangible thing, or it can be a presentation of a solution to a problem or answer to a driving question. By creating a product, students make what they have learned tangible and thus, when shared publicly, discussible. Making student work public is an effective way to communicate with parents, community members, and the wider world about PBL.

Throughout the book, I have referred to Matt's way of learning as both hands-on and project-based, because the assignments in which he excelled often involved projects. Matt ultimately thrived in CTE courses, which contained some elements of PBL (as defined by BIE), but not all of them.

What was key for Matt was the opportunity to "test-drive" careers. CTE students can try out and learn essential skills in culinary arts, animal science, cosmetology, and information technology, among others. They can serve as pathways to other professions, from auto technology to mechanical engineering and forensic science to biotechnology.

The CTE program aligns with the National Career Clusters Framework, an organizing tool for curriculum design and instruction designed by Advance CTE. The framework is structured into sixteen career clusters:

- Agriculture, Food & Natural Resources
- Architecture & Construction
- Arts, A/V Technology & Communications
- Business Management & Administration
- Education & Training
- Finance
- Government & Public Administration
- Health Science
- Hospitality & Tourism
- Human Services
- Information Technology
- Law, Public Safety, Corrections & Security
- Manufacturing
- Marketing
- Science, Technology, Engineering & Mathematics
- Transportation, Distribution & Logistics

Each cluster contains curriculum designed to teach the knowledge and skills essential for students to navigate more than seventy-nine career pathways. The framework bridges secondary and postsecondary programs and helps students create individual study plans tailored to the career that interests them.

Although CTE can be integrated with college preparatory courses (as offered at Arlington Tech), it also offers students paths, including licenses and certifications, to well-paid technical careers. Those who earn associates degree have a wide array of options, like air traffic control, radiation therapy, or computer programming. Not every student is determined to pursue extensive college degrees, but students considered "at risk" or "disadvantaged" have a greater success rate completing high school when they are enrolled in technology education, school-to-career, and other CTE programs.

There is a growing need to fill jobs in STEM fields, but not enough students preparing for them. Exposing students to STEM options, through practical, hands-on learning experiences in CTE programs, could chart a course that otherwise might not have been taken. If Matt were taking automotive courses at the Career Center now, he would have several work-based training opportunities through local dealerships; academically, he could have earned up to eleven college credits toward a NOVA Automotive Technology Associate Degree, since several of the automotive courses are dual enrolled. Over the years, many college-bound students have taken courses in the automotive program to apply what they learn in their STEM classes.

On the other hand, if Matt had stayed in the traditional school system, labeled as emotionally disturbed and confined to the Interlude program, the results of his projective testing from many years ago might have turned out to be true. He very well might have chosen the easy way out in life, choosing jobs where there was little risk of failure.

In post-secondary technical school, Matt thrived in an environment where he could apply his book knowledge about car parts and systems to know what skills and tools to use to repair a car. His career choice as an auto technician required him to think on his feet and move all day—the perfect combination for Matt, particularly given his history of sleep problems in a traditional classroom.

Matt's career path did not plateau at becoming a master auto technician, though the position required eight rigorous Automotive Service Excellence (ASE) certifications. Ten years after starting auto technology classes at the Career Center, he became a successful business owner. Despite the alphabet soup of school labels that defined him by his "learning deficits" rather than his strengths (and all the other obstacles he faced along the way), Matt beat the odds.

But asking every student to beat the odds isn't the answer.

We need to reform the system.

As proud as I am of Matt's success, his story is bigger than just his own achievements in the right program and career. Ultimately, what we've learned and want to share is how and why hands-on, project-based learning can be transformative for all students. "Instilling a passion for learning by doing" is the mission statement of the Career Center but it should be the goal for all school programs. Applied academics works because it recognizes and values the strengths in each individual student, and then builds on those strengths.

My family had to fight for something every student deserves and should be able to consider a basic right. All children should have access to the pathways that will allow them to reach the heights of their human potential. Education should invite exploration of the real world around us. It should spark children's individual, unique creativity, and harness their hearts and minds. Every child should be given the tools to open the box of untapped possibilities and go beyond it.

▪ RESOURCES ▪

While by no means an exhaustive list, these are some of the organizations and materials I find most crucial to understanding…

1. Getting Smart (http://www.gettingsmart.com/topics/project-based-learning/): A learning design firm that partners with educational foundations and organizations and schools to advocate and promote project-based learning. Their current campaign, "It's a Project-Based World," includes a blog series, podcast interviews, publications, infographics, and speaking engagements that are an excellent educational jumping-off point for anyone interested in learning more about PBL and real-world applications.

2. Buck Institute for Education (BIE) (http://www.bie.org/): A nonprofit organization that creates, gathers, and shares practices, services, and products to encourage use of PBL in all grade levels and subject areas.

They set the gold standard for PBL, and their support and guidance scales all levels of the educational system, from teachers to schools to districts.

3. Association for Career & Technical Education (ACTE) (https://www.acteonline.org/): The largest national association in the United States that is dedicated to career-preparation education. They provide professional development resources and organize networking opportunities and events for individuals and CTE programs.

4. Advance CTE (https://www.careertech.org/): The longest-standing national non-profit that represents and provides a collective voice for the directors and leaders responsible for secondary, postsecondary, and adult CTE across the United States and U.S. territories. They research, monitor, and advocate for policies and legislation to promote CTE; collect state and national data on the value of CTE to students, employers and the economy; and cultivate best practices through the National Career Clusters Framework and Common Career Technical Core, a set of common CTE standards.

5. Wrightslaw (http://www.wrightslaw.com/): The leading website about special education law and advocacy. It specializes in information to help parents, educators, advocates, and attorneys work with the school system to ensure the best services for children with disabilities. It also produces several legal publications and publishes an online blog; over the years, I found it to be an invaluable tool as I tried to find a program that worked for Matt. The weekly newsletter features articles on special education eligibility, effective IEPs, and rights and benefits under Section 504 of the Rehabilitation Act of 1973 and Individuals with Disabilities Education Act (IDEA).

6. 2e: Twice-Exceptional Newsletter (www.2enewsletter.com/): A bi-monthly electronic newsletter for the parents, teachers, and counselors of children who are both highly able and have learning challenges. They provide important information and resources for raising, educating, and emotionally supporting twice-exceptional children.

7. Narcolepsy Network (https://narcolepsynetwork.org/): A national patient support organization that raises awareness and promotes research and development for the understanding and treatment of narcolepsy.

8. Career Pathways (https://www.nationalskillscoalition.org/state-policy/career-pathways): The state initiatives of the National Skills Coalition to promote allowing children and adults to combine work and education while obtaining postsecondary credentials. They advocate and support legislative policies that align basic education with job training and support, either through the establishment of new programs or tuition assistance.

9. Eye to Eye (https://eyetoeyenational.org/): A coalition to empower and teach self-empowerment techniques to students with learning and attention issues. They provide mentoring programs, speakers and events, and leverage new technology to support children and transform cultural perceptions of learning differences.

10. Center for Universal Education – Brookings Institution (https://www.brookings.edu/center/center-for-universal-education/): A leading policy center dedicated to influencing global policies to provide universal quality educations to all children. They conduct extensive research on how governments can make better use of their existing financial resources to improve education, develop new ideas to address inequality of educational access, and teach global decision-makers on the most effective strategies for expanding quality education.

11. Edutopia (https://www.edutopia.org/): A foundation dedicated to researching and identifying best practices to transform K-12 education so that all students can apply the knowledge, attitudes, and skills they develop during these years into their future careers and adult lives.

12. Davidson Institute for Talent Development (https://www.davidsongifted.org/): A private foundation that supports the education and development of profoundly gifted children with resources ranging from summer programs and scholarships to both a physical and online high school program for students who score in the top 99.9% in IQ and achievement tests.

▪ ABOUT THE AUTHOR ▪

Paula Lazor is a parent advocate and the host of *Education Innovations*, a radio program on hands-on, project based learning on WERA 96.7 FM (wera.fm). She earned a B.A. in Journalism at Indiana University of Pennsylvania and an M.A. in Writing at Johns Hopkins University. In her previous career, she covered domestic policy issues for a legal publication in Washington, D.C. She lives with her husband in Arlington, VA.

▪ACKNOWLEDGMENTS▪

Writing Beyond the Box was a hands-on project in itself, and would not have come about without the knowledge, encouragement, and support offered by so many along the way.

I owe a special thanks to Mascot Books, especially my editor, Lauren Kanne, who made the process of polishing prose and clarifying the message of this book an enlightening experience (and even fun!); Senior Acquisition Editor Maria Abram, who believed from the start that this story could help parents whose children were struggling in school; Director of Author Services Kristin Perry, who kept the train running on time; and the CEO and publisher, Naren Aryal, for his enthusiastic support of my book project.

I am most grateful to Arlington Career Center (ACC), which helped prepare a pathway for our son when it looked like all doors were closed. The Arlington Public Schools system prides itself in offering a wide range of education programs, and since 2004, those options have grown, much to the benefit of K-12 students. It has been my privilege to meet many APS students, dedicated instructors, and administrators. I am especially inspired by the commitment to hands-on learning shown by ACC Principal Margaret Chung, Arlington Tech Coordinator Catherine Steinmetz, and parent advocate Alisa Cowen.

Transitioning from full-time reporter to book author had its challenges, but the M.A. in Writing program at Johns Hopkins University taught me the important elements of storytelling over the course of my "five-year academic plan." I owe a special thanks to then Writing Program Director David Everett and many of my writing instructors, especially Susan Fierston, Cathy Alter, Sue Eisenfeld, Tim Wendel, Bill Loizeaux, and Ed Perlman (grammarian extraordinaire). Also indispensable were my reader, Morgan Swanson, and the "as you revise" critiques shared by classmates in our writers' workshops. And, because of the inexplicable way life works, Raima Larter, a Hopkins alum I had never met, but who announced a Mascot book deal on our Hopkins Scribes Facebook page, was instrumental in leading me to contact the (now mutual) publisher.

I also thank WERA 96.7 (wera.fm) for providing me and my expert guests a radio platform to shine a light on the multiple ways that students learn and make connections between education and future careers. Arlington Independent Media (AIM) Executive Director Paul LeValley and Director of Community Relations Jackie Steven personify community radio's commitment to give voice to its citizenry, a dedication that is reflected in the tireless work of its many volunteers, including the producers and technical engineers.

To those whose loving support and encouragement to write this book never failed to push me along, I give special thanks to my long-time soulmates Kathy Davenport, Carla Reichard, Chris Stunkard, Leigh Mallis, Deb Kyle, Sherry DeGeralamo, Christine Schott, and Audrey Sember. I also extend heartfelt thanks to dear friends Judy Clark, Val James, Tina Rafalovich, Ellen Ratner, Nancy Ognanovich, Linda Kenyon, Linda Voss, Deb Schule, Susan Hussar, Paula Wolfson Stevenson, April Ryan, and Lem Truong. There are many others who showed up at just the right time and do not realize the seeds they planted, among them Jim

Egenrieder; Libby Garvey; Nancy Van Doren; Jan MacLeod; Michael Shea; Carl Cannon; and the OLQP gospel choir, that sang just the right songs at just the right time.

I can never give enough thanks to my sister, Stephanie Longstreet, whose faith and encouragement to write this book helped in more ways than she can ever imagine.

And most importantly, I want to thank my family. This book would not have been written without their love and support. There is a great risk in doing a book like this, and I tried my utmost to tell our story without invading their privacy or asking them to relive it. Focusing on how one person overcame the odds doesn't make that person the sole hero. In this story, there is no star performer; no one in this family is a member of the supporting cast.